Searching for Arthur
... finding Arthwys

Alistair Hall

Raven Fell Limited *Publishers*

First published in 2025 by Raven Fell Limited

Every effort has been made to trace and contact all copyright holders. A CIP catalogue for this book is available from the British Library.

ISBN 9781068610974

Edited by Kat Harvey, Athena Copy

Graphics by Room for Design

Printed and bound in Berwick upon Tweed by Martins

Raven Fell Limited, Berwick upon Tweed

HIBERNIA
MANAVIA
SEGONTIUM
MONA
YR WYDDFA
ITUNOCELUM
ERECHWYD
ISCA DUMNONIORUM
ISCA AUGUSTA
DEVA
WENLOCK EDGE
VIROCONIUM
WRIKON
VILLA OCTAVIUS
DURNOVARIA
LINDINIS
BREMETENNACUM
MAMUCIUM
GLEVUM
CORINUM
CRAPEN
SORVIODUNUM
LETOCETUM
BADON
DERVENTIO
VENTA BELGARUM
VECTIS
CLAUSENTUM
CAMBODUNUM
RATAE
DANUM
ISURIUM
BRIGANTIUM
LACTO DURUM
EBORACUM
Gainnion
Ypwines Fleot
NOVIOMAGUS
GALLEVA
CAUSENNIS
LINDUM
VERULAMIUM
LONDINIUM
DUROBRIVAE
Crecganford
Wippeds Fleot
CAMULODUNUM
DUROVERNUM
VENTA ICENORUM
RUTUPIAE
BONONIA
GAUL

BRITANNIA IN THE MID FIFTH-CENTURY

Contents

Introduction

In 2019, I published a book called *The Battle of Mount Badon, Ambrosius, Arthur and the defence of Britain* in which I outlined a number of discoveries which I believed might assist with the identification of the legendary King Arthur. A great deal has been written about this subject, but prior to the second millennium I had never read a single theory sufficiently convincing to tip the balance in favour of Arthur being a real historical figure. However, this changed for me between 2000 and 2019, when the evidence progressively unravelled, and I began to realise that there was a pattern and structure behind the information in the sources.

On reflection, I presented my findings in my first book in a rather cautious style and hesitated to positively identify who I believed was the proto-Arthur. This was through my inexperience as a writer rather than any lack of confidence in my discoveries.

Since that time, I have written two historical fictions *Bears in the North*, published in the US as *The Genesis of Arthwys*, followed by *The Rise of Arthwys*. Both books follow the family of the northern warlord Coel Hen, and map the victories and tragedies of the most likely candidate for a proto-Arthur. Aside from thoroughly enjoying writing with the freedom of fiction, the research for these books further convinced me that the northern warlord named Arthwys, listed in the family tree of Coel Hen, is the most likely candidate for the Arthur mentioned as the battle leader in the *Historia Brittonum*. I have therefore written this book to support that claim. But the case is complex and will require the readers to maintain their trust through to the final chapter, if the theory is to be fully understood. There are a few authors who propose Arthwys as a proto-Arthur, and the immediate criticism of that proposition is always the different spelling of the names, so it is important I dispel the validity of that argument from the outset.

In simple terms, neither name was recorded in writing for nearly four centuries, so both spellings come from spoken phonetic memories which were perhaps relayed through the known bardic tradition of the Celts. Pronunciation of names is also a mystery, so I think we can be comfortable that Arthur and Arthwys could easily be the same person, provided we can show their lifetimes, careers and regional achievements match up in the overall pattern of events that are known to have befallen Dark Age Britain.

There are many who say this is a tired old debate that is better left out of our history books, but once you have read this book, you too will see why this is a mistake. There is a distinct parallel between events in fifth-century Britain and the developing history of Europe at that time, and I believe that Arthwys' victories are what convinced the Romans to recruit an army of Britons to fight the Visigoths in the dying throes of the Western Empire. There appears to have existed a much greater level of contact between the Empire and ambitious Romano-British magnates in Late Antiquity than was previously thought, and there was palpable optimism following the Battle of Mount Badon for a reunited Christian Empire that we now know was so cruelly dashed by Roman military failure on the Continent and the subsequent end of the Roman Empire.

The research for this book has consumed much of my spare time over the last two decades, but there is a sense of achievement to being able to present a coherent and realistic solution to one of history's great mysteries, a challenge that seemed insurmountable when I first put pen to paper. The task would have been impossible without the help of so many patient collaborators – you all know who you are… Thank you.

Alistair Hall
September 2025

I

The background and sources to Arthur and the Battle of Mount Badon

The many tales of King Arthur and his knights of the Round Table are all based upon an enthralling medieval romance. Many attempts have been made to prove or disprove the historicity of these legends, leading to strong opinions on both sides of the argument. The view from conventional history is that Arthur is no more than a myth. This is because only one piece of provable history appears in the legend – a major confrontation between sub-Roman Britons and the Saxons called the Battle of Mons Badonicus (Mount Badon). Unfortunately, the more reliable source for Mount Badon fails to even mention Arthur. There have been many attempts to locate where this battle occurred, but so far, not one potential site has proved conclusive.

It was a bitterly cold day in January 2000 when I first began to think that I may have spotted a contender for the location of this famous but elusive battle. I had been travelling up and down the M1 motorway on long journeys, and my mind would often wander to my interest in history. A friend had bought me Alistair Moffat's *Arthur and the Lost Kingdoms* for Christmas, and I had not been able to put it down. This book examines Arthur's links to the Borders of Scotland and the subject of Arthur's battles was at the forefront of my thoughts that day.

Mons Badonicus is mentioned in three ancient annals – in particular, the account by Gildas, who wrote in Latin in the early sixth century – and I had begun to realise that finding an accurate location for this battle would be a good starting point for anyone hoping to discover more about King Arthur.

My journeys often took me past the highest point on the M1, known as Bardon Hill, and on this particular morning, it was shrouded in a frosty mist. Rising up from the Vale of Trent to 912 feet above sea level, Bardon Hill dominates a region known as Charnwood Forest, and the motorway passes close by its summit. I had driven past the hill countless times, but this day, I was reflecting on what I had read over Christmas. The similarity of the names suddenly struck me, in particular, the spelling. There are many Bardens but only one Bardon, and I made a mental note to review Bardon Hill as a possible Arthurian battle site. The description of a 'Mons' by Gildas, the chief source of this event, certainly fitted this peak, but I thought it might be too simple a solution and one which must have already been considered by others.

I have read many books on Arthur and was quite familiar with his different guises and traditional locations. My first thought was that it was just a coincidence, and Bardon Hill was probably nowhere near where a major defeat of the Saxons could have occurred, but when I subsequently studied the Ordnance Survey map of the region, I was intrigued. Three miles to the east is Beacon Hill, a Bronze Age hillfort, which, at 814 feet above sea level, is almost as high as Bardon Hill. An ancient trackway called the Salt Way can be traced all the way from the Wash past Beacon Hill and seems to terminate on the slopes of Bardon Hill. Most intriguingly, to the south of Bardon summit, there is an area known as Battle Flat, and I subsequently determined that no one knows which battle occurred here to give the area its name. However, although this was interesting, it was hardly conclusive. After all, there are many hills with hillforts around the country on ancient paths with better connections to the legends.

Gildas does not even mention Arthur in connection with the battle he calls Mons Badonicus and implies it was the successful end to a campaign by the sub-Roman warlord Ambrosius Aurelianus. Arthur is not associated with the battle until some four centuries later. With this in mind, I scanned the map and spotted some possible further evidence connecting the area with the Battle of Mount Badon. Seven miles to the north, close by Breedon on the Hill, lies Ambro Hill. There are only a few Ambro place names. Most are south of Oxford, and it is theorised that they may be associated with Ambrosius Aurelianus. I had not yet found a connection with Arthur, but it was looking increasingly likely that I might have stumbled upon Mons Badonicus.

It has taken years of research in my spare time to gather sufficient evidence to substantiate this theory. After more than twenty years, I have tracked down enough information to show that the Battle of Mons Badonicus could well have been the successful end to a long campaign led by a 'leader of battles', whose name was Arthwys.

I have loved history and archaeology all my life. My specific interest in Roman Britain began to develop from the age of sixteen, not from school lessons but from a combined interest in fell-walking and local history. It is through this interest in the topography of ancient Britain, followed by the occupation patterns of Imperial Rome, that

I have come to understand its significance in the interpretation of the history of post-Roman Britain. The internet, particularly Google Earth, gives us huge access to knowledge and images of the national terrain, but modern living has left us blasé about the ease of travel. Motorways and bridges that overcome massive obstacles and span estuaries have numbed our senses to the barriers that used to exist to travel, and also to the significance of regional territories and their frontiers in the first millennium. Our economic reliance on roads and railways to move goods similarly diminishes our understanding of the importance of inland waterways and coastal shipping. Our ancestors looked at the landscape in an entirely different way.

I have visited as many ancient sites and monuments as I have been able to over the years, and since my work required national travel, it enabled me to indulge my hobby.

My interest in Arthur was first fired by a trip to Tintagel aged eleven, where my father bought me a modern version of Thomas Malory's *Le Morte D'Arthur* which I treasured. Shortly thereafter, I read T H White's *The Once and Future King*. The late fifties and early sixties saw the worlds of art and entertainment mine history for subject matter, providing my imagination with rich pickings. *The Adventures of Robin Hood* ran on TV from 1955–1960. The late Roger Moore was Ivanhoe in a successful TV series from 1958–1959, and Disney released the cartoon *The Sword in the Stone* (1963). Famous movies such as *Richard III* (1955), *Ben-Hur* (1959), *El Cid* (1961) and *Cleopatra* (1963) similarly stoked my interest in the history of the first millennium and the medieval period. I have no doubt Ridley Scott's *Gladiator* (2000) will have inspired many a budding Roman historian in the same way.

In the late eighties, I spent a great deal of time in Wiltshire and the rest of the South West and visited Glastonbury, Cadbury Hill and Tintagel a number of times. Their connection to the fabled King Arthur never seemed right to me. Glastonbury Abbey as the reputed site of Arthur's grave has long been discredited, yet the South West still clings to its hero. It is this confusion, arising from the conflation of legend, literature, and scant history, mixed up with medieval religion, that bedevils a proper analysis of the events of the fifth century.

My interest in this subject has lasted decades, and I now have hundreds of books covering a period from the Roman invasion through to the eighth century. I have enjoyed them all, even those verging on fantasy or making outlandish claims about King Arthur. The most recent and more serious attempts to analyse the legends usually end up doubting Arthur's historicity. Modern archaeology plays an important role in the interpretation of early history and has come to take precedence over recorded myth. Historians have, in consequence, become much more cautious, leading to a rather bland, reductionist view of the fifth century. As a school pupil, I was taught there was an Anglo-Saxon invasion, but current archaeology suggests a good deal of acculturation between Britons and Anglo-Saxon elites who are said to have influenced fashion, since some Saxon burials have proved to be indigenous Britons.

As a result of this science, historical conjecture is frowned upon, making it much less likely that academics will ever attempt anything other than a superficial review of those sources which are considered myth. In my opinion, this is a mistake. Archaeology can tell us nothing about the big events unless a dig is in precisely the right spot. There is an opportunity here to take a more forensic view of the sources and reconsider the opinion of earlier historians whose work could now be considered fallible. We live in an age where fake history abounds, and caution is hugely important when making absolute conclusions or sweeping statements of fact, but this shouldn't mean that philological guesswork and measured conjecture have to be banned.

In the early nineties, I read *The Age of Arthur* by Dr John Morris. His book reads as if Arthur is a proven historical figure. While it is true that, for an academic, he got a little too much behind his man and wasn't clear about the evidence he conjectured, the academic backlash to Morris' book rather stifled historical research, leaving the field open to populist studies of Arthur written with an opinion about one thing or another – a regional preference for his battles or simply casting more doubt on his historicity. Geoffrey of Monmouth's *History of the Kings of Britain* which includes tales of Arthur is, after all, nothing more than a story, yet it is a book that is hugely important to the early development of literature and was the first attempt at giving structure to an existing legend. Many authors include 'King Arthur' in the title of their work for commercial reasons, and although he is considered by some to be a diminished historical figure, he's still a crowd-puller.

For me, the description of the known events of the period in the sources available are explicit. There was murder and mayhem as Picts, Saxons, Irish Scotti and brigands took advantage of a poorly defended Britannia, safe in the knowledge that a weakened Rome was too busy defending itself from barbarian hordes roaming the Continent to spare any manpower to defend its island frontier. These events were followed by civil wars and then federate rebellion. This was an intense period of unrest, culminating, I believe, in the Battle of Mount Badon, the outcome of which appears to have been the stabilisation of the region, an end to the disorder, and the agreement of some form of partition. Such a politically advantageous outcome would seem to indicate a coordinated campaign more in keeping with national Romano-British politics than the warmongering of later regional kings, and rather indicates the battle occurred in the last throws of the Empire and therefore much earlier in the Dark Age timeline than is often believed. This earlier date for the Battle of Mount Badon and the accompanying theory about a structured campaign leading up to it and a stabilisation of relations following it would lend greater weight to an earlier Arthur and the developing view from archaeology that the sixth century was a period more geared towards consolidation than war in the areas where Anglo-Saxons had settled and continued to arrive.

The sources

There are a few sources for the history of the fifth century, but there is very little that can be relied upon with any confidence. Despite continued scrutiny by academics and writers, it seems to me that a considerable amount of topographical and social context has been overlooked in their interpretation. Finding more cohesion between seemingly unrelated accounts of what could simply be differing regional perspectives on the same events is likely to prove worthwhile. How often do we hear of the London view, the Scottish perspective, the view from the North? Roman Britain consisted of different tribes from regions with different terrain. There were different challenges for each. Some areas were rich, some were poor, some were occupied by troops, some were terrorised, some were even the source of the terror. Some Britons retained power and authority, many were slaves. Moreover, there were confusing shifts of power throughout the period, which intensified after AD 410. Separating fact from legend is, to say the least, challenging.

Gildas

Gildas was a monk writing in the early sixth century and is the only known contemporary source for the events that occurred in Britain at that time. He is best known for his scathing religious polemic *De Excidio et Conquestu Britanniae* (On the Ruin and Conquest of Britain). Part one of this work provides a narrative history of Roman Britain right up to his own time and mentions Ambrosius Aurelianus and the Battle of Mount Badon but does not mention Arthur. Part two consists of a condemnation of five British kings thought to be in control of the South West, Wales and West Midlands at his time of writing. Here again, there is no mention of Arthur. This work was not published until the sixteenth century and is a reconstruction of early manuscripts. Most later sources contain some reference to Gildas – Bede, in particular, whose own interpretation gains much respect from historians.

Dating when Gildas wrote and perhaps establishing where he wrote is the key to synchronising the whole period. As I will explain later, my own topographical research has led me to firmly believe that Gildas wrote much earlier than is usually thought. Guy Halsall, in his book, *Worlds of Arthur: Facts and Fictions of the Dark Ages*, has re-analysed Gildas and also believes an earlier date is more relevant. We are extremely fortunate that *De Excidio* has survived and that it provides traceability in every record or chronicle that followed. Gildas alone casts light on the effect of the end of the Roman Empire on Britain. Little else was written down for two hundred years, so dating and understanding Gildas is extraordinarily important to the interpretation of the history of this period.

Historia Brittonum (The History of the Britons)

This is a history of the British people that was written around 829 and survives in various recensions that date from after the fourteenth century. Sometimes referred to as Nennius, the name of the monk to whom the work is attributed in later copies, it is a miscellany of origin myth, legend and genuine history. The work contains the first written record of Arthur's detailed battle list, which includes Mount Badon, and we will review this in detail later. It is believed that Geoffrey of Monmouth gleaned most of his history from this source.

The *Historia Brittonum* is a collection of synchronised and sometimes synthesised historical material, which is generally considered less reliable than Gildas and Bede, and this is where the academic doubts about Arthur mostly arise.

Annales Cambriae (The Annals of Wales)

This is a compilation of chronicles derived from diverse sources at St. Davids in Dyfed, Wales. The earliest copy was written by hand in the twelfth century. It consists of a series of numbered years from 445 to 977, noting significant contemporary events against each relevant year. More source information for Badon and Arthur is available here, but it is suspected that Geoffrey of Monmouth's *History of the Kings of Britain* influenced some entries.

The Anglo-Saxon Chronicle

A collection of annals in Old English which was created in the ninth century, probably in Wessex during the reign of Alfred the Great (871–899). There are nine different copies relating to the different areas in which they were compiled. The earliest starts with Caesar's invasion of Britain. The oldest is the *Winchester Chronicle*. An important early edition was printed in 1692 by Edmund Gibson. The *Chronicle* is the single most important source for history in Anglo-Saxon times.

Historia ecclesiastica gentis Anglorum (The Ecclesiastical History of the English People)

Written by the Venerable Bede in 731, this is a history of Christian churches in England. Divided into five books, the *Historia* covers the history of England from 55 BC to its completion in AD 731. Bede was a careful historian and relied almost entirely upon Gildas for the early Anglo-Saxon information. Consequently, there is no mention of Arthur.

Genealogies

There are many Welsh and Anglo-Saxon genealogies to consider as well as the *Bonedd Gwŷr y Gogledd*, known in English as the *Descent of the Men of the North*. Carvings on the Pillar of Eliseg, which are recorded but no longer legible, and the Vortiporigis Stone, now in Carmarthenshire County Museum, provide important evidence for Welsh dynasties.

Y Gododdin (The Gododdin)

A medieval Welsh poem consisting of a series of elegies to Brittonic warriors who died at a battle at Catraeth in about 570. It is traditionally ascribed to the bard Aneirin. One stanza compares an Arthur to a Gwawrddur and is often claimed to be the earliest reference to the Arthur of legend. The location, period and combatants mentioned in the poem are hugely important to gaining an understanding of the status quo of northern warlords towards the end of the sixth century and also provide clues to the likely distribution of the stories about Arthur and the Battle of Mount Badon.

Notitia Dignitatum (The List of Offices)

A document of the late Roman Empire that details the administrative organisation of the Eastern and Western empires. It is a unique record that describes several thousand offices from the imperial court to provincial governments. It is considered accurate for the Western Roman Empire in the 420s. This is a particularly useful reference for the likely disposition of Roman troops in Britain around the turn of the fourth century, particularly in relation to the *Dux Britanniarum* and the *Comes litoris saxonici* military appointments, which may have continued for a period in post-Roman Britain.

Chronicles and hagiography

There are a number of Roman Empire-wide chroniclers and historians who had something to say about either pre- or post-410 events affecting Britain. These include Marcellinus, Zosimus, Sidonius Apollinaris, Orosius, Prosper of Aquitaine, Jordanes, and the Gallic Chroniclers of 452 and 511 whose names are now lost. There is also a considerable amount of relevant hagiography, including St. Patrick, St. Gildas and St. Germanus.

The history of the period covered by this book is complex, and I am particularly grateful to all the authors whose work I have plundered to help explain it. These are listed in the bibliography where I suggest some important reading that has proved most influential in the completion of this work.

II

Religion, saints, legends and literature

We no longer believe in giants, wizards, dragons, or swords with magic qualities, but the legends and myths of Arthur employ them all. Saints, miracles and the Celtic Church are similarly drawn into these fabulous tales, sometimes to justify purpose, but often to simply add mystery, creating an intoxicating medieval mix.

We are indeed fortunate to live at a time when science and technology provide many of the answers to the questions about life, death and the universe that challenged medieval thinking. History now provides a perspective on religion, resulting in more tolerance than our forebears felt able to accept, and in Western culture, blind faith, when it occurs, has become more of a personal choice. During the late twentieth century, the Christian Church was criticised for its doctrines on sexuality, its refusal to ordain women and its handling of sexual abuse cases involving the clergy. It is no wonder church congregations have diminished. Yet, it is not so long since church leaders were as powerful as kings and governments, influencing events at international level.

Most people of my generation will remember Archbishop Makarios III who was at the centre of Cypriot politics and was elected the country's first president, holding office during the turbulent period between 1960 and 1977. As founding father of modern Cyprus, he regularly featured in news reports in the 1960s on our black-and-white TV set. More recently, Ayatollah Khomeini, who was at the centre of the Iranian Revolution of 1978–1979, demonstrated the power of religion with an Islamic fundamentalist power grab of the country, becoming supreme leader with global consequences that reverberate to this day. Theocracies are unusual in the world now, although we have recently witnessed the rise and fall of the self-styled terrorist group ISIS. Driven by medieval religious fundamentalism, powered and policed by modern weaponry, with a staggering reach through information technology, this group was able to carve out territory in the troubled Middle East.

I digress from the Dark Ages to make the point that religion has been the world's most powerful influencer until quite recently, and it has been the principal lens through which we interpret events of the past. Medieval Christianity was near fever pitch in its zeal; we only need to look at the grandeur of York Minster or think of the fervour of the Crusades to remind ourselves of that. The alluring medieval literature that made Arthur a famous legend not only flirted with religion but also benefitted from the information technology of the era – the printing press. The advent of early printing saw tales about Arthur widely distributed long before John Wycliffe had translated the Bible into English. Celtic Christianity and the so-called Age of Saints became thoroughly interwoven with Arthur's legend which, at the time, must have made it seem to be irrefutable history.

As a boy, I was required to attend church every Sunday during school term-time with the consequence that I have never attended voluntarily since. I have, however, always received my daily bread and perhaps should bear that in mind! My understanding of the history and development of the Church is therefore limited to what I have read. I am fortunate to own a copy of Nora K. Chadwick's *The Age of the Saints in the Early Celtic Church.* Chadwick masterfully explains the isolation of the Celtic Church after the collapse of the Roman Empire but emphasises it never stepped outside the framework of the Roman Church and remained completely orthodox. However, as a result of its remote position, Celtic Christianity clung to early practices in matters of ritual. Furthermore, local conditions within far-off regions produced considerable differences in the funding of the Church and what form its buildings and establishments took. The predominance of monastic foundations in Celtic Christianity also contributed to the developing differences in organisation and ritual compared to the Continent.

This divergence became a matter of growing bitterness and misunderstanding, lasting right up to the eighth century, often resulting in accusations of separatism and even heresy. Those who, like Bede, looked to the authority of the Roman Church, represented since 537 by the Archbishop of Canterbury, had no sympathy with or understanding of Celtic Christianity, even though there was never any theological divergence. Arthurian literature made much of these early differences, often inferring arcane practices, Druidic influence and even the use of magical powers – such as those conferred upon Merlin, Arthur's legendary wizard who is variously depicted as both a shaman and hybrid Christian, enabling him to foretell such events as the quest for the Holy Grail. Certainly, monasticism, and the more severe ascetism, appear to have been widely practised by the anchorites who chose some strange and remote western locations from which to worship their god.

Chadwick succinctly summarises the real history of the famous schism between the Celtic and Roman Churches:

> *In 597 St. Columba died and St. Augustine landed in Canterbury. The coincidence is a dramatic one. St. Columba, the greatest saint of the Celtic Church, is the founder of the Order which had spread from Donegal in Northern Ireland to Iona, and from there had established in Northumbria the form of Christianity which was virtually Irish, monastic in organization, and to all intents and purposes independent and self-governing though perfectly orthodox in belief. The clash between the two Churches was bound to come. The form of Christian organization introduced into Kent by St. Augustine was unlike that of the Celtic Church. It made no claim to be either independent or self-governing. It was in all matters directly under obedience to Rome. But while the Celtic countries shared to the full the orthodox views of the Church of Rome, their remote position made them conservative. They were failing to keep pace with modifications in the Continental Church. To the Irish people and the members of the Columban Church in Britain, a sudden change in their church government, a modification in their ecclesiastical system, involving a reduction of monastic prestige, would have involved an economic revolution. The Welsh, for their part, feared and disliked the suggestion of direct control from Rome through a bishop of Canterbury under a Saxon king. They were suspicious of the political implications. They liked their own ways, the*

traditions handed down to them by their own 'seniores'.

Bede's Ecclesiastical History concentrates closely on this theme within the larger framework of the Conversion of Britain and the foundation of Christianity in our islands. Whether from lack of knowledge or from lack of interest, Bede says nothing of the conversion of Wales or Ireland to Christianity. He never mentions St. Patrick or Armagh and dismisses in a sentence the statement (derived from Prosper) that Celestine sent Palladius as the first bishop to the Irish believing in Christ. He relegates the foundation of Whithorn to an aside. His concern with the Christianity of Ireland and Scotland is limited to the Columban Church. His theme throughout is the Roman mission – first the two preliminary missions of St. Germanus (derived by Bede from the Vita of St. Germanus by Constantius) and then the real opening of his theme with the mission of St. Augustine from Pope Gregory to King Æthelberht of Kent and the foundation of the other English bishoprics, and the conversion of Northumbria. The conversion of the Northumbrian king, Edwin, he attributes – contrary to Celtic sources – to Bishop Paulinus of Canterbury. He moulds his narrative henceforth around the Paschal Controversy, and the gradual progress of the Celtic Church towards inclusion in the Roman Order. The consummation is reached towards the close of the Ecclesiastical History in the glowing panegyric and requiem on the English monk Ecgberht, who had, after long toil, brought the Columban Church into conformity with the Roman Order.

The British Church had been a source of uneasiness to the head of the Church in Rome for a long time. It had been the stronghold of the Pelagian heresy, and we have seen the anxiety with which Celestine, the bishop of Rome, viewed the speculative thought of Britain, and the care with which, through the missions of Palladius and of St. Germanus, he had 'sought to make the pagan island Christian and the Christian Island Catholic'. Now, a century and a half later, with the establishment of a powerful Teutonic kingdom in Kent under Æthelberht and his Frankish Christian wife, Bertha, Pope Gregory realized that the moment had come for a fresh effort towards complete unity in the institutions of the western Church. To this end Bede relates two distinct campaigns from Rome. The first had been made about the beginning of the seventh century under St. Augustine of Canterbury against the British Church in the west; the second was made in the time of Bishop Wilfrid at the Synod of Whitby in 663, when the issue turned on the dating of Easter, in which the Celtic usage had not adopted the practice of the Roman Church as fixed by Victorius of Aquitaine in 457. The celebration of this, the greatest of all Christian festivals, on divergent dates by the adherents of the Celtic and the Roman orders in Britain was an obvious disadvantage, and a natural point on which the struggle for unity focused.[1]

The Celtic Church must have felt collectively affronted. It had succoured its flock through years of heathen aggression and persecution, devoting its very essence to Christianisation and worship, only to be delivered into the hands of Saxon bishops who were not only comparatively recent converts but also now in control as the representatives of the Roman Church. St. Wilfrid, in particular, was seen as divisive – in effect, refusing to accept that any British bishops had been validly consecrated. He was certainly controversial and, in many respects, remarkable, as a read of the *Life of Wilfrid*, written by Stephen of Ripon in the eighth century, will show. I have myself experienced takeovers by large corporations in which I had no faith at all, so I empathise with the Celtic Church. It was not until circa 1147 that St. Davids, Llandaff and then Glastonbury submitted to the Province of Canterbury. By this time, legends about the Holy Grail and Joseph of Arimathea visiting Britain had already begun to circulate, adding an air of mystery to Celtic Christianity and making the schism appear more doctrinal than it actually was.

Hagiography – otherwise known as the documenting of the lives of the saints – contains a number of mythic encounters between the saints, Padarn, Cadoc, Carannog, Illtud and Gildas, and Arthur. While this is not history, the tales have interest in showing the various traditions that began to surround Arthur, even before Geoffrey of

[1] N. K. Chadwick, *The Age of the Saints in the Early Celtic Church* (London: Oxford University Press, 1961), pp 119–121.

Monmouth wrote *The History of the Kings of Britain.* They are all gleaned from medieval records, and the following stories will have influenced some of the detail in Geoffrey's book.

Padarn meets Arthur when the king chances upon the saint's cell. Arthur covets Padarn's tunic, but the saint tells him it is only fit for a person in clerical office. Arthur leaves but returns in a rage, intent on taking the tunic. The saint makes the earth open which swallows Arthur up to his chin until he begs pardon.

Cadoc's father was a Glamorgan king called Gwynllyw and his mother was known as Gwladys. In the *Life of Cadoc*, written by Lifris in 1086, Cadoc's parents are said to have absconded so as to marry against the wishes of Gwladys' father, King Brychan, who pursues them. The fugitives meet Arthur and his knights, Kei and Bedwyr, gambling on a hilltop. Arthur is enamoured of Gwladys, but his knights remind him that it is custom to aid the needy and distressed. So, the three of them defend the runaways. Later, when Cadoc is Abbot of Llancarfan, Arthur is seeking a man who has killed three of his knights. Cadoc hides the man for seven years, then persuades Arthur to accept arbitration. On the banks of the Usk, he, with other monks, offers to compensate Arthur with a hundred cows for the dead knights. Arthur insists that each cow must be red and white. Cadoc enchants an ordinary herd to correspond with Arthur's demand, but when Kei and Bedwyr lead them over the ford, they turn into bundles of fern. Arthur, suitably humbled, dedicates the spot as a sanctuary.

Carannog is said to have crossed the Severn Sea following a floating stone altar which he loses sight of. He meets Arthur in Somerset, who is looking for a ravaging serpent. Arthur promises to find out where the altar has come ashore, in return for aid against the serpent. The saint prays; the serpent is easily tethered and presented to the king. Arthur produces the altar which he had been trying to use as a table, but everything put on it was flung off. He gives the saint land near to where he came ashore – thought to be Carhampton – and later builds a church there.

Illtud is said to have founded a divinity school which trained many saints including St. David. Stories about his life hold that he was a cousin of King Arthur and served him as a young soldier.

Caradoc of Llancarfan composed the *Life of Saint Gildas* in about 1136 and wrote in the vein of the romances. Arthur is king of all Greater Britain, much loved by Gildas. But Gildas' twenty-three brothers will obey no lord and resist the king's authority, especially the eldest, Hueil, who keeps raiding from Scotland until Arthur kills him on the Isle of Man. Gildas, then in Ireland, is deeply grieved, but on his way to Rome is reconciled with Arthur who undergoes penance. Later, Gildas is at Glastonbury writing his history. Melvas, King of Summer Land, who has carried off the wife of the king, takes her to a marsh-enclosed sanctuary. After a year, Arthur discovers where she is and brings all the forces of Devon and Cornwall against Melvas, but Gildas and the Abbot of Glastonbury make peace between the kings.

These apocryphal tales are an intoxicating mix of myth and Christianity. It is no wonder that they became source material for medieval romances and were given historical credence. A good example of this credence was witnessed in 1113 by a party of canons from Laon who were on a visit to England. They carried a shrine containing the relics of Our Lady of Laon, hoping to raise money to rebuild their cathedral. From Exeter, as they went westwards, they were told that they were on the very land of King Arthur, and they were shown Arthur's Chair and Arthur's Oven. Then, at Bodmin, an argument arose between one of the canons and a man with a withered arm who had come to be healed: 'Just as the Britons are wont to wrangle with the French on behalf of King Arthur,' says Hermann de Tournai, who tells the tale, referring here to the Breton wars. The cripple maintained that Arthur still lived, and the argument became a brawl. An armed crowd rushed to defend the honour of Arthur and bloodshed was not easily averted. Our Lady of Laon did not heal the cripple.

This event, which predates the great expansion of Arthurian romances, shows how deeply a memory of Arthur had sunk into the minds and hearts of the Celtic peoples of Wales, Cornwall and Brittany, keeping it alive through their long struggles for independence. Arthur still lived – as a raven or a chough, as leader of the Wild Hunt, as a Maimed King, as a Warrior Chief guarding treasure in a hollow mountain. He was waiting in the otherworld lair of Avalon, he was Lord of the Antipodes (another form of the otherworld). There are many sites where he is located as the Sleeper awaiting the Trumpet that calls the last battle, the final achievement of freedom. For example, it is said he sleeps in the cave of Craig-y-Dinas in Glamorgan; his men are hidden on Yr Wyddfa (Snowdon); he lies under a cairn in Bwylch y Saethau where he fell driving his enemies from Cwmllan (doubtless taken as Camlann). He lies in the hollow hill at Cadbury in Somersetshire; under Richmond Castle in Yorkshire; under Sewingshields

Crags near Hadrian's Wall in Northumberland. Some say he sleeps in a vast cavern under the Eildon Hills. In medieval days, crusaders believed he lay under Etna in Sicily.

In time, however, Arthur became more than a mythical leader fated to bring victory and freedom to the Bretons or the Welsh. Through Geoffrey and the romance writers, he became European property, the medieval king under whom life rose to its noblest height of glory and fulfilment. The *Prophetiae Merlini* (Prophecies of Merlin), written by Geoffrey of Monmouth in about 1135, were taken very seriously right up to the sixteenth century. Certain events, such as the sinking of the *White Ship* in 1120, when the son of Henry I perished, were said to have been foretold.

The extraordinary legend of Arthur was fully exploited by the romances, in particular by Sir Thomas Malory. Arthur became portrayed as a universal figure, no longer fighting just the Anglo-Saxons but taking on the mighty Roman Empire – a worthier foe. In overthrowing the Roman Emperor, and in driving on like Alexander into Asia itself (as he does in the medieval tale *Culhwch and Olwen*), he became a universal champion. As it turns out, the crumbling Roman Empire may have been aware of the Britons' victory at Mount Badon and the request from Emperor Anthemius for Riothamus to bring his army across to the Continent and join his campaign against the Visigoths probably contributed to the legends.

When William Caxton printed and published Malory's *Le Morte d'Arthur* in 1485, he wrote a preface justifying his reasons for so doing. There appears to have been some debate because:

> *... divers men hold opinion that there was no such Arthur and that all such books as been made of him been but feigned and fables, because that some chronicles make of him no mention ne remember him nothing, ne of his knights.*

However, Caxton, who in his day was a mighty press baron with a populist eye, wisely decided otherwise, justifying his decisions as follows:

> *Then, all these things considered, there can no man reasonably gainsay but there was a king of this land named Arthur. For in all places, Christian and heathen, he is reputed and taken for one of the nine worthy, and the first of the three Christian men. And also he is more spoken of beyond the sea, mo books made of his noble acts, than there be in England; as well in Dutch, Italian, Spanish and Greekish, as in French. And yet of record remain in witness of him in Wales, in the town of Camelot, the great stones and marvellous works of iron lying under the ground, and royal vaults, which divers now living hath seen. Wherefore it is a marvel why he is no more renowmed in his country, save only it accordeth to the word of God, which saith that no man is accept for a prophet in his own country. Then, all these things foresaid alleged, I could not well deny but that there was such a noble king named Arthur, and reputed one of the nine worthy, and first and chief of the Christian men. And many noble volumes be made of him and of his noble knights in French, which I have seen and read beyond the sea, which been not had in our maternal*

tongue. But in Welsh been many, and also in French, and some in English, but nowhere nigh all. Wherefore, such as have late been drawn out briefly into English, I have, after the simple cunning that God hath sent to me, under the favour and correction of all noble lords and gentlemen, enprised to enprint a book of the noble histories of the said King Arthur and of certain of his knights, after a copy unto me delivered, which copy Sir Thomas Malory did take out of certain books of French and reduced it into English.

And so continued the development of the tales of King Arthur 'the once and future king'. John Steinbeck, a titan of twentieth-century English literature, began writing *The Acts of King Arthur and his Noble Knights* in 1956, and although unfinished, it was published in 1976. Like myself, as a boy he was given a copy of Malory which he credits with not just his fascination for the English language but also his sense of right and wrong. I treasured the book my father bought me in Tintagel in 1964, and I have been fascinated by the mystery and its likely history ever since. By contrast, my father never quite understood my interest, but like so many of his generation who suffered the rigours of the Second World War, he considered history mostly painful reflection. It is perhaps for reasons similar to this that Britain lost the real history of the so-called King Arthur. So, who might he really have been?

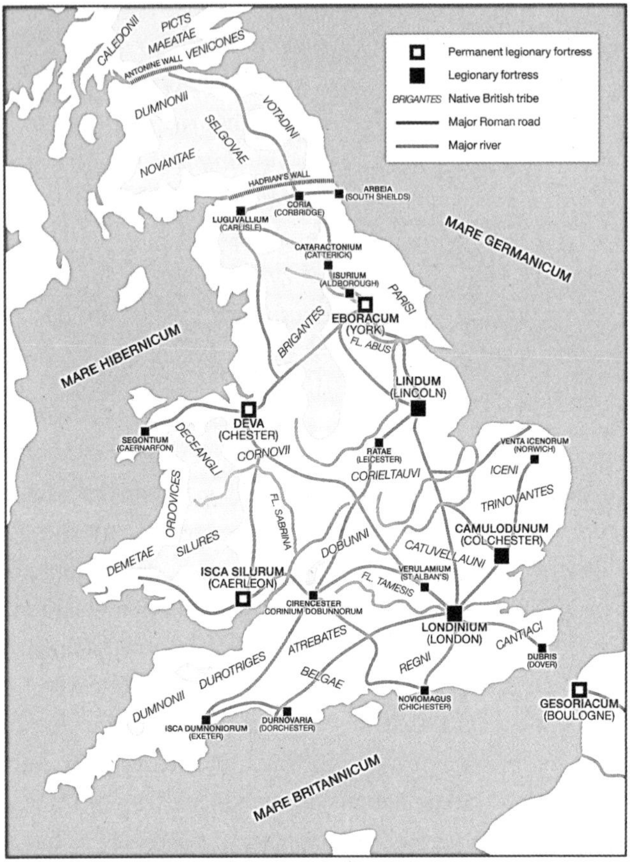

Map 1: Roman Britain, circa AD150

Roman Britain was never a settled territory. Maps showing Roman roads and towns may seem to indicate the advance of Roman culture and society, but this was far from the truth. The Caledonni and Picts were never defeated. The Selgovae and Votadini remained hostile, confirmed by the necessity for, and location of, Hadrian's Wall. The Brigantes were not defeated until the end of the first century and went on to rebel several times. Yorkshire was still garrisoned in the fourth century as was northern Wales. The Iceni rebellion under Boudica is famous for the destruction of Camulodunum, Londinium and Verulamium and was only suppressed through the genocide of the tribe. Other famous rebel leaders include Calgacus (Caledonii), Caratacus (Catuvellauni) and Venutius (Brigantes).

III

A brief history of Roman Britain

If we are to find Arthur and his battles, it is important to understand the history of late fourth- and fifth-century Britain, when Roman imperialism broke down and the invading Anglo-Saxons had not yet consolidated their kingdoms

The Battle of Mount Badon occurred sometime during this period at a place that has never been properly identified. It was credited as a victory for the Britons, staying the advance of the nascent Anglo-Saxon kingdoms for a considerable period. Most historians agree that the battle was a genuine event, but beyond that, little more can be added that is provable. It has always been apparent to me that locating the correct battle site and placing it within an accurate time frame, could well be the key to bringing the true history of the fifth century into sharper focus.

The Battle of Mount Badon was undoubtedly the most significant encounter on British soil in a century, but its association with the legendary King Arthur befuddles clinical assessment of its date and location. Finding the battle site without consideration of Arthur might be considered unthinkable by some, but skewing research to accommodate the legend is equally unacceptable and garners little support from academics. A unifying and overarching solution has remained elusive, and perhaps it is the resulting mystery that has become the legend's charm.

It is intended that this book should be written in such a way to allow anyone approaching this period for the first time to understand and follow its course. I am aware that many readers will already be well-versed, if not expert, in the Dark Ages, but

I hope to hold your attention through my telling, because with only subtle reinterpretation of the sources and significant topographical analysis, I will show you where and how a broader national context can be detected. I believe I have determined that Badon was fought at a much earlier date than most commentators suggest, at a time when the Roman Empire was still in existence and hopes for its future were at the highest point for fifty years. A return to an ordered Christian life was the goal, and overcoming the encroaching heathens was the only way to achieve this.

Roman Britain was never a settled territory, so it is as well to begin by sketching out all that happened following the Claudian invasion in AD 43. By the year 47, the Romans held the lands to the south of the Fosse Way. Control over Wales was initially delayed by Boudica's uprising in 60. Then the conquest continued further into Britain under the command of Agricola (77–84) who invaded north of the Forth estuary.

By the end of the first century, the Roman Empire had control of the lowlands as far north as southern Scotland and had subdued the hill tribes in Wales, though there was still trouble among the Brigantes of Yorkshire. Towns were being built across the south, with York, a military headquarters, the most northerly major site. It might well seem from this rate of progress that it would not have been long before the Romans would hold the whole island and be on their way to invading Ireland. But by 100, a serious setback seems to have occurred in the north because we know garrisons were withdrawn from there. When the frontier was re-established, it was by the building of Hadrian's stone wall, running from the Tyne to the Cumbrian coast (circa 122–128). Under Antonius Pius, the line moved north again, and a turf wall was built roughly along the earlier Forth–Clyde boundary, but before the end of the second century, the Antonine Wall, as it is now known, had been abandoned. Septimius Severus, in his expedition of 208–211, made the last effort to dominate the whole island. He failed, though his settlement in the north secured peace for a couple of generations.

The third century was a time of deep and violent change for the Empire in general, although Britain did not fare as badly as most other provinces. The Roman Empire was convulsed by barbarian invaders, rebellions and imperial pretenders, and there was a check to Britain's municipal life and its economic bases. Britain became a member of the so-called Gallic Empire (259–273), established by the rebel Postumus Aurelian who reunited the Empire, but soon afterwards, a usurper, from Britain, Bonosus, tried unsuccessfully to split the Empire, proclaiming himself Roman Emperor at Cologne. Probus defeated him and sent his own governor to Britain, who similarly revolted and, in consequence, was assassinated at the Emperor's orders. To help keep things under control, irregular troops consisting of Burgundians and Vandals were sent across the Channel. It is believed these troops stayed in Britain, presenting early evidence of Germanic settlement.

Later in the third century, the failing imperial power showed in the increasing attacks by pirates, Franks and Saxons, who filled the Channel. In 285, Diocletian sent his co-Emperor Maximian, to deal with the barbarians in revolt on the Rhine. Maximian built up the Channel fleet under the commander Carausius, who followed up his successes by declaring himself Emperor of Britain and North-West Gaul. His position was so strong that he had to be tolerated until 293 when the imperial forces, under Constantius Chlorus, took Boulogne. Soon afterwards, Carausius was murdered by his finance minister, Allectus, who was himself easily defeated by Constantius Chlorus.

Carausius had previously done much to start off Britain's coastal defence system that now emerged in strength, with great bastioned fortresses set from the Wash to the Isle of Wight along the coast known by the Romans as thc Saxon Shore. A similar but lighter defence system was also built for the west (for example, at Cardiff and Lancaster), because from about 275, the Irish had been raiding South and North Wales. These developments were typical of steps being taken throughout the Empire to construct massive defences all along threatened frontiers.

Diocletian had begun a general reorganisation of the government that was carried further by Constantine the Great who, after the death of his father Constantius Chlorus at York, set out from Britain and successfully staked his claim to the Empire. The provinces were now grouped in larger units, dioceses under *vicarii*, with separation of civilian and military powers. Britain was divided into four provinces, each under a *vicarius*, who in turn was under the praetorian prefect based at August Treverolum (Trier). To offset the emphasis on garrison defence, a mobile field army was built up. Out of this rearrangement came a Duke (*Dux*) of the Britons at York, and a Count (*Comes*) of the Saxon Shore. The Empire's capital was moved from Rome to Byzantium, and Christianity was adopted as the religious and ideological expression of the state in its new form.

The Emperors were clearly attempting to bring order to a society which had undergone drastic changes. The tenant farmer, *colonus*, was tied to the soil; government controls were extended over practically the whole of economic life which was gathered into corporations; bureaucracy grew in intricacy and power. A new class of landlords, *potentes*, emerged out of the civil wars of the previous century, drawing wealth from the tenants who gave their service in the form of labour and bore the main tax burden.

The cities in Britain, which had for the most part relied upon the wealth of the middle classes, known as *curiales* and *decurions*, began to decline. Municipal life was in a bad way. No longer the urban administrator class working in cooperation with the government, the *decurions* became a subjected class, forced to carry out imperial tax and expenditure policy under steadily more difficult conditions. This decline was multi-faceted, varied from region to region, and was often the result of local conditions such as raiding.

In about 306, there was trouble in northern Britain from the Picts, and from the fourth century, at least, the Irish Scotti were attacking from the Bristol Channel to the Clyde. In about 342 to 343, the Emperor Constans I was in the north fighting, eventually making a treaty with concessions that doubtless involved permitting Picts and Scots to settle inside the Roman area. He was murdered in 350 by Magnus Magnentius, a Briton or Teuton, who seized power and was hailed in Gaul, Spain, Britain and even Italy. In Britain, he was supported by the *vicarius*, Martinus. When Magnentius was defeated in 353, the new Emperor Constantius II sent an emissary, Paulus Catena (Paul 'the Chain'), who put down the usurper's British partisans with much cruelty.

The year 360 saw more incursions in the north, which were met by a field army under Lupicinus, the *magister militum* of Emperor Julian, although it is thought he was given the posting to keep him out of the way. He was arrested when he returned to Gaul a few months later. Then in 367 came an alliance between Picts, Scotti and Attacotti – an obscure folk who later provided crack troops for the Empire. Together, it appears, with the Saxons and Franks, they made a concerted attack called the Barbarian Conspiracy. The *Comes* of the coastal defences was killed, probably in Gaul. The *Dux* was immobilised, and the Wall fell through the treachery of scouts.

Count Theodosius was sent to restore order. The wall system had been wrecked, and so it was perhaps now that the method of using local tribes as federate allies was introduced: the Damnonians of Strathclyde and the Votadini of Lothian and Northumberland. Some inland forts, however, were still strongly held – Piercebridge and Malton, for example, with York as their centre, and Caernarvon in North Wales, near important copper deposits. The shore forts were still garrisoned, and signal stations were set up along the Yorkshire coast and elsewhere to warn of approaching raiders.

Under Valentinian I, the Alemannic tribe of the Buccinobantes, from near Metz, was settled in Britain as a frontier troop under their king, Fraomar, who became tribune, or commander. No doubt they were stationed in the north, but there is no trace of them in documents such as the *Notitia*.

In 378, the Empire suffered a great disaster at Adrianople in the east, when it was finally made clear that the old legions were of no avail against heavy mounted troops – the Goths, in this instance.

In Britain, 383 saw another secession. A Spaniard, Magnus Maximus, who had first visited Britain with Theodosius, had returned in 380, probably as a *Comes* or *Dux*. After defeating the Picts and Scots, he now led the main troops of the island over to Gaul, defeated the Emperor Gratian, and made himself Emperor of Britain, Gaul and Spain until he was killed in 388. The final imperial expedition to Britain was made by the Vandal general, Stilicho. The poet Claudian claims there were victories over Pict and Scot, and mentions the naval successes from 395 to 399. But while Stilicho was able to mount a punitive campaign, he lacked the resources to augment the British garrison, struggling even to maintain the status quo.

In the face of increasing danger to Rome from Alaric, the King of the Visigoths, Stilicho withdrew a legion, and in 402 defeated Alaric at Pollentia. Claudian's poem, *Gothic War*, leaves little doubt about Rome's increasing fears for its security:

> *First hurry the neighbouring troops, with loyalty proved by Raetia saved and Vindelicia's plunder. Next the legion left to guard remotest Britain that had checked the ferocious Scot and watched in wonder strange tattoo-marks on faces of dying Picts. Even the legions that faced the blond Sigambri or held the Chatti and wild Cherusci under, now turned this way their threatening arms and left the Rhine a sole defence; the fear of Rome.*

We are now on the verge of the decisive changes that turned Roman Britain into sub-Roman Britain, and already some points have come up that are important for our understanding of those changes. Firstly, the tendency towards secession, which, though undertaken in the name of usurpers to the imperial title, must have induced a growing sense of independence in Britain. Secondly, the increasing numbers of *foederati* and *laeti* (local militia) which put arms in the hands of Britons and gave their chieftains an increasing sense of power, both military and administrative. Thirdly, Christianity, which spread rapidly among the Britons and across the Empire. Major figures such as Constantine the Great, Ambrose and Magnus Maximus were fervently Christian. By the end of the century, Romano-Britons would have little in common with an Empire in turmoil, other than a shared belief in salvation. Dr John Morris drew attention to a tract known as *De Vita Christiana* dating to about AD 411 which may have been written in Britain by a bishop called Fastidius:

> *We see before us many instances of wicked men, the sum of their sins complete, who are being judged at this present moment, and denied this present life no less than the life to come... Those who have freely shed the blood of others are now being forced to shed their own... Some lie unburied, food for the beasts and birds of the air. Others have been individually torn limb from limb. Their judgements killed many husbands, widowed many women, orphaned many children, leaving them bare and beggared... for they plundered the property of the men they killed. But now it is their wives who are widowed, their sons who are orphans, begging their daily bread from strangers.*[2]

The Church's power, wealth and political influence were on the rise. The Kingdom of Heaven offered much more promise than the Roman Empire, and Christianity was providing a platform that enabled the opinions and creed of great men to be heard and considered. Martin, Pelagius, Patrick, Germanus and Gildas are just some of the names from this period. In our modern world of science and technology, we are somewhat removed from the cohesive power of religion. Fundamentalism is now seen as a pejorative noun, but

---

[2] John Morris. *The Age of Arthur: A History of the British Isles from 350 to 650* (London: Phoenix Giant/Orion, 1998), p 45.

in the fifth century, it was about to provide the Roman Britons with the necessary strength to face their barbarous pagan enemies and turn the tide of events.

IV

The enemies of Roman Britain, and the Barbarian Conspiracy

In recorded history, the Barbarian Conspiracy shines a spotlight on the plight of Roman Britain following an immense civil war among the Roman elite on the Continent. The incursions by Picts, and rebellions in Britain, brought Count Theodosius and two future Roman generals, both of whom later became Emperors and ultimately enemies, to the diocese. Order and defence were restored, but continuing civil and barbarian wars on the Continent emboldened Britain's enemies to intensify their raiding.

In 367, the formidable Emperor Valentinian received reports from Britain that a combined force of Picts, Attacotti and Scots had attacked and compromised the *Dux* Fullofaudes. The tribes had crossed the frontier in force and were ravaging the countryside. At the same time, Saxons and Franks were harrying the coast of Gaul, and the death of the *Comes* Nectaridus was reported. This combination of attacks had not been anticipated by the Romans and was a huge blow to imperial prestige. Professor Salway analyses the leadership that the plan, known as the Barbarian Conspiracy, must have required:

> *... the events of 367 imply at least one very capable and well-informed military mind on the barbarian side. But they imply more: a leader with the personal reputation and persuasiveness to weld such disparate peoples into a league to take*

common action, if only for an operation, and perhaps even more remarkable to keep the news of such a plan secret from the Romans.[3]

It is not known who this coordinator was or whether the attacks achieved his objectives. Professor D. P. Kirby, in his book *The Earliest English Kings*, notes the efficient military organisation of the Germanic barbarian tribes of the Alemanni:

Ammianus Marcellinus records how in the year 357 the Alemanni on the continent were led into battle by ten petty kings, under the command of five kings, under the direction of two commanders. So structured a hierarchy will surely not have been without parallels during the complexities of a transmaritime military operation in Britain.[4]

Certainly, the barbarians, thanks to the shock of the attacks, were able to plunder the countryside on a grand scale. But was there more behind this coordinated attack? We shall recount and interpret what the Romans discovered about the Barbarian Conspiracy after clarifying the people and tribes involved.

Military expansion by the Romans arguably led to the disparate peoples beyond the borders responding with a form of tribal militarism. Each chieftain would have a retinue of elite warriors rewarded with honour, feasting and moveable wealth – usually obtained by raiding the Roman Empire. Tribes formed into confederacies at first

[3] Peter Salway, *Roman Britain* (London: Book Club Associates/Oxford University Press, 1982), p 376.

[4] D. P. Kirby, *The Earliest English Kings* (London: Routledge, 1994), p 16.

to resist Roman expansion, then in time, these confederacies formed into kingdoms. By the fourth century, land-based military expansion by the Romans had turned into a defence of those lands already taken, using mobile troops based in military installations, while naval defence and response had proved to only have limited capability against the constant piracy and seaborne raids.

Barbarian kingdoms were beginning to see and exploit Roman weaknesses, and the Empire's mounting dependence upon barbarian troops and officers, while helping to avoid casualties in civil wars, had inadvertently introduced problems with external security. Professor Salway explains this as follows:

> *In the west, inside the empire Germans were already appearing as generals in the Roman armies on equal terms with Romans. The day was not far off when they would hold certain of the great offices of the Roman state. Their position could indeed be equivocal: in the next century such figures as Theodoric could at one time hold high rank under the Empire, at another be carving out vast kingdoms to be dominated by their barbarian followers.*[5]

So, who were the barbarian enemies of Roman Britain?

The Picts

The Picts' origin, language and society remain a topic of fierce debate in Scottish history. Their name is first mentioned in a late third-century poem, and *picti* is taken to mean 'painted ones'. When Tacitus describes Agricola's

---

[5] Salway, *Roman Britain*, p 376.

campaign in the late first century AD, he refers to a confederacy of tribes collectively named the Caledonians who were heavily defeated at Mons Graupius. Thought to inhabit the north and east Highlands, the Picts spoke, it is believed, a form of Brittonic Celtic. As fierce and organised enemies of the Romans, they commanded respect to such an extent that Hadrian's Wall and the Antonine Wall were constructed, and in the later Dark Ages, their society continued to develop along militarist lines. Their culture has produced intriguing carvings with unique Pictish symbols which are not yet fully understood.

The Scotti

Scotti is the Latin name for Gaels. First attested in the third century, it referred to the people of both Northern Ireland and north-west Britain, who were judged as presenting an increasing threat to the Roman Empire. Later, the name Scotti came to refer to those people speaking Gaelic in northern Britain only, hence Scotland. Their kingdom was known as Dal Riada. The hillfort of Dunadd is thought to have been their capital. Their reputation as seafaring raiders intensified in the fourth and fifth centuries, and they likely played a pivotal role in the Barbarian Conspiracy.

The Attacotti

The reference to the Attacotti by Ammianus is interesting. Dr John Morris states that the name is British (or even Pictish) for 'very old people'. He adds that St. Columba met on old man who came to Skye and spoke a tongue neither Irish nor Pictish.[6] It is fascinating to muse on the possibility this tribe may have been the surviving aborigines who built the brochs and duns.

Following the Barbarian Conspiracy, it appears that the Attacotti were conscripted into the Roman army and the *Notitia* places one unit in the Diocese of Illyricum, attested to by a contemporary funerary dedication to a soldier of the 'unit of Atecutti'. St. Jerome, in his treatise *Against Jovinianus*, says that he was told the Attacotti ate human flesh.

There are various proposed homelands for the Attacotti. Some say Ireland, but I believe they must have been squeezed in between the Scots and the Picts. In the 1990s, my wife Debbie and I spent some time walking the Scottish Munros (mountains over 3,000 feet). One of our most thrilling experiences (although Debbie does not remember this quite so fondly) was getting caught in a serious blizzard halfway along the ridge of the Five Sisters of Kintail. Forced to turn around, darkness fell, and we just made it off the mountain before the Kintail Mountain Rescue set off to find us. This is a remote and beautiful part of the Highlands. Connected by Loch Duich to the sea (and to Skye), Kintail is a region with much folklore. There are brochs thereabouts and paths worn into rock which are thousands of years old. Place names such as Attadale with the Attadale River in the Attadale Forest may well preserve a memory of the Attacotti. Ben Attow (3,385 feet) overlooks this entire area, which incidentally encompasses

[6] Morris, *The Age of Arthur*, p 190.

the Falls of Glomach, the most magnificent (and highest) waterfall in the British Isles.

More recently, in 2021, I was exploring the Borders of Scotland and came across a magnificent fortification known as Edin's Hall Broch. This is the best preserved of three brochs, all built after the initial occupation by Rome in the region of Trimontium, otherwise known as Newsteads near Melrose. There are about 570 broch sites in Scotland, almost all of which are in the far north and built at least fifty years before the Roman occupation. The origin of these Borders brochs is a mystery, and since no frontier existed in this region, we may assume that the Romans knew the occupants. I have wondered if the Attacotti were army recruits or *foederati* long before the Barbarian Conspiracy and that these fortifications could have been the strongholds of their tribal leaders. The tribe might even have been the *Areani*, the name of the scouts known to have betrayed the Empire. It would be a mistake to look north from Hadrian's Wall and assume that the region beyond was wild and completely untamed by Rome. We know that Roman roads penetrated far to the north, and Romanisation was attempted even beyond the Antonine Wall. Most importantly, this was a huge military zone where the army's equipment and techniques were on full display and tribal allies were sought and trained.

The Franks

The original Franks are generally accepted as the tribes living on the lower and middle Rhine. The name only appeared in the third century and is first associated with raids into Roman territory. However, the tribes were long associated with the Empire. In 288, Maximian defeated the

Franks and moved them into Germanica Inferior (Lower Germany). In 292, Constantius is recorded as defeating the Franks who had settled at the mouth of the Rhine. It is likely that the name 'Franks' was extended to include coastal Frisians. The Franks were sometimes allies and sometimes enemies of Rome. The Salian Franks were first mentioned by Ammianus who described their defeat by Julian in 358. They were allowed to remain in Texnandria (Antwerp region) as *foederati*. The *Notitia* lists their soldiers as *Salii.* Some decades later, they controlled the River Scheldt as pirates and disrupted supplies to Britain. The Salian Franks are generally seen as the predecessors of the Franks who pushed south-west into what is now modern France.

The Saxons

In the context of the Barbarian Conspiracy, the Saxons raiding Gaul and possibly Britain were seafaring tribes from north-west Europe. Their ethnicity is unclear, and although settlements between the rivers Wesser and Elba, bounded by Bremerhaven, Bremen and Hamburg, have been identified as Saxon, I doubt the origin of these North Sea raiders can be so specific.

Their reputation as sea pirates was so profound that it prompted the Romans to create a military zone called the *Litus Saxonicum* (the Saxon Shore) and was most probably the impetus behind the creation of the Saxon Shore forts and defences started during the usurpation by Carausius. Joint Saxon and Frankish raids were frequent, and one wonders whether the Romans were able to determine which tribe was mounting an attack at any one time. Angles, Jutes, Saxons, Frisians and Franks were all remarkably similar and their territories were not yet nation states. I believe use of the word *Saxone* by the Romans was all-embracing for German seafaring raiders and pirates, very much like the term Vikings came to describe all Nordic raiders. It is interesting to note that the Finnish word *Saksa*, which is a derivative of *Saxon*, refers to all Germans.

We will come back to the Saxons in detail, particularly with respect to the complex problem of the Anglo-Saxon migration.

The Barbarian Conspiracy

Whether or not the intense raids by the Saxons and Franks on Gaul were part of the Barbarian Conspiracy in Britain, or just a coincidence, remains a mystery, but the Romans seemed to consider it a combined threat. After some initial manoeuvring and intelligence-gathering, Severus, the *Comes Domesticorum*, was sent to the coast of Gaul with a small force. He was recalled, and Jovinus, the *magister militum*, was sent in his stead, probably to engage the Saxons and Franks. Jovinus wrote to Valentinian requesting reinforcements, whereupon Jovinus was also recalled, probably to continue his part in a campaign along the Rhine which had much higher priority.

In the end, the Saxon threat became so serious the Emperor decided upon a task force as the solution. He selected four first-class units from the field army (the Batvia, Heruli, Jovii and Victores) and placed one of his most capable generals, Theodosius, in command.

It seems likely that the war to defend the *Limes Germanicus* (German frontier) was the root of the Barbarian Conspiracy. In 365, the Alemanni had crossed the Rhine, and the two Roman generals sent to engage them were defeated and killed. Valentinian was distracted from responding with his planned punitive campaign because of the barbarian attacks in Gaul. The general Jovinus was proving effective at recovering ground against the Alemanni, and Valentinian had spent the entire winter of 367 gathering a massive army for this campaign. Macrian, King of the Bucinobantes, tried to confederate all the north German and Alemannic tribes against Rome and may have instigated the raids by the Saxons and Franks which at least delayed Valentinian's campaign.

Theodosius landed at Richborough and waited while his force assembled. He advanced to London, eliminating bands of barbarians on the way, and his unexpected arrival was met with much rejoicing. He immediately restored the army, pardoned deserters and arranged for an official named Civillis to take over as *vicarius.* He had brought the able General Dulcitius to take over as *Dux* and was accompanied by future generals, his nephew Magnus Maximus and his son Theodosius. These operations included naval warfare against the Saxons, helping to relieve some pressure on Gaul. By 369, Theodosius had, according to Ammianus, restored cities and forts. A substantial programme of re-equipping and remanning was underway.

There had been much treachery in the north, and it appears that the *Areani* (or possibly *Arcani*, meaning 'secret ones'), a *foederati* army unit whose duty was intelligence-gathering and communication for the Romans, had misled and betrayed the *Dux*, Fullafaudes. There had followed coordinated attacks by barbarians by land and sea on both the east and west coasts. Once the

Roman forces had retreated, deserted or been defeated, the barbarians had broken up into raiding parties seeking the booty they had been promised. The speed with which Theodosius moved is likely to have been the key to his successful out-manoeuvring of so many of these bands of brigands.

However, it was clear the defence strategy in the region needed to change. Estuaries were a weakness and required not just naval defence but also land-based forts. The new base at Bitterne, on the Itchen by Southampton Water, may be evidence of this change in policy, along with the implementation of the coastal warning systems on the Yorkshire coast from Filey to Huntcliff, possibly coordinated from Malton.

Assessing what naval solutions were enacted is difficult. The threat of sea raids was a constant thorn in the Western Empire's side, but defending against a campaign on the scale of the Barbarian Conspiracy was never in the planning, despite the mounting threat from increasing raids. The Theodosian programme recognised this flaw and sought not only to anticipate such future events but also strengthen the ability of towns and cities to resist roaming raiding parties. A rigorous reorganisation of the army was therefore undertaken.

The *Areani* were abolished, and Hadrian's Wall appears to have been repaired and regarrisoned. The army in Britain had been suffering from low morale for a decade following the retribution wrought by Paul 'the Chain' upon the demise of Magnetius, added to which, senior officers had been unable to cope with continued barbarian incursions. Valentinian, an able commander, was concentrating his efforts on the Rhine region from Trier, and although he was acutely aware of the position in Britain, he had not addressed the problem soon enough.

Theodosius encountered more problems than just barbarians and brigands, however. A number of Roman exiles, in particular a certain Pannonian named Valentinus, had attempted to gather a substantial party in Britain and persuade some army commanders and their troops to mutiny. Theodosius crushed this conspiracy, and Valentinus was executed, although the recriminations were purposefully limited to the chief perpetrators so as not to further damage morale. Whether Valentinus was an arch-perpetrator or just part of the general chaos is difficult to establish. It rather looks as if his rebellion was a reaction to the barbarian attacks.

Following the restoration of order, Theodosius declared that a fifth province had been 'recovered', which he named Valentia. Theodosius' military planning would have demanded more robust effort in the north, and therefore, Valentia would have been a territory north of Hadrian's Wall administered from Carlisle. I hesitate to say how much territory, but it likely included the Strathclyde Britons and the Borders region. This new province allowed for a different sort of troop deployment. The Wall was still important, but Valentia was to be the buffer zone, a plan which would chime with Valentinian's own policy on the Continent of pushing beyond the Rhine frontier and building forts. This development led to the establishment of more effective native frontier troops led by their tribal leaders, so laying the foundations for the likes of Coel Hen.

Their work complete, Count Theodosius, Maximus and Theodosius left Britain in 370, and evidence would seem to show, they were campaigning against the Alemanni in 371, in Illycrium in 372 and Mauretania in 373. In 375, Valentinian died, and Gratian, his son, became Emperor in the west. At this time, Count Theodosius was in Africa, whereas Magnus Maximus was campaigning near the Danube. Theodosius, by now *magister militum*, was arrested, taken to Carthage and executed. His son was sent home to the family estate in Spain. No reasons are known, but we may speculate that he posed a threat to the new regime or that a plot was discovered to which Theodosius the Younger and Magnus Maximus may well have been privy. The next time we hear about Magnus Maximus, he is back in Britain in 381 campaigning against the Picts and Scotti. Theodosius the Younger, however, was recalled in 378 by Gratian following the defeat of his uncle Valens by the Goths at the Battle of Adrianople. He was first appointed *magister militum*, and then, in 379, following military success, Theodosius was appointed Gratian's joint Augustus in the east. The Emperor's choice was remarkable. The entire Roman Empire was being run by a twenty-year-old in the west and a thirty-two-year-old in the east.

Whether Maximus or Theodosius blamed Gratian for the fate of Theodosius the Elder is not known, but I suspect they both did. However, single-minded pragmatism saw Theodosius the Younger become the central figure in Roman history for the rest of the century, whereas the hubris of Maximus led him to take some radical steps.

V

Magnus Maximus and his arrangements for the defence of Britain

Maximus returned to Britain to campaign against the Picts but turned the posting into a launch pad for an expedition to the Continent in which he successfully usurped the throne of the Western Empire. To achieve his objectives, he first reorganised the defence of Britain by devolving military authority to key British dynasties. The earliest Brittonic genealogies give Maximus the role of founding father for dynasties including those of Powys, Gwent and Galloway. The leadership of this devolved military authority appears to have been granted to Vitalinus in the south-west and Coel Hen in the north. The descendants of these men went on to dominate Britain's defence for at least a century.

The period commencing with the Barbarian Conspiracy in 367 through to the defeat and execution of Constantine III in 411 probably shaped the future of the British Isles more than any other prior to 1066. The selfish and ruthless actions of a series of usurpers wrought mighty consequences on Roman Britain and its close neighbours, eventually culminating in the expulsion of the Roman officials – an action which spread to Armorica (Brittany) and Gaul, and effectively signalled the end of Roman Britain.

The first of these usurpers was a general called Flavius Magnus Maximus Augustus. He was born in Gallaecia, on the estates of Count Theodosius to whom it is claimed he was related. No single Roman had as great an impact on

British and Armorican history and folklore as Maximus, and his Welsh name, Maxen Wledig, featured in Welsh poetry for many centuries. He may have returned to Britain as early as 378, and it was likely he was already planning his usurpation of the Emperor. Maximus' ultimate success as a usurper can be attributed to three elements. Firstly, careful planning – he was, after all, a senior Roman general and, doubtless, a brave soldier. Most, if not all, of his decisions hereafter were taken with his usurpation campaign in view. Secondly, resources – it is difficult to estimate the extent to which he depleted the army in Britain. Professor Frere summarises:

> *His expedition involved the evacuation of many of the forts still held in Britain; the garrisons concerned were apparently those of the western Pennines and North Wales and included Legio XX from Chester. These positions were never re-occupied. He is often credited with the final evacuation of Hadrian's Wall, but this view can no longer be maintained... The troops which Maximus took with him were no doubt rewarded with promotion into the field-army; and, indeed, the Notitia preserves a record of the Seguntienses – apparently the former garrison of Segontium (Caernarvon) – among the auxilia palatina in Illyricum. If they were thus raised in grade, it is unlikely that their return to Britian was envisaged; and there arises the question what arrangements*

were made by Maximus to fill the vacuum caused by their departure.[7]

Thirdly, authority – the Theodosian reorganisation had removed any doubts about Rome's intentions and capabilities. The army was once again well-resourced, and Maximus arrived back in Britain with his reputation intact. Furthermore, he had no need to curry favour with the magnates – this was an army matter and the Christian Empire was in peril. It therefore comes as no surprise that he managed to impress his Roman colleagues and the British tribal leaders. He is long remembered as a hero in Celtic poetry, folk memory and tradition. Gildas even recounts that Maximus was accompanied to Gaul by a large number of British volunteers, many of whom never returned and are said to have settled in Armorica.

Maximus appears to have positioned his headquarters at Segontium (Caernarvon). This was an interesting choice. I have stood on the quayside of the River Seiont and looked out towards Anglesey and was in no doubt that the Menai Strait would have provided a safe and easily defended haven. There was a naval base at Holyhead and the network of connections provided by the Irish Sea is extensive, not just for military purposes but also for domestic and international trade. Mynyad Parys (Parys Mountain) in north-east Anglesey has been constantly mined for copper from about 4000 BC through to the present day – an example of a Roman copper cake from here can be seen at the British Museum. This trade will have been ongoing and required protection. The Romans,

[7] Sheppard Frere, *Britannia: A History of Roman Britain* (London: Book Club Associates/Routledge and Kegan Paul Limited, 1973), p 361.

throughout their occupation, had exploited the mineral resources of Britain – as we will note with lead mining in the Pennines later. In fact, the whole of Wales was susceptible to raids from Irish Scotti and required naval and military protection. Moreover, coastal communication with troops at Chester and Carlisle could be easily maintained from Maximus' base in North Wales. Maritime communication will also have been important for the northern tribes and militia that were stepping up to defend the frontier.

According to legend, Maximus even seems to have found time to marry into a notable British family – quite which one is difficult to say. In the Welsh poem *The Dream of Maxen Wledig*, which is found in the thirteenth-century collection of Welsh Triads known as the *Mabinogion*, the wife of Maximus, named as Helen or Elen, is the daughter of a chieftain who is given sovereignty over Britain. This rather suggests the family of Vitalinus, grandfather of Vortigern. However, I doubt his romantic pursuits genuinely influenced his choice of Caernarvon as a headquarters, despite what we read in this ancient poem.

Despite the bardic tradition suggesting Maximus was considered a hero by the Welsh, in truth, he was a ruthless Roman who was just there to take advantage of valuable resources. The location he chose for his headquarters was likely more to do with boosting his planned secession than any romantic or heroic notions. The prying eyes of the Empire's spies would certainly have experienced difficulty watching and interpreting the comings and goings in Caernarvon.

Before I summarise my understanding of Maximus' arrangements for the usurpation, I shall first explain a dating template that will help provide a framework upon which many of my assumptions rely.

For some time, I have been convinced that the conventional history of the fifth century has been manipulated to accommodate legends. I am not the first to suggest a revised reckoning of the key fifth-century dates. Indeed, it is common for many authors to push the date of Gildas' *De Excidio* as far back as possible to the 540s. This is usually to accommodate the notion of King Arthur battling Saxons in the south-west. As I noted earlier, Gildas mentions the Battle of Mount Badon, which is variously dated between 493 and 516. This book challenges this assumption, preferring circa 512 for Gildas and circa 469 for Badon – a full generation earlier. In the Introduction, there is a table of dates that approximate key events with key leaders and support the assumptions in this book. I hope it helps readers to understand the pattern of events and unscramble some of the obscure chronology.

The Northern Frontier

About this time, military control of the entire north seems to have been in the hands of Coel Hen (Coel the Old). North of Hadrian's Wall (perhaps in Valentia), there appears to have been treaties with the Strathclyde Britons, and the Votadini/Gododdin. South of the Wall, which was still garrisoned, Coel Hen's role appears to have mirrored that of the *Dux Britanniarum*, which the *Notitia* indicates was still extant. This commander really was the Old King Cole of nursery rhyme, and as the *Descent of the Men of the North* indicates, his descendants and successors dominated northern Britain for a further century. The threat of the Irish, Scotti, Picts and Saxons had unified the north into a formidable frontier. The Picts would never again find it easy to invade by land with the Wall garrisoned, although their naval threat continued to grow and their sea raids intensified.

The appointment of Coel Hen likely occurred after the Theodosius reorganisation, or perhaps upon the return of Maximus. History does not specifically record this, but later legends and traditions accord him the title *Guotepauc*, meaning ‘Protector’. He was most probably an existing tribal leader with extensive Roman military experience who was already a trusted figure. The authority conferred upon both Coel Hen and his south-western counterpart, Vitalinus, by Maximus was a progressive attempt to reduce the extent of the Roman troops required to protect and control Britain.

Gildas makes no reference to Coel Hen but records three Pictish wars around this time, indicating an embattled frontier. It is important to note that Gildas' knowledge of northern matters was poor. *De Excidio* describes how, after Maximus took away all the military forces and a vast quantity of the youth of the country, the frontier was defenceless. The helpless Britons appealed to the Romans, and they sent a legion which expelled the raiders. According to Gildas, the Britons then built a wall of turf, but the raiders broke through again. Once again, the Romans expelled the raiders, but this time helped to construct a stone wall which was again attacked by raiders using hooked weapons to pull defenders down from the wall. Gildas also claims the Roman occupation, about which he is extremely vague, ended with Maximus. He makes little distinction between Scots and Picts, both of which he believed to be *gentes transmarine*, that is ‘people beyond the sea'. This imprecision smacks of hearsay, and contrasts markedly with his detailed knowledge of events in other places, Wales in particular.

Prior to these events, Coel Hen was clearly privy to Maximus' plan as they must both have agreed upon the relocation of the warrior chieftain, Cunedda, from Manaw Gododdin (Lothian region) to North Wales to counter the Irish raiders who would certainly return once Maximus departed. These decisions followed the successful Maximus campaign against the Picts, so he may well have fought alongside both Cunedda and Coel Hen.

The genealogies show that Cunedda was married to Coel's daughter Gwawl, and both Coel's and Cunedda's ancestors appear to have had Roman ties, titles or descriptions. But my chief purpose here is not to establish their pedigree, rather it is to give Cunedda's historicity a second chance, because many historians discount the significance of this event, and I'm not sure why.

The manipulation of barbarians as *foederati* was becoming commonplace across Europe. Maximus made the decision to relocate Cunedda's tribe with the full authority of the Empire, and the movement of these people was across territory under the control of Coel Hen who, it seems, may also have retained overall military control of North Wales.

The *Historia Brittonum* states:

> *Maelgwn the Great King ruled the British in Gwynedd, for his ancestor (*atavus*) Cunedda, with his eight sons, had come from the North, from the country called Manaw Gododdin, 146 years before Maelgwn reigned and expelled the Irish from these*

countries with immense slaughter, so that they never again returned to inhabit them.

This statement is perhaps accurate in its dating but not its hindsight. King Maelgwn is known to have ruled at least Gwynedd and was a contemporary chided by Gildas. If we count146 years from 380, it takes us to 526 which is towards the end of Maelgwn's reign and, therefore, does not undermine my proposed date for Gildas, who was clearly writing about his early period. However, the Irish Scotti returned time and again, even settling on the Llŷn Peninsula. Another Irish tribe, the Deisi, were similarly settling in South Wales in the late fourth century. Although, perhaps, weighed against the problems in the east, this could be counted as a success, and may even have occurred by arrangement – after all, settlers are better than raiders. Vortipor, a Welsh king, a contemporary of Maelgwn, was a descendant of the Deisi and appears to have also held an honorific title of Protector.

There is a missing generation in Cunedda's family tree, but nearly everything else fits, and there is no reason to suspect this positioning of *foederati* was invented. The tradition itself implies a Roman decision. Maximus was clearly covering his imminent departure, and it is highly unlikely that any later leader would have either the authority or even an interest to deploy northern Gododdin to this region. So, welcome back to the fourth century Cunedda!

The Army

It is extremely important for anyone seeking to understand the Roman world that they should be clear about the power, authority and ruthlessness of the Roman army and its commanders. The men in charge had literally fought their way to the top, and their self-assurance, pride and arrogance went far beyond anything we might encounter from leaders today. Such men could inspire blind loyalty, and a soldier never questioned their duty. The army could make or break Emperors and was capable of genocide with impunity whenever and wherever it was required.

Let us attempt to put the size of the Roman army in Britain into context. Overall, the general population of Britain was probably never more than two million (London 30,000), whereas the inhabitants of the City of Rome alone numbered one million. Here I quote from Robin Fleming in *Britain after Rome: The Fall and Rise, 400–1070:*

> *The army stationed in northern Britain was very large, more than 40,000 men at its height, or about an eighth of the imperial army. This level of garrisoning required the expenditure of something on the order of a sixteenth of the total imperial budget each year, although Britain itself was only one of forty Roman provinces. An army of this size required not only immense outlays of state funding, but constant provisioning with a wide range of goods – food (in particular grain), clothing, arms, transport animals, building materials – some supplied by local communities, but much brought from further afield. During the height of the principate, the army contracted supply agents and transporters from provinces across the Channel to provision it with much of the food and matériel it*

needed. These commodities, as well as goods for indigenous British markets, followed inland waterways across Gaul to the Rhine and then on into Britain.[8]

Add to this the 20,000 or so officials required to support all this, and we start to see that the army was the economy. In consequence, sweeping decisions by army commanders had immense impact.

Professor Salway mentions how, following 367 and the restoration by Theodosius, a decision was made to switch northern military pottery orders to a supplier in Malton, so-called 'Crambeck Ware'. The former supplies had come from Dorset, and the switch demonstrates how military decisions could so easily affect regional economies. Salway summarises as follows:

It is not known whether the war had largely destroyed the former main factories or whether costs were now being cut by reducing transport distances. It may indeed be that long distance transport, especially by sea, was now much more risky, or that opportunity was taken to change an arrangement that had gone unchallenged for nearly three centuries, though there were now much more convenient sources of supply.[9]

I draw attention to the scale and consequence of military policy decisions for two reasons.

---

8 Robin Flemming, *Britain after Rome: The Fall and Rise 400 to 1070* (London: Penguin, 2011), p 99.

9 Salway, *Roman Britain*, p 645.

Firstly, it is clear that there was a considerable amount of cross-Channel, coastal and inland waterway activity. This must have brought a substantial number of continental sailors to Britain and vice versa. The Tyne, Tees, Humber, Wash, Crouch, Thames and Medway estuaries in particular will have maintained contacts with the Franks, Frisians and Saxons. I have read a suggestion that the so-called 'Saxon Shore' was named for the presence of all these people, and I can see much justification for this. It is highly likely, therefore, that German settlers might be found all around these estuaries and inland waterways from an early date and were probably sailors settling there after finding British wives.

Secondly, the Humber estuary, River Trent and Lincoln areas were critical for the army. Lindum Colonia, at the top of the Fosse Way, was first a legionary fortress before it became a place of settlement for retiring soldiers. York then took over as the principal legionary fortress in the north. The Humber estuary was therefore crucial to trade and to the army on both shores. There were many German auxiliaries in the Roman army in the fourth century who perhaps felt it suited them to take their retirement citizenship in or around Lincoln. Ammianus mentions that, in 372, Fraomar, a deposed king of the Alemanni, was transferred to Britain as a military tribune to command a Roman unit of Alemanni already stationed there. Clearly, there was an increasing number of Germans, Saxons and Frisians as yet culturally and ethnically ambiguous who were settling in Britain, in this region in particular but also around the estuaries.

The failure of the army following the shock of the Barbarian Conspiracy led to unparalleled reorganisation.

In his book, *Worlds of Arthur: Facts and Fictions of the Dark Ages*, Guy Halsall studies Gildas and re-evaluates the purpose and structure of *De Excidio*. He arrives at a possible reinterpretation that the *tyranius superbus* (proud tyrant) mentioned by Gildas is not the legendary figure from the 430s named as Vortigern by Nennius but actually Magnus Maximus. Gildas blames the 'proud tyrant' for introducing the 'hated ones', by which he meant the Saxons. This is an important revision, but Professor Halsall does not attempt to interpret how, where or when this occurred because, as you might expect, he steers well clear of guesswork and legend.

It seems to me that either Theodosius the Elder or Magnus Maximus (or both) identified the vulnerability of South Humberside and engaged an Angle seafaring tribe as land-based and seaborne *foederati*. This tribe's descendants became the kings of Lindsey. I suggest that these amphibious *foederati* were brought under the control of the Count of the Saxon Shore. Their role was to defend the Humber and the passages south, and to assist with troop movements. Their subsequent involvement in the Saxon rebellion of the 440s is uncertain, since the Angles are not recorded anywhere as raiders. But it is clear that, despite the apparent success of the Theodosian campaign, Pict and Saxon raiders were emboldened at this time. Barbarian intelligence regarding the Britons had never been better and their campaigns, based on stealth, sought to take advantage of the weaknesses in the Briton's defences.

It is interesting to note that the Picts and Saxons were recorded as a simultaneous threat and might even have been working together, perhaps following their joint success in the Barbarian Conspiracy? However, it is more likely that the raiders acted independently.

Britain's profusion of estuaries and creeks must have been impossible to patrol. With all this in mind, the Roman defence strategy becomes clear. Through signal stations down both the north-west and north-east coasts and fleet detachments at Holyhead and perhaps Scarborough or Bridlington in Yorkshire, it was possible to measure, counter and engage an approaching threat. North of the Humber, a military response to an incursion could be coordinated from Malton. However, south of the Humber, where a variety of routes would allow raiding parties to penetrate as far inland as the Midlands, the risks multiplied.

It was clear to the Romans that naval defence was becoming essential, given Britain's coastal exposure. In the fifth century, naval warfare intensified everywhere, particularly in the Mediterranean. A conflict of interest must surely have developed with respect to the planned usurpation by Maximus, since a fleet would certainly have been required not only to transport the army to the Continent but also to support the land-based campaigns. The army never returned, and perhaps the Roman fleet suffered a similar fate.

An understanding of what arrangements Maximus left in place is crucial in establishing the political landscape that generated the Briton military commanders who fought in the Saxon uprising and the battles that led up to Mount Badon. We might expect that Theodosius' reorganisation was intended to conform to the *Notitia*. Indeed, this may well have been the plan for proposed troop deployments. However, both Theodosius and Maximus were capable, progressive army commanders and doubtless considered all options after the Barbarian Conspiracy, including the employment of *laeti*, *foederati*, and *limitanei*. Then, when Maximus returned with his mind set on usurpation, he made changes that suited his plans. He was already familiar with the regions and their chieftains, and although this is impossible to establish, his British wife may well have influenced and helped him.

Constantine the Great had completed the separation of provincial military and civil offices, and these arrangements appear to have continued. Britain was split into five provinces, and new military arrangements were in force. It is likely that the civil administration was required to similarly adapt but within the pre-existing structure. A comprehensive analysis of the *Notitia* may one day help us understand this period better, although the rapidly changing fortunes of the Roman Empire must have undermined the relevance of the information to such an extent that it was almost immediately anachronistic. The *Notitia* certainly could not have foreseen the secession of Maximus. Nonetheless, all the evidence suggests the continuity of civil administration into the early fifth century, and a *vicarius* was still in office in 406.

When Maximus departed for Gaul in 383, the diocese of Britain appears to have been left as follows:

The North – Britannia Secunda and Valentia

These provinces were under the control of the *Dux*, most probably Coel Hen, with regular troops based at York and Malton. The Wall had been regarrisoned, probably by *limitanei* who were possibly supported by some *foederati* and local levies. The appointment of a trusted Briton as

Dux was progressive, and his influence with the regions to the north would have been an important factor. I have often wondered if the reason for the creation of the fifth province, Valentia, was to provide Coel Hen with an administrative base from which to make arrangements and treaties with such regions. York was some distance, had its own priorities, and had failed to deal with the Barbarian Conspiracy. Perhaps the *Areani* had been associated with York and trust was not yet restored. Most of this arrangement was likely the work of Theodosius, but it is interesting to note the subsequent cooperation between Coel Hen and Maximus with respect to Cunedda and the abandonment of some Pennine forts which the Romans had garrisoned to control the Brigantes. It would appear Coel Hen had this tribe's respect.

The West – Britannia Prima

This huge area encompassed every region west of a line running from the Mersey to Poole in Dorset but excluding Devon and Cornwall (Dumnonia). This province included Chester, Wroxeter, Gloucester, Cirencester, Bath and all of Wales. It appears to be the region where Maximus' changes had the greatest impact.

Gwynedd may have been annexed to the authority of Coel Hen for military reasons. Certainly, good relations were apparently maintained between Gwynedd and the Pennine regions throughout the fifth century. The rest of the province most probably became the responsibility of another trusted Britain named Vitalinus of Gloucester, grandfather to Vortigern. He became, without doubt, the most important Briton in the west. His responsibilities must have extended to not only relationships with Welsh chieftains but also to Dumnonia. Much like Coel Hen, he probably had a foot in both camps, and perhaps his ancestors were chieftains of the Dobunni. It is impossible to know if he held an army position, but we may surmise it likely. About this time, an additional command known as the *Comes Britanniarum* was established. It was a mobile force consisting of six cavalry and three infantry units which was designed to support frontier troops in fending off the increasing number of barbarian raids. This unit would have proved ideal for the defence of this province with its long coastline and difficult terrain.

The East – Flavia Caesariensis

This province consisted of Lincolnshire, Derbyshire, Nottinghamshire, Leicestershire, Warwickshire, Norfolk and Suffolk with Lindum Colonia as its provincial capital. The region, as noted earlier, was likely subject to ongoing settlement but was also most susceptible to barbarian raiding. There are indications that Anglian *foederati* were engaged to defend the Humber and routes south. This remit may have been extended later to include the Wash. The area was otherwise under the control of the Count of the Saxon Shore.

The South – Maxima Caesariensis

This province included Londinium as the diocesan capital, the location of the headquarters of the *vicarius*. The coastal region ran from Harwich around to Poole and consisted of the Home Counties, Sussex, Hampshire and Oxfordshire. This area was similarly susceptible to barbarian raids and was home to many of the Roman magnates and landlords with conspicuous wealth. The region was the military responsibility of the Count of the Saxon Shore.

While the above regional analysis is largely supposition, it provides a basis of understanding for the events that unfolded later in the fifth century. In particular, it demonstrates the extent to which military authority was devolved. It is not surprising that Welsh dynasties reference Maximus as their founder and, in part, explains why the legends arose. The initial success of Maximus' usurpation campaign, following an apparently successful campaign against the Picts and Saxons in 381, is considered a high point in British morale and self-confidence. It would be three generations before the Britons had reason to feel this way again.

Significant Empire-wide events

378 Goths defeat Emperor Valens at the Battle of Adrianople

383–388 Magnus Maximus, Emperor. He was initially accepted by Theodosius I and elevated his son Flavius Victor to Co-Augustus in 384. Maximus was defeated at the Battle of Save, captured and executed in Aquileia. His son was murdered in Trier by the Frankish general Arbogast.

375–392 Valentian II, Western Roman Emperor.

391 Theodosius I bans paganism, making all sacrifices illegal and closing all temples.

392 Arbogast murders Valentian II.

394 Eugenius (with his general Arbogast) defeated at the Battle of Frigidus by Theodosius. Eugenius was executed. Arbogast committed suicide.

393–423 Honorius, Western Roman Emperor.

395 Death of Theodosius I. Arcadius, Eastern Roman Emperor.

402 Stilicho defeats Alaric who withdraws from Italy.

405 Stilicho defeats Ostrogothic army at Fiesole near Florence.

406 Suebi, Vandals and Alans cross the Rhine.

406 Marcus elevated to Augustus by the army of Britain, murdered by the army.

407 Gratian elevated to Augustus by the army of Britain. Deposed and murdered after four months.

408 Death of Arcadius. Theodosius II, Eastern Roman Emperor (aged 7)

409 Stilicho arrested and executed.

407–411 Constantine III elevated by the army of Britain and recognised by Honorius as Augustus in 409. Captured and executed in 411.

410 Rome sacked by Alaric.

410–411 Rescript of Honorius.

411–413 Usurpation of Jovinus in Gaul.

VI

Usurpers ad nauseam followed by immense turmoil

The history of Britain during the latter years of the fourth century is inextricably linked to that of the Roman Empire. From 382 to 410, there was a period of momentous change and immense violence. In particular, the decline of the Western Roman Empire, through constant civil war and barbarian incursion, piled tragedy upon tragedy. The purpose of this chapter is not to recount the history of the decline of the Western Roman Empire, interesting as it is, but to track the impact of its decline on Britons living and fighting within it.

In the twenty-seven years to 410, there was a confusing array of rebellions, usurpers and civil wars in the Western Roman Empire. The Britons endured savage barbarian attacks from every direction – Irish Scotti and Scotti down the west coast, Picts in the north and Saxons down the east coast. Then, in 405, the High King of Ireland, Niall of the Nine Hostages, raided along the south coast. During this period, all signal stations down the north-east coast were destroyed, perhaps by seaborne Picts. Raiders were becoming bolder, and their harassment was relentless. Back when Maximus had embarked with his army for Gaul in 383, Rome still considered Britain an extremely important diocese, and Britons, by and large, regarded themselves Roman subjects. But, by 410, the importance of Britain to the Empire had diminished significantly, and as a result, Britons were completely disillusioned.

Much of the impact of the aforementioned significant Empire-wide events on the British diocese was felt through the withdrawal of troops from British shores in various stages.

The army that crossed into Gaul with Maximus never returned. It had become customary for victorious commanders to offer clemency to their opponent's troops in exchange for service, and according to Dr John Morris, Theodosius I had a reputation for this. There is evidence of military settlement in northern Brittany in place names such as Pagus Legionensis. Furthermore, as Professor Salway notes, the *Notitia* records a unit called Seguntienses (Caernarvon) which was based abroad in Illyricum (northern Balkans).

Gildas refers to three Pictish wars before the middle of the fifth century. The first started after Maximus invaded Gaul and lasted 'many years'. It may not have abated until the diocese submitted to Theodosius when a task force was sent, which is recorded by Gildas as the arrival of *legio*. This may well have occurred in 390 upon the reinstatement of Valentinian II but before the usurpation by Eugenius. Professor Salway notes the change in Roman strategy in respect of frontier assaults:

> *Many forts were abandoned or lightly held, others, notably legionary fortresses, were given more powerful defences but occupied by units reduced in size. Fortified granaries also make their appearance, presumably so that an invader could be prevented from seizing military supplies or living off the land. Towns were remodelled to act as impregnable strongholds during an invasion and as*

springboards from which the main Roman striking forces could launch a counter-attack after an enemy thrust had exhausted itself. We should therefore not be surprised if reliable evidence one day appears for the presence in Roman Britain of organized barbarian allies around the end of the fourth century (more probably outside the cities than within), for regular frontier garrisons undergoing reduction but not total elimination, for the provision of fortified stores (perhaps in old forts), and for mobile field-units based in towns or other strong-points. This was, of course, a pattern to which the earlier refortification of the towns and repair of frontier forts, which we accepted as most likely the work of the elder Theodosius.[10]

By 398, the poet Claudian refers to the Vandal general Stilicho's naval success over the Saxons and Irish Scotti. The Picts were also beaten, but this appears to have been via a land campaign. This report has been linked to the second Pictish war mentioned by Gildas, but it is not known if Stilicho came to Britain to lead this campaign. Between 395 and 406, two *vicarii* were appointed to the diocese, most likely by Theodosius I and then Honorius. Their names were Victorinus and Chrysanthus, and both were Christian, the latter subsequently became a bishop in Constantinople. This suggests Rome was still in control right up to 406, despite all the raiding. However, in that same year, the army in Britain became agitated by the barbarian invasion of the Rhine frontier and eventually

[10] Salway, *Roman Britain*, pp 405–407.

elevated a soldier, Constantine, to Augustus. The reasons behind this secession are not fully understood and may be linked to soldiers concerns for the security of their homelands or perhaps their wages. Constantine proceeded to cross into Gaul with the army, further reducing the garrison in Britain. Constantine III was accepted by Honorius, but his campaign soon became embroiled in the political crisis gripping the Empire.

More troops were withdrawn under a British general, Gerontius, who secured Hispania but subsequently revolted, adding to the crisis. At the same time, Alaric's Goths piled increasing pressure on Rome. Initial victories were followed by significant defeats with massive consequences for almost everyone. It is thought that, at this time, the *vicarius* had already departed Britian, and so the Britons rebelled, expelling all Constantine's Roman officials.

One source for these events is Zosimus, a Greek historian who lived in Constantinople at the end of the fifth century, and his note of what happened next in Britain is graphic:

> *The barbarians from beyond the Rhine [Saxons?], ravaging everything at will, drove both the inhabitants of the British Isle and some of the peoples of Gaul to secede from the Empire of the Romans and live in independence, no longer obeying the Roman Laws. The people of Britain, therefore, took up arms and braved every peril, freeing their cities from the attacking barbarians. And the whole of Armorica, and other provinces of Gaul, imitating the Britons, liberated themselves in*

like manner, expelling the Roman officials and setting up a civil policy according to their own inclination. The secession of Britain and of Gallic peoples took place during the time of Constantine's usurpation, the barbarians rising up in consequence of his neglect of the government.

On the Continent, Stilicho was assassinated in 409. Alaric sacked Rome in 410, which was a staggering blow to imperial prestige. In 411, Constantine was executed. In Britain, a Gallic chronicle tells us:

The multitude of the enemy so prevailed that the strength of the Romans was enormously diminished. The provinces of Britain were laid waste by an incursion of the Saxons.

By the eighth century, the compiler of the *Historia* described the event as follows:

The Britons overthrew the dominion of the Romans, neither did they render tribute to them, nor receive their kings to rule over them, nor did the Romans dare to come to Britain to rule any longer because the Britons had slain their leaders.

This was the end of nearly 400 years of Roman rule. Zosimus tells us of a letter from Honorius to the cities of Britain in which he told them to undertake their own defence. This is known to history as 'the Rescript of Honorius'. Procopions, another Greek scholar from the Eastern Roman Empire, writing in the 540s, notes in his work, *History of the Wars*:

Constantine was defeated in battle. But in spite of this the Romans were never able to recover Britain, which from that time onwards continued to be ruled by tyrants.

After 410, Roman occupation of Britain effectively ended, and the early fifth century should only be considered sub-Roman – a term that distinguishes the difference between direct rule and mere influence. The challenges faced hereafter by the Britons were their own to resolve. Interaction with the Empire and Roman thinking continued though, and there was, in some quarters, a hope of reunion, but it was never to be.

Although 410 is considered a significant moment in history for the Britons, the same cannot be said for the remains of the Roman Empire which rapidly continued its terminal decline. When Magnus Maximus departed Britain to stake his claim, the Empire was still intact, albeit under mounting pressure. However, the Limes Germanicus, which followed the Rhine and the Danube, would shortly collapse under the strain of Alan, Suebi and Vandal advancement in the west and Goth, Visigoth and Hun incursion from the east. It is hard to picture this mass movement of extremely large tribes, formed into armies, moving across vast swathes of Europe, sacking towns and cities and partitioning territory.

By the time Aetius tenuously held the reins of authority in the Western Roman Empire on behalf of the child Emperor, Valentinian III, and his mother Galla Placidia, barbarians were in situ across the Empire. Franks, Burgundians, Alans and Goths were 'settled' in Gaul and Spain, while the Vandals had crossed into Africa and would come to dominate Carthage and the Mediterranean. The rise of the Huns in Central Asia had been remarkable, and their movement west was one of the pressures that forced Germanic tribes to move west and south. Britain, with its raiders and Anglo-Saxon settlers, was just a side show to all this. Only the Second World War has created similar turmoil, displacement and uncertainty.

VII

Late Antiquity in Britain

There is little history to recount between 410 and 430, although this must have been a period that saw the consolidation of the power and authority of the Brittonic chieftains, in particular, Vortigern. We also begin to note the name of a young Roman, Ambrosius Aurelianus, who appeared to claim hegemony over the tribal territory of the Belgae.

Many writers mostly skip from 410 to 429 which is the next date of note, being a visit to Britain by St. Germanus to address the heresy of Pelagianism. Sometimes this is also a point at which it is considered necessary to look back at Britain's pre-Roman tribal history to try to establish the Celtic credentials for Britons likely surfacing now that the yoke of Rome had been cast off, making room for a sort of Celtic resurgent tribalism. This is then followed by Vortigern, Ambrosius and, eventually, Arthur appearing out of the mists of legend to fight Saxon invaders. I am certainly heading in this general direction – but with as little mist as possible. In particular, I believe there was much more political structure to this period than is usually implied.

The term 'Late Antiquity' refers to the period between the decline and fall of the Western Roman Empire and the Middle Ages and is often used by historians to track continuity between the late Roman Empire, the early Byzantine Empire and the early Middle Ages. Detecting where Rome resonated in the face of the societal collapse generally associated with this period helps to analyse cultural continuity. It is most relevant to the Continent and perhaps less so at the frontiers where change was rapid and destruction more final. To establish a much less ambiguous interpretation of fifth-century history, it is essential that we consider the impact of events in relation to Late Antiquity and perhaps look to the Continent for insightful comparisons. Professor Ken Dark makes this comment in *Britain and the End of the Roman Empire*:

> *Standard views of the end of Roman Britain seem flawed and open to reinterpretation. Reliable written sources suggest that fifth- and sixth-century British society and culture retained far more of the Late Roman past than has usually been supposed, and did so within a political framework inherited from the fourth century. Although the diocesan administration may have been swept away in the first decade of the fifth century, the provincial structure may have survived until the end of the century. Archaeological evidence lends support to [St.] Patrick's picture of the survival of Romano-British rural society into the mid-fifth century, and to Gildas' account of the employment of Germanic troops in mid-to late fifth-century Britain. Their rebellion may have collapsed the provincial structure and permitted them to take over parts of eastern Britain.*[11]

Gildas, reflecting upon the turbulence of the fifth century, hints at this continuity:

---

[11] Ken Dark, *Britain and the End of the Roman Empire* (Stroud: Tempus Publishing, 2000), p 57.

But the cities of our land are not populated even now as they once were, right to the present they are deserted, in ruins and unkempt. External wars may have stopped, but not civil ones. For the remembrance of so desperate a blow to the island and of such unlooked for recovery stuck in the minds of those who witnessed both wonders. That was why kings, public and private persons, priests and churchmen, kept to their stations. But they died; and an age succeeded them that is ignorant of that storm and has experience only of the calm of the present.

If we examine the start of Late Antiquity in Britain, we can find clues that may lead to evidence for this continuity and, in consequence, set the stage for later events. Each region, polity and faction has to be considered – in particular, the emerging Late Roman warlords who took centre stage mid-century. Britain's enemies and allies similarly require a thorough review so that their objectives in a shrinking Roman Empire are better understood.

It is rare indeed when researching this period to identify the career of a civil servant. I mentioned a Victorinus appointed as *vicarius* of Britain just after the start of the fifth century. Remarkably, a chronicler called Rutilius met this man in Tuscany. Victorinus had retired as a Count of the Third Class to Toulouse where he held property. When Ataulf the Goth (brother-in-law of Alaric) took the city in 413, Victorinus fled with his household to Tuscany, where he recounted his experiences to Rutilius:

His wisdom was bright when life was prospering duly and still it shone unquencht in hardships now. His virtue's known to Ocean and to Thule, and all the fields ferocious Britons plough. He earned the esteem that grows each steady hour: the Prefect's deputy, with self-checked power. On the far edge of habitable parts he ruled as if at the active centre of things. The more the merit to have wooed the hearts of men whose hatred would incur no shame. Now Count of the Sacred Palace he's become but mocks in his dear country-lair at fame.

There is a bitterness to the last line which hints at the frustration of the consequences of civil war and military failure by the Romans. So, we must first reconsider what was meant by the expulsion of the Roman officials in 409.

British magnates and Roman nobles

Throughout Roman occupation, property ownership in Britain developed much along the lines of the rest of the Empire.

Latifundium refers to very large villa holdings. There had been an economic trend for consolidating property ownership into fewer owners, mainly Roman senators and the Emperor himself. Pliny the Elder at one point claimed that half of the province of Africa was in the hands of six people which may have been rhetorical exaggeration, but it makes the point. In second-century Britain, Emperor Antoninus confiscated much of the Brigantes territory 'for himself', according to Pausanias, a Greek geographer, thus referring to an area covering most of the north.

Between 200 and 350, there would have been little change to ownership as property passed through inheritance. Imperial confiscation in the latter half of the fourth century was a terrifying prospect for any magnate.

The usurpation by Magnentius subsequently resulted in confiscation and cruel revenge wrought throughout the Gallic and British nobility, and were it not for the weak leadership of Valentinian II (and many other pressing matters) such retribution may also have occurred following the secession by Magnus Maximus. The bloody rebellions of the army, resulting in the murders of Marcus and Gratian in 406, followed by the usurpation by Constantine must have alarmed everyone in Britain with a vested interest. Not only was Britain being abandoned to the relentless raids of Picts and Saxons, but the British magnates, by implication, were also facing the threat of being held responsible for this bloody campaign.

These secessions by Marcus, Gratian and Constantine remain a curious chain of events and may well have been almost entirely to do with soldiers attempting to secure their own wages, since they had not been paid. The later involvement of a British general, Gerontius, might suggest army solidarity, but this is only one senior figure who joined the fray seeking power for himself. The local militia probably remained at their posts. So, who ejected the Roman officials?

Zosimus reports the expulsion occurred not just in Britain but also Armorica and some parts of Gaul, and he connects it with the successful repulsion of barbarians. The events in Armorica were more likely linked to the activity of the *bacaudae*, who were peasant and slave insurgents, often led by brigands and disaffected former soldiers. Uprisings between 409 and 417 were unlikely to be connected to Britain. We have already seen how quickly Victorinus was able to move his residence from Toulouse, and I suspect that Britain's Roman officials were feeling equally stateless following the usurpation. If the army had not been paid, perhaps their plight was similar, and they may well have left of their own accord.

I believe that the answer to this question may be found through deeper interpretation of 'the Rescript of Honorius' where the Emperor told the British people to defend themselves. Zosimus gleaned much of his Western history from Olympiodorus, an Egyptian Greek who wrote twenty-two books on the Western Empire from 407 to 425. He was sent on a diplomatic mission by Honorius to the Black Sea and later lived at the court of Theodosius II. 'The Rescript of Honorius' is seen by most historians as a reply to a request from the Britons. I wonder if Olympiodorus was aware of this initial communication to Honorius which was likely a request for military support with offered appeasement.

The contents of 'the Rescript' were likely to have been thoroughly disappointing for those Romano-Britons living in the east and south-east, whereas the north and west, with their recently devolved military power, will have been much less concerned by this development. Gildas implies that, at about this time, the Britons fought back against the Picts and Scots and inflicted a 'massacre' that resulted in a period of respite. This may well be correct but could also be an explanation by Gildas for a period of prosperity rather than a significant military success.

So, the expulsion of the Roman officials begins to look more like positive spin from both Britons and the Emperor and was perhaps considered a temporary arrangement. Later chroniclers, in hindsight, make it appear more absolute, as that is what it proved to be.

I have yet to read a satisfactory account of the twenty years from 410 to 430 in Britain. We know what happened centre stage:

After yet another usurpation by the Gaul senator Jovinus, which lasted only two years (411–413), Flavius Constantius took revenge on Stilicho's murderers and gained supreme command as *magister utriusque militum.* After successes against the Goths, he became Patricius and, in 417, married Emperor Honorius' sister, Galla Placidia, by whom he had two children, Valentinian and Honoria. He was proclaimed co-Augustus in 421 but died seven months later. Honorius died in 423, and Ioannes seized the purple with the support of the general, Castinas. Both men fell from power when an eastern army returned the infant Valentinian III and his mother to the Western throne in 425.

In Britain, there is no record of the immediate reaction, which has led to speculation that the diocese may have endured for a short while. Initially, there must have been a period of expectation that an army would land, accompanied by Roman officials, and that everything would go back to how it was previously, perhaps something along the lines of the Theodosian restoration. Senior British officials and magnates will have feared, but expected, this outcome. Of course, nobody could guess who the Emperor might be or what retribution might follow. This tension may have lasted as much as five years, and presumably, Britons stayed alert to this and, by and large, 'kept to their stations' and way of life as described by Gildas. Nonetheless, there is no doubt that urban life continued its massive decline, and many villa holdings were abandoned or perhaps worked in different ways.

There is also real confusion with respect to the army. The *Notitia* suggests a reduced garrison, but this is most probably bureaucratic inertia with regards to record-keeping and, in fact, the garrison no longer existed. Military defence will have initially followed an adapted Roman pattern, but as time passed, it surely adapted to a form of regionally organised protection, based on obligation and experience. In many respects, the devolved military arrangements of Maximus were ideal preparation for this outcome and provided a structure that ensured a shift in power to the north and west.

However, the east and south-east were extraordinarily vulnerable and ultimately were only in a position to barter their wealth for defence or lose it to raiders. Anyone with a vested interest in these regions must have constantly prayed for the Romans to return – raiding certainly continued, but now there were no legions to push the Saxons back beyond the borders, with the consequence that they stayed and settled. Without military defence, there was no option but to tolerate this accelerated settlement.

Perhaps, initially, the Anglo-Saxons could not believe their luck and were less inclined to undermine their new-found opportunities by making the mistake of upsetting the neighbours. This might be another reason for Gildas' reported period of prosperity. The Anglo-Saxon people were river and seafaring traders with a tendency towards piracy. A settlement closer to the prosperous Roman Empire with extensive coastline and estuaries was eminently preferable to being surrounded in their homeland by hostile tribes, principally the Huns. Germanic tribes throughout Europe were being displaced as a result of the rise of the Hunnic Empire, and we have already discussed how barbarian leaders had become astute in their anticipation of Roman strategy, military capability and response, and how they adapted accordingly, so it comes as no surprise that settlers from these displaced tribes now started to flood into the east of Britain.

This better explains why raiding diminished and, also, how various Anglo-Saxon tribes coalesced and settled such a large area so quickly. In many ways, the militaristic north and west will have preferred this development to a return of the Romans, but to the cives of the south and east, it was a sign of defensive and military failure and a challenge to both Christianity and the Roman way of life hitherto defended by the legions. An entry in the *Anglo-Saxon Chronicle* for 418 states:

> *In this year the Romans collected all the treasures which were in Britain and hid some in the earth so that no one afterwards could find them and some they took with them into Gaul.*

This suggests some form of evacuation which may well have resulted from an indication that Rome might not be returning soon. Following the defeat of Constantine III, the Western Roman Empire had lost much of Gaul to the barbarians. In Britain, the absence of the army made the economy shrink, ironically leading to a surplus, and with no taxation, this further adds to an explanation of Gildas' period of prosperity. Coinage was less scarce in this shrinking market, and many countrywide silver hoards of clipped *siliquae* reveal that this still served as money in provincial communities until as late as 430. When

Germanus visited St. Albans in 429, he found a prosperous region with residents 'conspicuous for riches, brilliant in dress and surrounded by a fawning multitude'. This was a brave face that belied the true position.

The family of Ambrosius Aurelianus

In the most repeated quote from *De Excidio*, Gildas mentions Ambrosius Aurelianus. While I will return to this person's impact on fifth-century history, it is important to place his family within their region and sphere of influence. Gildas writes that he was a gentleman:

> *... who, perhaps alone of the Romans had survived the shock of this notable storm: his parents, who had certainly worn the purple, were slain in it. His descendants in our day have become greatly inferior to their grandfather's excellence.*

So, who was Ambrosius Aurelianus? Gildas is clear – he was a Roman and his father was an emperor or at least of senatorial rank. Later, it becomes apparent from the *Historia* that Ambrosius and Vortigern were considered rivals. Much like Magnus Maximus, Ambrosius has become a legend. The *Historia* records fantastic tales of the fatherless boy, Ambrosius (Emrys in Welsh) predicting the location of a battle between a white and red dragon. This legend is recounted in many books on the period, not least because the red dragon became the symbol of Wales. Ambrosius' family forbears could well have been Belgic nobles of note.

Aurelius Ambrosius (340–397), otherwise known as St. Ambrose, Bishop of Milan, was probably the most influential ecclesiastical figure of the fourth century. He was raised in Gallia Belgica. His mother was a member of the Roman family *Arelii Symmach*, so he was cousin to Q Aurelius Symmachus, the famous orator. His father was another Aurelius Ambrosius, the Praetorian Prefect of Gaul from 337 to 340, in effect chief aide to the Western Emperor, Constantine II.

It is tempting to make a connection between Ambrosius of the fifth century and this famous family whose connections to Britain may go even further back. There are many place names that may be associated with the name Ambrosius concentrated around West Sussex, Hampshire and Wiltshire. Sir Barry Cunliffe, in his book *Britain Begins*, says this is the former territory of the Belgae, a group of immigrants from Belgic Gaul, who in the first century BC, according to Julius Ceaser, 'came to raid and stayed to sow'. The Romans located their capital at Winchester (Venta Belgarum). Later, Commius, a refugee from Caesar's war in Belgic Gaul, fled to Britain to 'join his own people' probably setting up a new centre at Silchester (Calleva). One of the chief Belgic tribes was called the Ambiani, and many of their coins have been found across the south of England. In Belgica, the Ambiani were based around the Somme, and their chief town was Civitas Ambianensium which is modern-day Amiens. This looks a very similar name to Amesbury and is most likely the reason for this concentration of 'Amb' place names. However, further north, there are place names that seem they could be directly attributable to Ambrosius of the fifth century.

All these connections are circumstantial and unproven, but I can't help seeing a logical link between the Belgae territory, the Ambiani, Ambrosius' political position, and the stellar Roman careers and position of these forbears. In their book, *Unroman Britain: Exposing the Great Myth of Britannia*, Miles Russell and Stuart Laycock discuss the post-Roman earthwork Wansdyke. This runs along a probable border between the pre-Roman tribes of the Dobunni and Belgae but also lies along a line of villas affected by fires which have been dated to the Late Roman period and may indicate tribal conflict. We should not forget the *Discordia*, mentioned in the *Historia*, between Vitalinus (Dobunni?) and Ambrosius (Belgae?), known as the Battle of Wallop which occurred sometime in the late 430s just to the south of Wansdyke. Perhaps a large chunk of the Belgae territory was consolidated into the hands of this noble and powerful Belgic family along the lines of *latifundium*?

Gildas clearly knew more about the background of Ambrosius Aurelianus than he recounts. The statement about his parents' death in this 'notable storm' may well refer to any of the wars and conflicts in Britain or on the Continent from 406 onwards. It is interesting to note that the legend references a fatherless boy which may indicate that his parents died at an early date and saw Ambrosius moved to the family's British estates for safety. If we were brave enough to interpret Gildas literally, we should really be looking to connect Ambrosius Aurelianus with a Roman emperor – the reference to his parents having 'worn the purple' explicitly indicating this. Geoffrey of Monmouth, who was certainly brave, made this assumption and cast him as a son of Constantine III. This was a fair guess in his day but proved unhistorical. However, there are two other Emperors worth considering. One is the late and often overlooked usurper Jovinus (411–

413) and the other is his brother Sebastianus. Their demise was certainly violent.

Following the defeat of Constantine III, Jovinus was declared Emperor at Mainz in 411. A Gallo-Roman senator, he was sponsored by Gundahar, King of the Burgundians, and Goar, King of the Alans. Jovinus kept his position in Gaul for two years, long enough to issue coinage that showed him wearing the imperial diadem and was supported by a number of local Gallo-Roman nobles who had survived Constantine's defeat. He may well have been the son of the Belgic-Roman, General Jovinus, who successfully pushed the Alemanni out of Gaul in 366 and was awarded the consulate by a grateful Valentinian I. Nothing is known of the usurper's family except that he elevated his brother Sebastianus to the position of co-Emperor. Ataulf, King of the Visigoths, decided to ally his forces with Honorius, and they defeated Jovinus' troops. Sebastianus was executed and Jovinus fled for his life but was besieged and captured in Valentia (Vallence, Drôme) and taken to Narbo (Narbonne), where Caius Posthumus Dardanus, the Praetorian Prefect of Gaul and loyal to Honorius, had him executed. Jovinus and Sebastianus' heads were afterwards sent to Honorius and mounted on the walls of Ravenna (before being taken to Carthage where they were put on permanent display with the heads of four other usurpers). Ambrosius would have been approximately thirteen years old when Jovinus was executed. It is possible that the father of Jovinus acquired Belgae property in Britain, and it is worth noting that Valentinian I based himself at Civitas Ambianensium (Amiens) with Jovinus in 367 during the Barbarian Conspiracy perhaps suggesting he held property there.

It would be extraordinarily interesting if *siliquae* of Jovinus were ever to be discovered in the West Sussex, Hampshire or Wiltshire regions, confirming a connection with Ambrosius. To my knowledge, the only such find is a gold *solidi* bearing the head of this Emperor, discovered near Ashford, Kent in 2004. Also interesting are two relatively recent finds at Patching, West Sussex in 1997 and Pewsey, Wiltshire in 2000, containing coins dating to the late fourth/early fifth century. In particular, the Patching hoard contains gold *solidi* of Honorius (whose reign extended to 423), his successor Valentinian III (425–55) and Theodosius II (Eastern Roman Emperor 402–50). Also present are eight *solidi* (and three silver *siliquae*) of the Visigoths which have only otherwise been found as solitary examples, sometimes converted to pendants, at Anglo-Saxon sites. This helps us to build a picture of a region still in contact with the Roman Empire and with coin still in use beyond the middle of the fifth century.

There is much debate over the generations of Ambrosius and it has been suggested that his father was involved somewhere in the sub-Roman hierarchy of Britain. We should not discount this, but Gildas says nothing further, and there is little else to indicate this apart from the name of the owner of some spoons which formed part of an immense treasure find. The hoard, found at Hoxne, Suffolk in 1992 and dated to after 407, contained many silver items with different inscriptions. Ten spoons were inscribed as the property of one 'Aurelius Ursicinus'. This find has led to theories that this may be the father of Ambrosius Aurelianus who was attempting to make his escape to the Continent. It is an interesting suggestion but somewhat random because the age of the spoons cannot be determined. The only clue to their age might be in their Christian monograms and symbolism. The owner of this treasure was certainly a wealthy Roman who was never able to recover it, which suggests departure or death with no heirs. But we know the dynasty of Ambrosius Aurelianus endured. Assuming Gildas wrote no later than 512, Ambrosius' grandchildren, to whom he refers, will have been his contemporaries, but we have no idea who they were or what became of them. The absence of any king list or noted descendants is frustrating, and were it not for Gildas, we might not know they existed at all.

However, a warlord of the 470s, to whom Sidonius Apollinaris wrote a letter, may well be the son of Ambrosius. He was known as Riothamus, and the sixth-century chronicler, Jordanes, refers to him as 'King of the Brittones'. His name is a Latinisation of the Brittonic personal name, Rigotamos, meaning 'great king'. As we will note next, the name Vortigern was most likely an epithet, and Riothamus may well be similar, so linking this king to his father, forebears and the region of the Belgae.

The family of Vortigern

There is almost as much written about Vortigern as there is about Arthur. He is the more historically provable of the two, but arguably both are legendary. Gildas first mentions a 'proud tyrant' who is responsible for the downfall of Britain by inviting in a band of Saxons as federate troops who revolted. Bede actually names the tyrant as Vortigern and, further, names Hengist and Horsa as the Saxon leaders. He adds that Horsa was killed in battle in East Kent and provides the brothers' genealogy along with a list of countries of origin for the Anglo-Saxons. The *Historia*, written in the ninth century, dramatically expands the information to include the career and failures of Vortigern, some of which are apocryphal tales. His connection with the west of Britain is derived from Gildas associating five regional kings within the sphere of his influence. Subsequently, Vortigern appears in several Welsh genealogies and also on the lost inscription of the Pillar of Eliseg.

There are many experts who have researched Vortigern, and I don't propose to question or challenge any of them. His apparent role in the defence and downfall of Britain makes him just as fascinating as Arthur, perhaps more so. It is generally accepted that 'Vortigern' was an epithet for his real name, since it means 'supreme king'. Considering all his mentions in the *Historia*, he appears to have been a divisive character who suffered from seriously bad press, and he is cast as much less straightforward than his rival Ambrosius Aurelianus. He may well have been associated with the pre-Roman Dobunni tribe, and his great-grandfather, Gloui, is said to have founded Gloucester.

The *Historia* provides the following genealogy: Vortigern, son of Vitalis, son of Vitalinus of Gloucester. This is the Vitalinus I mentioned earlier in connection with *Britannia Prima* and whom I believe held special status in the west at the time of Maximus, much like Coel Hen in the north. It is interesting to note that both Vitalinus and Coel Hen handed down their positions of authority to their sons. In early medieval terms, they might be considered regional federate overkings, but as sub-Romans, they appear to have held responsibility for the defence of Britain, with the honorific title, Protector, a role that carried obligations that were still being fulfilled two generations later. Whatever their remit, they were two of the most powerful men in the land and both their families had been indulged and appointed by Emperor Maximus.

Vortigern's real name may also have been Vitalinus. There is evidence that a Vitalinus was twelfth Archbishop of London, but this may not be relevant except in confirming the family's firm Christian credentials. Vortigern's succession is complicated and depends upon which genealogy you choose to follow. Vortimer, his eldest son, is sometimes omitted, and this has led to speculation that Vortigern and Vortimer may have been one and the same. While Vortimer suits the epithet better, I don't think this is likely. The interceding generations work better with Vortimer as the son, and both are recorded valiantly fighting the Saxons in the mould of proud Protectors.

We do know that Vortigern was to come under immense pressure, as the *Historia* relates:

> *It came to pass that after this war between the British and the Romans, when their generals were killed, and after killing of the tyrant Maximus and the end of the Roman Empire in Britain, The Britons went in fear for 40 years. Guorthigirnus (Vortigern) then reigned in Britain. He had cause for dread, not only from the Scots and Picts, but also from the Romans, and a dread of Ambrosius.*

There should be no doubts about the stature of Vortigern or his family. Glevum (Gloucester) is surrounded by the most lavish villas ever excavated in England, and it seems likely that his actions to protect Britain were not those of a power-seeking usurper but more that of a patrician fulfilling his obligations. This is a different picture to Welsh legend, and some historians consider that his legacy has been poorly understood and perhaps denigrated to undermine his descendants.

The family of Coel Hen

Coel Hen would be unknown to history were it not for his mention in heroic poetry, the Harleian genealogies and the late pedigrees known as the *Bonedd Gwŷr y Gogledd* (*Descent of the Men of the North*). The latter is an extremely interesting collection of northern descendants who become more traceable through each generation. The names provide some insight into, inter alia, the Brittonic kingdoms of Rheged, Elmet and Edyn. Some of the descendants named cross-check to Celtic heroic poetry which helps to confirm that Coel Hen was the likely progenitor and less of a legend than he first might appear. Coel Hen means 'Coel the Old' and he is also known as Godebog (Guotepauc) which means Protector. He is often associated with the pre-Roman tribe, the Carvetti, mostly because of his assumed territory around Carlisle and his influence with the Strathclyde Britons.

There is also a possibility that he was a surviving leader of the Brigantes, the great northern tribe that plagued the Romans because there is some doubt about the significance of the Carvetti. They are not mentioned in Ptolemy's *Geography*, and only a small number of late inscriptions infer their existence. By contrast, the Brigantes controlled a huge area – most of the north stretching from 'sea to sea'. It is unlikely that a small tribe could hold sway over neighbours such as the powerful Votadini, whereas the Brigantes certainly could. It is interesting to note that Coel's successors quickly established themselves throughout the north in a preordained manner. Simple inheritance could not secure such entitlement. It certainly appears as if the major tribes, and perhaps, with them, territorial claims, were resurfacing in sub-Roman Britain – I have already mentioned similar activity by the Dobunni and the Belgae further south. Furthermore, the cooperation between Coel and Magnus Maximus with respect to the abandonment of Pennine forts implies not just firm territorial control but perhaps a degree of self-regulation in the former Brigantian territories.

During the early stages of the Roman military campaigns, distinction was made between two Brigantian leaders – Cartimandua, who cooperated with the invaders in the south of the territory, and her former husband, Venutius, who led the resistance from further north. The defeat of the Brigantes took decades, and a series of Roman marching camps from Stanwick (the Brigantes *oppidum* south of the Tees) to the Eden Valley and Carlisle region may suggest the line of a Brigantian retreat to the north-west of their territory, even perhaps beyond the frontier line of the future Hadrian's Wall.

Three of Coel's descendants are particularly interesting. First, his grandson, Mor, features in place names across the north from Morley in West Yorkshire to Morland in Westmorland. This underpins the extent of the area still under the family's control two generations later. Mor's son, Arthwys, will have been a contemporary of Riothamus, and as I will go on to show, looks very much like the proto-Arthur. Urien of Rheged, a sixth-century descendant, is well attested in the poetry of Taliesin, who also references Coel in several of his poems. Aneirin, who is generally considered to have written *Y Gododdin*, references Arthur, Coelings and Godebog (Celtic name for Coel Hen).

Most of the territory controlled by the Coeling dynasty was later absorbed into Rheged, a Brittonic-speaking kingdom which was briefly annexed by Northumbria before 730 and, thereafter, Cumbria, while the north-west Pennines remained under the influence and control of Strathclyde Britons until the beginning of the eleventh century.

According to the University of Oxford's 'People of the British Isles' project, Rheged left a distinct genetic heritage in Cumbria, the west Pennines and the West Riding of Yorkshire. The name Cumberland derives from Cymry, meaning 'the citizens'. The Brittonic language of Cumbrian resonates in northern sheep-counting systems, and Welsh Cumbric place names are evident across the north. I regularly walk Penhill in Wensleydale, Pen-y-ghent, near Settle, and Blencathra, near Penrith, where 'eccles' and 'egles' place names are evident throughout the northern landscape, so denoting the presence of an early church and helping to map Christianity's progress before Bede.

The visit of St. Germanus

One of the few recorded events of the early fifth century is a visit to Britain by Bishop Germanus of Auxerre with his companion Lupus, Bishop of Troyes. Apparently, envoys had been sent from Britain complaining about the spread of a heresy known as Pelagianism. Prosper of Aquitaine, an opponent of the heresy, wrote in his chronicle under the year 429:

The Pelagian Agricola, son of the Pelagian bishop Serverianus, corrupts the churches of Britain by insinuating his doctrine. But at the suggestion of the deacon Palladius, Pope Celestine sends Germanus bishop of Auxerre as his representative, and after the confusion of the heretics guides the Britons to the Catholic faith.

Pelagianism was a Christian belief that original sin did not taint human nature, and that mortal will was capable of choosing good or evil without divine aid. This was considered contrary to the teachings of the Church and branded a heresy at the Council of Carthage in 418.

Constantius of Lyon wrote about the life of Germanus, *Vita Sancti Germani*, in 480. The mission was successful – Germanus and Lupus were able to debate with the Pelagians and 'great crowds' came to listen. Germanus visited the shrine of St. Alban, performed some miracles, and even took command of a hostile engagement with Saxons and Picts who had come to raid. This is known as the 'Alleluia Victory', taken from the battle cry that Germanus told the soldiers to shout in order to surprise the raiders.

Constantius' report of events provides an insight into Late Antiquity Britain that would otherwise be unknown. It is interesting to note that St. Albans was still functioning as an urban centre. Germanus is said to have cured the daughter of 'a man of tribunician power', suggesting the continued presence of senior civilian or military personnel, a clear indication of continuing sub-Roman organisation. We are told the Pelagians flaunted their wealth in resplendent clothes and were surrounded by a mob of flatterers. Clearly, this was a typical Roman debate among people concerned for their religion and institutions which suggests both a level of contact with the Continent and a host of magnates still maintaining their *romanitas*. The beleaguered Britons, however, were still suffering raids and seemed to lack the courage and military expertise to do anything about it.

St. Patrick

This famous Irish saint was the son of a regional British villa owner called Capernius who belonged to the local *decurionate* class from which municipal council members were drawn. Patrick was captured in a raid in the early fifth century and taken to Ireland as a slave, where, after six years, he escaped. He returned home, whereupon his father, who was also a deacon of the Church, implored him to stay at home and undertake public duties known as *munera*. Dates and locations are disputed, but it is accepted as an event that occurred in the first quarter of the fifth century. Here is a small villa owner continuing to conduct his affairs in traditional Roman style but under the extreme pressure of seaborne raids. It is no wonder that the ruling classes of Britain sought a strong leader well placed to deal with these external threats.

There are many different proposed dates for the accession of Vortigern as this leader, but it appears that he had taken up this role by the mid-420s and was attempting to control the defence of Britain.

VIII

A brief summary of the usual view of the history of Britain 430 to 470

Conventional history suggests the Saxons first arrived in Britain as federate troops in the 420s and then rebelled in the late 440s, fighting battles against Vortigern and then Vortimer in Kent until 465. Thereafter, the war continued until sometime between 493 and 516 when they were defeated by Ambrosius at the Battle of Mount Badon.

I will challenge some of this in later chapters, but for readers who may not be familiar with the conventional history of this period, it is best to first outline the standard view.

Gildas describes how, after a period of prosperity up to the 420s, during which raids by the Picts and Scots had been subdued, the attacks started again at a time when the country was suffering an outbreak of plague. In response, Vortigern invited bands of Saxons to settle as *foederati* in the east of Britain. They were granted monthly rations, *epimenia*, and an amount of corn, *annona*, and their role was to protect the east coast from the Picts. This was initially a success. More Saxons arrived, negotiating further supplies. This continued for some years until the Saxons complained that supplies had become insufficient and rebelled against the Britons, laying waste to the countryside and towns alike.

The narrative suggests that Vortigern's policy of bringing in Saxons was opposed by those magnates who were hoping for Rome's return. They appear to have purposefully cut off supplies to the Saxons in an attempt to send the settlers home, and this may have sparked the revolt. Vortigern, by contrast, had no desire to see the Romans return, and prior to the revolt had invited even more Saxons to counter raiding Picts. Vortigern's policies were discredited and war was waged with the Saxons for many years.

British resistance rallied under Ambrosius Aurelianus, after which, battles were won, sometimes by the Britons and sometimes by the Saxons, until eventually the Britons won a resounding victory at the Battle of Mount Badon which is widely thought to have been fought between 493 and 516. After this, there was a long period of peace. Bede concurs with this version of history, adding a little more about the background to the Saxons. The *Historia Brittonum*, attributed to Nennius, provides more information, but also more legend, in particular referencing Arthur's battles and presence at Mount Badon.

Gildas, Bede and Nennius all indicate that there were two important stages to the *Adventus Saxonum*. First, the initial settlement and deployment of *foederati* and, thereafter, their rebellion.

Bede suggested that the initial Saxon landings were in 449. This is later than the date calculated using the *Historia*, but it is helpful because it clearly indicates Bede was really in the dark about it all. He was not alone – we shall see in the following chapters how little the settlers themselves knew about their own heritage.

A Gallic chronicler noted in the year 442 that: 'The British who to this time had suffered from various defects and misfortunes are reduced to the power of the Saxons.' This might indicate the rebellion, and by about 446, the panicking pro-Roman magnates were appealing to Aetius

– the Roman *magister militum* in the west, who was campaigning in Gaul – for Rome's help. Gildas records:

> *The miserable remnant sent a Letter to Agitius, a man of high Roman power, speaking as follows: To Agitius in his third Consulship the Groans of the Britons. And after some remarks they complain: The barbarians drive us into the sea, the sea drives us into the barbarians: between these two kinds of death we are cut down or drowned.*

'Agitius' is taken as Aetius who was shortly to face a most serious threat to the Western Roman Empire: Attila the Hun. With this in mind, he was assembling troops, veterans and federate allies in preparation while engaging in a political stand-off with the Emperor and his mother, so he was rather too busy to help. Intriguingly, the above quote hints at the rising sea levels of the period, which is factual and may have played a part in events. The Humber estuary and York had most likely flooded.

So, the generally accepted view of Britain's political position between 430 and 470 is a period of internecine war between Saxons and Britons, underpinned by a flood of Saxon immigrants, until the Battle of Mount Badon halted the western advance of the Saxons for a period.

The evidence from archaeology seems to support Gildas. Roman lifestyle disappears during this period, and towns and villas are abandoned. Coins cease to be minted, and small groupings of wooden huts appear, usually in new locations.

The burial methods in the cemeteries of these settlers are initially cremations which then give way to inhumations and include grave goods from German culture. I have already explained that German settlers were undoubtedly arriving from an earlier time and that this may well have provided momentum to the accelerated settlement of Germans in the east of Britain, and we know the earliest settlers were in eastern England because large cremation cemeteries have been found in East Anglia, Lincolnshire, the East Midlands and East Yorkshire. The earliest urns are Anglian, and according to Barry Cunliffe in *Britain Begins*, Saxon urns can be quite closely dated to between 380 and 420, implying mass movement of families into Britain in the first decade of the fifth century. He adds that, by the second half of the fifth century, the distribution of female brooches firmly indicates links to Anglian and Jutish regions. Elsewhere, particularly along both sides of the Thames, the settlements appear to be made up of Saxon and Frankish *foederati*. Men are buried with weapons and belt fittings of Late Roman origin. This is interpreted as there being a need to mount a defence of the Thames as far west as Oxford. A completely different settlement occurs in Kent. These are Jutes who, once established, forged strong links with the Franks on the Continent. Barry Cunliffe summarises:

> *By the middle of the fifth century, then, a number of disparate Germanic groups had settled in the south-east of Britain, some invited, others not. More were to follow in their wake. A careful study of the pottery used in Britain compared to that of the continental homelands leaves little doubt that the stream of incomers was continuous. Communities of Anglian origin favoured the areas around the wetlands of the Wash, while Saxons were concentrated in the*

Thames valley, the south Midlands, and the Hampshire-Sussex region. In this way the basis of the Anglian and Saxon kingdoms of England was laid.[12]

Rome never returned and had itself collapsed in the west by 480. Of course, the important passages of Gildas have been read and reinterpreted time and again, but it seems strange that such an intense rebellion and war was only concluded by a battle some thirty years later. Gildas knew the precise date for the Battle of Mount Badon – it was his birth date, and he was writing about it some forty-three years and one month since the victory. So, determining when Gildas wrote *De Excidio*I would at least solve that puzzle.

However, determining if an Arthur was involved would be better served if we could locate the region in which the battle was fought. I reached a straightforward conclusion many years ago. If Badon was a battle in the south, then it must be connected to the Saxon campaign that occurred in the early years of the sixth century. If it was in the north, then it would have to have occurred at the tail end of the Saxon rebellion and wars, a whole generation earlier. In my opinion, Gildas could not have been writing any later than 512, meaning the Battle of Mount Badon could have been fought no later than 469, which is a significant revision to conventional history, moving the battle back in time by thirty years. But the proposed northern site for the Battle of Mount Badon is not the only credible reason to support this shift in time, as I shall go on to explain.

---

[12] Barry Cunliffe, *Britain Begins* (Oxford: Oxford University Press, 2013), p 421.

Fifth-century table of events with key leaders

The table below is an attempt to unscramble the history of fifth-century Britain. Most of the events, names and dates cannot be reliably proven. Bede, Nennius in the *Historia Brittonum* and, later, Geoffrey of Monmouth tried to sequence events by recounting traditions in a linear way leaving historians with a hotchpotch to decipher. It becomes apparent that the *Adventus Saxonum* described by Gildas is only part of a huge settlement of *foederati* that began much earlier and probably about the time of the usurpation of Maximus. This is difficult to prove but seems to make complete sense and better explains the so-called "Saxon invasion". All the names below come down to us as assumed leaders in several regions. Some may have been family connections others will have been successors. Each name is placed in the decade where it seems likely they were most prominent, which is sometimes referred to as their "floruit".

		Romans/ Ambiani	Dobunni	Brigantes/ Carvetti	Déisi	Votadini (Wales)	Angles	Jutes	Saxons West	Saxons South
370	Barbarian Conspiracy		Vitalinus							
380	Theodosian restoration	Jovinus (General)		Coel Hen						
390	Usurpation of Maximus				Triphun	Cunneda	Finn	Whitgils	Gewis	
400	Raiding intensifies Stilicho		Vitalis							
410	Constantine III Rescript of Honorius	Jovinus / Sebastianus		Ceneu						
420	Period of surplus *Adventus Saxonum*				Aircol	Ceretic	Friothulf	Hengist	Esla	
430	Raiding intensifies		Vortigern							
440	Battle of Wallop	Ambrosius		Mor						
450	Appeal to Aetius Saxons rebel				Cunorius	Einion Yrth	Freuleaf	Aesc	Elesa	
460	Saxon War		Vortimer							
470	Ambrosian fightback. Battle of Mount Badon	Riothamus	Pascent	Arthwys						
480	Expedition of Riothamus Western Roman Empire ends		Britu		Vortipor	Cadwallon	Winta	Octha	Cerdic	
490	Camlann Arthwys dies		Riocatus							Aelle
500	Saxons begin southern expansion	Natanleod		Eliffer/ Pabo						
510	Gildas. *De Excidio*					Maelgwn	Cretta	Oisc	Cynric	

The Descent of the Men of the North

The *Bonedd Gwyr y Gogledd* is a Middle Welsh tract which gives the names of rulers of the old Brythonic North in the sixth century. The text was composed in the twelfth century but the earliest surviving manuscript is late thirteenth century. There are two dynasties included, that of Coel Hen and that of Dyfnwal Hen of Alt Clut (Strathclyde). The table below shows the descendants of Coel Hen who appears to be the progenitor of the houses of Rheged (the Northern Pennines, Cumberland and Westmorland), Eidyn (southern Scotland up to Edinburgh) and possibly Elmet (the North and West Ridings of Yorkshire). The table suggests that Mor and Arthwys became powerful overlords and that dynastic friction was likely to occur as territory became divided amongst descendants. Myth and legend surround many of the names and some became famous through poetry, such as Urien of Rheged. However, the late date of the manuscript and the absence of any other corroborating evidence means these genealogies cannot be relied upon and we can only speculate when these leaders were active and what part they played in history.

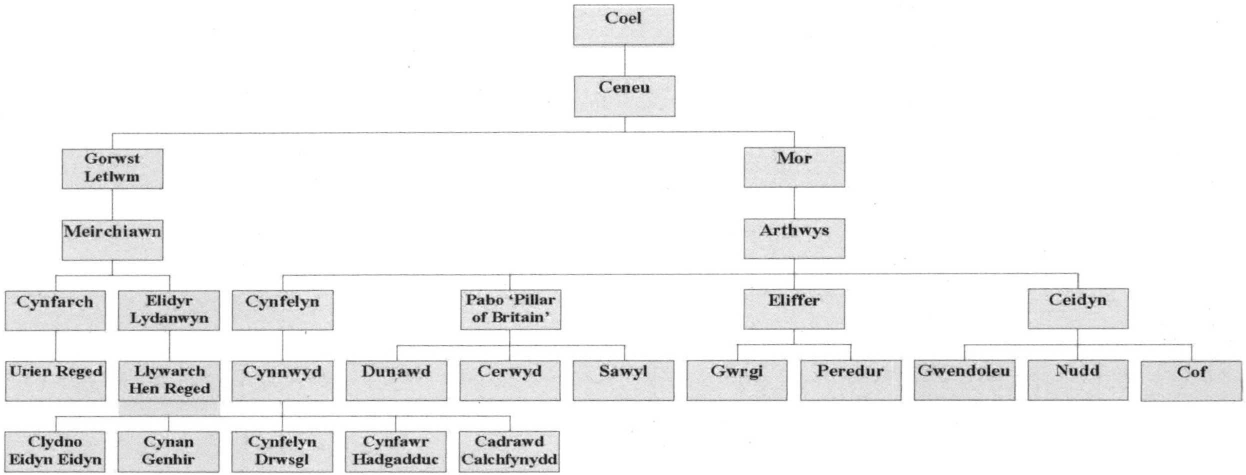

IX

Why Britain's fifth-century hero could have come from the north

If there was an Arthur who was commander at the Battle of Mount Badon in about 469, who might he have been? Tradition and, later, Geoffrey of Monmouth hold he was a prince or a king. Most historians now set him aside as a myth, but with this reassessment of the date and location for this battle, one candidate, who may well qualify as the source of the legend, now comes to light.

I confess to a lifelong interest in King Arthur in all his forms and guises. The Arthur of the *Historia Brittonum* is an important component of the Battle of Mount Badon and must be given due consideration alongside Ambrosius Aurelianus. After reading countless books and theories on the subject, I still believe the following quote, in *Roman Britain and the English Settlements* by R. G. Collingwood and J. N. L. Myres, best summarises this chapter:

> *... the historicity of the man can hardly be called in question. The fact that his name in later ages was a magnet drawing to itself all manner of folk-lore and fable, and that an Arthurian cycle grew up composed partly of events transferred from other contexts, no more proves him a fictitious character than similar fables prove it of Alexander or Aristotle, Vergil or Roland. It tends rather to prove the opposite. The place which the name of Arthur occupies in Celtic legend is easiest to explain on the*

hypothesis that he lived, and was a great champion of the British people.[13]

This chapter is predominantly about northern Britons and their leader Arthwys, great-grandson of Coel Hen, who may well be the source of all this intrigue and was likely involved in the Saxon wars and the Battle of Mons Badonicus. The *Historia* is a miscellany which cannot be relied upon to the same extent as Gildas. However, it is generally believed to contain historical content, even in the sections that are considered to contain a considerable amount of folklore. There is an important passage describing Arthur's battles, which I will detail in the later chapter on the Saxon rebellion and wars, commencing:

> *Then in those days Arthur fought against them [the Saxons] with the kings of the Britons, but he was commander in the battles.*

Earlier in the narrative, when describing the valiant campaigns of Vortimer, the *Historia* notes:

> *... and then they [the Saxons] fought against the kings of our people; sometimes they were victorious and extended frontiers, at other times they were defeated and driven out.*

Both these passages clearly show that coordinated campaigns were undertaken. We know from Gildas that the proud tyrant (Vortigern) attempted to control and resolve the rebellion, and that, ultimately, Ambrosius

---

[13] R. G. Collingwood, and J. N. L. Myres, *Roman Britain and the English Settlements* (Oxford: Clarendon Press, 1937), p 321.

rallied the 'miserable remnant', but where do the Coelings fit in?

Doubtless, the north endured further warfare with the Scots and Picts, but this is barely recorded. However, the 'kings of our people' is an explicit and inclusive statement. The genealogy of Coel Hen, tentative as it is, suggests both Mor and Arthwys were alive around the time of the Saxon wars. This is obviously guesswork, but Mor could have been fifty in 450, with his son, Arthwys, aged twenty. This fits with a proposed involvement of Arthwys at Mount Badon in 469.

It has often been suggested that 'Arthur's battles' in the *Historia* is a remnant of a northern heroic poem. This may well be so, but establishing the source is difficult. The compiler was writing in about 829, probably in North Wales, so it may be likely that this, and other sections relating to the Saxon rebellion and wars, were taken from various northern sources and folklore. There appears to have been a degree of cultural and Christian exchange between the kingdoms of Elmet, Rheged, Strathclyde and Gwynedd. This is evidenced by early post-Roman inscribed stones from Wales and by the inference of chapel dedications, and it is therefore reasonable to assume that these domains were initially allied under the direction of Coel Hen. While it is recognised that the compiler of the *Historia* steadfastly followed *De Excidio*, perhaps his other sources presented conflicting versions, some of which he names:

> *Then Talhaearn, 'Father of the Muse' was renowned in poetry; and Aneirin and Taliesin and Blwchfardd*

and Cian who is called 'Wheat of Song' were illustrious all at the same time in British Poetry.

Only the poems of Aneirin and Taliesin are known to history. The *Historia* therefore may well contain elements of many bardic sources with perhaps a northern view of the Saxon rebellion and wars. Geoffrey of Monmouth, who wrote the *History of the Kings of England*, drew much of his background information for King Arthur from the *Historia*, creating the myth with which we are all familiar. He purposefully turned Arthur into a national leader, equivalent to the kings of his day, holding court at recognisable medieval locations. But if Arthur truly existed in history, the location of his battles and his intent are the keys that will unlock the mystery to his identity. I hold an opinion that quite a lot of modern authors who refer to the *Historia*, or 'Nennius', when writing about Arthur, either miss important points or have not read the manuscript themselves.

I am not a Latin scholar but I have been fortunate to benefit from David Dumville's translation of the *Historia*. It seems to me that it is not too difficult to assess where the compiler is recording folklore compared to where he is reporting events of more substance. There is a 'Nennius' debate that centres around the theory that the compiler decided to first reconcile his sources before going on to synchronise the history. He might have known Arthur's campaigns against the Saxons were in the north, but Gildas implies that the southern-based Ambrosius Aurelianus was the victor at Badon, and Bede infers that the Saxon wars were, for the most part, in Kent, as does the *Anglo-Saxon Chronicle*. To avoid confusion, the compiler therefore separated his information about the famous Arthur, giving him pride of place, while also enhancing the story with folklore that had evolved around and about Wales in the intervening four centuries.

It is unfortunate that Arthur's battle list does not immediately follow the section on Vortimer, because this left historians, including Geoffrey of Monmouth, with the impression there was a significant passage of time between the two and that the battle list represented his lifetime achievements, whereas it was more likely Vortimer and Arthur's battles formed the parts of a single campaign, contemporary to the Saxon wars. The sources for the *Historia* must have been a fascinating mix, and the compiler himself may have had difficulty judging the correct sequence, as well as sorting the facts from the folklore. We should not therefore dismiss any of it. In particular, I believe that the elements the compiler considered genuine history are those laced with place names, which was a method of presenting 'evidence' for each event.

No maps of Britain are recorded as existing in the early ninth century, and very few people had much idea of whereabouts in the world they were. Sailors and travellers were held in high esteem and their tales of adventure were popular fireside entertainment. The journeys undertaken by the Romans and, in their wake, the Church made travel appear easier than it really was. For example, we are told that Germanus of Auxerre came to Britain twice from Armorica and later visited Ravenna where he died. St. Patrick is said to have been enslaved by Irish pirates and taken to Ireland from Britain. He escaped, studied in Auxerre, visited Tours and received his tonsure at Lérins

Abbey on an island off Cannes in the Mediterranean, all before returning to Ireland! The organisation of the pan-European Roman Church remains impressive, and as they say, all roads lead to Rome. However, in truth, the fear, danger and uncertainty of the Dark Ages undermined easy movement, and as communities became less able to travel, they became more neighbour-by-neighbour orientated. The hagiography of other saints describes how challenging their journeys became, and while some elements of trade continued, strangers were mostly perceived as a threat.

Place names were therefore extraordinarily important in describing locations for Dark Age travellers and were established with the intent of inferring location and sometimes ownership or hegemony. On the one hand, we worry about synthetic history, but on the other, we fail to rise to the challenge of properly establishing place name evidence within context, preferring to wait until something is dug out of the ground. Theories about Arthur often utilise place name interpretation, and range from the serious to the somewhat creative. Most are easily set aside when a strict regime of relevant topographical, historical and archaeological evidence is applied.

In the north, we have tended to accept that Arthur is a southern myth, but every now and again, there is an article or a book that rediscovers Arthwys of the Pennines, often justified by the inference of 'Camelot' from Rivet and Smith's identification of two Roman forts: Camulodunum at Slack, near Huddersfield, and the yet to be located Cambodunum, near Leeds. There are also old associations with Arthur at Richmond Castle in North Yorkshire, Pendragon Castle near Kirkby Stephen in Cumbria and Sewingshields milecastle on Hadrian's Wall, all in the former territory of Rheged. The Scottish Borders has its own collection of myths, place names and associations with Arthur and Merlin.

None of this adds up to very much when compared with the weight of association around the likes of Cadbury Hill, Tintagel and Glastonbury, except we are not so much looking for a man as a polity or, I should say, a kingdom.

We know that the Old North was still a Roman province in 400, but two hundred years later, we detect from heroic poetry that it had fractured into kingdoms. This could have been through inheritance, and given the loyalties that are possible to infer from genealogies, this seems most likely. By 580, we can identify Elmet as a kingdom, incorporating all West Yorkshire and extending west through Craven to the Ribble and north to the Nidd about this time. Urien of Rheged appears to have been in control of all territory west of the Roman road known as Dere Street, a much larger area.

This is all Coel's former territory, and we can surmise it did not fragment until the early sixth century. The distribution of 'Mor' place names suggests it was still largely intact in 450, although East Yorkshire and possibly York appear to have slipped from the family's control after the Saxon rebellion and wars. Elmet certainly looks like a Brigantes remnant. As powerful as they were, the Brigantes never sought to dominate eastwards beyond the Vale of York. The East Riding of Yorkshire, prior to the Romans, had been the domain of the Parisi, and it is interesting to note how quickly this region acculturated with the Angles in the late fifth century.

The Brigantes proved to be lots of trouble for the Romans. The episode between Cartimandua and her consort Venutius in 57–69 was just the start. In his book *Rome against Caratacus: Roman Campaigns in Britain, A.D. 48–58*, Graham Webster favours Barwick-in-Elmet as the location of Cartimandua's *oppidum* (large, defended Iron Age settlement). Tacitus recounts how Queen Cartimandua with her husband Venutius oversaw a powerful client kingdom loyal to Rome. The British resistance leader, Caratacus, sought sanctuary with the Brigantes after defeat by the Roman Ostorius Scapula in Wales but was handed over to the Romans in chains. Venutius and Cartimandua divorced, and while the queen remained loyal to Rome, her ex-consort revolted in about 52, establishing his *oppidum* much further north, possibly at Stanwick, close by Scotch Corner. The rebellion was quelled, but Venutius rebelled again in 69, and this time Cartimandua had to be evacuated. The Brigantes were not subdued for many decades.

There is no doubt that Barwick was an important tribal centre; the village is surrounded by the most remarkable earthworks, somewhat obscured in places by later medieval additions. Unfortunately, Barwick has never been excavated or properly protected until recently. It is sad to see an industrial estate cutting into the ditch to the north of Hall Tower Hill. Wendel Hill, the adjacent Iron Age enclosure, has modern buildings all over it. The two combined are sixteen acres, a large area. Hereabouts are several earthworks, called the Aberford Dykes, which are mostly Iron Age. Becca Banks, perhaps the best known, faces the north-east and cuts across the Roman road (the old A1 trunk road through Aberford). Woodhouse Moor Rein, another earthwork, looks like a continuation of Becca Banks and can be traced almost as far as Sherburn-in-Elmet. From the air, it is possible to detect other east-facing linear earthworks closer to Barwick.

In his 1904 guide, *The Old Kingdom of Elmet*, Edmund Bogg drew a map of Barwick-in-Elmet which reveals the extent of this formidable hillfort. Hall Tower Hill is the remains of a motte-and-bailey castle built by the Norman De Lacy family. This not only demonstrates continuous occupation but also indicates an ongoing need to control the locals. Norman fortresses such as this were about subjugation. Not far from Barwick is an area called Arthursdale which is close by a 'Pendas fields', although I was unable to locate either of these on the 1867 Ordnance Survey map. However, the battle of Winwaed, fought between Penda of Mercia and Oswia of Bernicia, is thought to have taken place on Whin Moor two miles east of Barwick.

The area around Cambodunum was always considered the crossroads of the north, and nearby battles have proved some of the bloodiest on English soil: Bramham Moor (1408), Towton Moor (1461) and Marston Moor (1644) are all within fifteen miles of Barwick-in-Elmet.

The local region was known to Bede as Loidis (Ledes or Leeds) and he mentions it in Book II, Chapter 14 of his *Historia Ecclesiastica*, noting a church erected by Edwin of Northumbria. There may have been an early Christian church in Barwick, since the churchyard was round and is raised, but there is only scant evidence for this. Bede's church is more likely to be the little church six miles away in Ledsham, elements of which are believed to go back to 700, which confirms its status as the oldest extant building in West Yorkshire. There is a famous south-facing Saxon door through which kings may well have entered. More recently, the discovery of a sub-Roman cemetery in 2023 at Garforth containing not only high-status graves but also Anglo-Saxon burials attests to fifth-century occupation in this area.

The Brigantes, and later Roman, settlements of Cambodunum, Isurium and Cataractonum all sit on a narrow magnesium limestone ridge which runs north to south in Yorkshire and more or less follows the A1 trunk road. As well as providing the people of the first millennium with a good defensive position, the three standing pillars known as the Devil's Arrows at Boroughbridge and the Thornborough Henges near Masham are evidence that the area also attracted Neolithic interest and occupation. There are even genuine reasons to believe that this route was used by Mesolithic travellers, so this region of the north has always played a prominent role in the history of Britain.

I have always questioned why the *civitas* of the Brigantes (Isurium) was sited at Aldborough, near Boroughbridge, because it is a long way from any of the known Brigantes forts. For a while, I wondered if it was a halfway point (bearing in mind the Cartimandua–Venutius schism). This was not an unreasonable conclusion to reach. But now I think I know why – Boroughbridge is the nearest access point to the Ouse which flows through York and into the Humber. The Nidd and Swale join forces just south of Isurium, making it eminently navigable. The Brigantes were renowned for their wealth, and they had access to one commodity that was in high demand by the Roman Empire: lead.

The lead mines of Swaledale, Nidderdale and Wharfedale were developed under the Romans and may well have been worked by slaves. The Romans were amazing plumbers, and while Britain was in the Empire, a significant trade existed which was shipped via the Humber. In the Middle Ages, lead was still shipped from Boroughbridge, and circa 660, St. Wilfrid is known to have arranged for the roof of his monastery at Ripon to utilise local lead – so we know production had continued. Two lead 'pigs' found at Heyshaw, near Greenhow Hill, in 1731 were inscribed with Emperor Domitian's Seventh Consulate and stamped with 'BRIG' for Brigantes. In 2007, Sir Thomas Ingleby of Ripley Castle sold one at auction for £36,000, while the other had been given to the British Museum in 1772. Barry Cunliffe notes the recovery of a cargo of lead weighing 22 tonnes from a shipwreck off Armorica where some pigs were similarly stamped 'BRIG', and these may well have originated from Isurium.

It is possible to walk from Swaledale almost directly to Boroughbridge without crossing a major river, and I am confident many such lead routes to Isurium existed in Late Antiquity. There were, most likely, attempts to continue production after 410, much like tin from Tintagel, but with the Anglo-Saxons choking the Humber and the Trent, there will have been hindrance and obstruction to both communication and trade.

This would have been one of several reasons for a powerful, northern Christian prince, such as Arthwys, to involve himself in the Saxon war. The Humber and Trent had become no-go zones, and the north-east and North Midlands were isolated and being held to ransom. But regardless of the negative effect on trade, the threat posed by the build-up of a mighty Saxon force just the other side of the Ouse would have been an untenable pressure on daily life.

With that in mind, could the area around Barwick-in-Elmet be a good candidate for the location of 'Camelot'? Well, the finds at Garforth in 2023 certainly help support that claim, and I live in hope that we may yet find further evidence for the elusive Cambodunum. I had always hoped that the Channel Four archaeology programme *Time Team* would show up in Barwick-in-Elmet, but they never got there. Perhaps the archaeologists still digging away in the East Riding searching for evidence of Anglo-Saxon assimilation might eventually agree to decamp to Barwick where they could find something interesting.

ROMAN BRITAIN'S ENEMIES AT THE CLOSE OF THE FOURTH CENTURY

Map 2: Enemies of Roman Britain, late fourth century AD

By the late fourth century, Roman Britain had been split into four provinces, and during this period, Barbarian raiding intensified. The above map indicates those tribes that were the likely culprits, some of which began to settle in Britain. The Romans established a military zone known as the Saxon Shore and built coastal forts along the east and south coasts. It is thought that, on occasion, Angles, Frisians and Franks worked with the Romans when transport by sea required additional boats, but 'Saxons' became the generic name for raiders and pirates, even though there was a diverse mix of seafaring tribes.

X

The English settlements

I spent an entire day trying to decide upon the title for this chapter. My first thought was to call it 'Who were the Anglo-Saxons?' This is an interesting question which I doubt the Anglo-Saxons themselves would have been able to answer. Only recently, I discovered the word 'Euhemerism' – the method of mythological interpretation which regards myths as traditional accounts of real incidents in human history – often used in relation to the Anglo-Saxon royal genealogies because, suspiciously, they all trace back to the god Woden! In short, these 'factual' accounts are considered mythical and, therefore, (to use that damning expression) 'cannot be relied upon'. Virtually all the sources for the Dark Ages fit this category to some extent.

My second thought was to call this chapter 'The Germanic settlers'. There can be no doubt that the fourth to sixth centuries saw increasing numbers of settlers arriving in Britain. Historians are no longer convinced this was the result of invasion, although the numbers make it appear such, and it cannot be denied that there were incidents of violence. But this rapid increase in population was likely multi-faceted and might well have occurred over a longer period than history books indicate. Perhaps the Gallic chronicler writing in 442 (who may well have been a Briton) was aware of a much greater concentration of Germanic settlers being present at that time, particularly on the east coast: 'The British, who to this time had suffered from various defects and misfortunes, are reduced to the power of the Saxons'.

This observation predated the Saxon wars, but it is an independent source and it might indicate how things were looking from across the Channel. We may one day discover that a greater density of settlers had already slipped into Flavia Caesariensis by this time, and that the raids recorded by Gildas were actually coming from much closer to home. With no legion to deter the enemy, this is highly likely. There is, therefore, a fair possibility that the Anglo-Saxons were already in control of huge swathes of the countryside and coastline even before the rebellion.

But I finally decided to call this chapter 'The English settlements' for two reasons. First, in honour of Collingwood and Myres' classic *Roman Britain and the English Settlements*, first published in 1936. Collingwood was criticised long after his death for his imaginative assumptions about Arthur, but his true legacy was the writing of a history of Roman Britain that combined archaeology and history with a unique philosophical perspective. Rightly or wrongly, I admire this style. Understanding history as it happened should not be constrained by fear of future discovery or reassessment. Secondly, it always seems to me that we behave as if we are reading and writing about foreigners, when in fact, the early Anglo-Saxons were the catalyst to the dawn of the great English nation.

Elements of settlement under the Romans

The tribes living in Britain at the time of the Roman invasion should be considered the baseline for the existing population here, although some were recent settlers themselves, such as the Belgae and the Parisi.

With the arrival of the Roman army came thousands of officials with their families, though Miles Russell and Stuart Laycock, in their book *Unroman Britain: Exposing the Great Myth of Britannia*, argue that Romanisation was mostly a veneer that peeled away quite quickly. This may be how it seems in the south, but the Celtic Church seems to have held the north together. Indeed, if it were not for Christianity, there might have been no sub-Roman measure to Late Antiquity Britain. In the north, early Christian churches are an indication of demarcation between the early Anglo-Saxons and the Britons. 'Eccles' and 'egles' place names come from the Welsh word 'eglwys' meaning church. The distribution of these places plots the likely boundaries between these separate cultures in the Dark Ages, and there are many in the north.

I have already outlined how cross-Channel transport and general trade had resulted in coastal and river settlements all the way around Britain. There is evidence for this everywhere. It is worth making the point again that the Romans established a military zone known as the Saxon Shore and that this may well have been called such as a result of the presence of Saxons on both sides of the Channel. All naval historians agree that Roman sea power had been run down to almost nothing by the late fourth century and this applies especially to the Western Roman Empire. Fleets for major campaigns had to be levied from the commercial sector, presenting opportunities for the seafaring Angles, Saxons and Frisians. For example, in 359, Emperor Julian organised a fleet of six hundred ships to transport corn from Britain to the Rhine, four hundred of which were specifically built for this purpose. Humber-based Angles and Frisians probably built and operated this fleet. Humber/Rhine traffic during the Roman Empire was significant in supporting both frontiers.

We should not forget the influence of slavery or indeed havens for escaped slaves on the population numbers. There would have been a high degree of slave ownership among the Roman occupiers, although I have never seen estimates of slave numbers in Britain. Not all slaves will have accepted their indentured status, and there is suggestion of *bacaudae* (rebels and escaped slaves) involvement in the Barbarian Conspiracy of 367 in Britain. We know *bacaudae* became a huge problem for Aetius, the Roman military commander on the Continent, who had to suppress whole armies of rebels in Armorica in 437 and 442 and in Spain in 443. There will also have been elements of *bacaudae* perhaps masquerading as Picts and Saxons, ultimately swelling the ranks of the settlers.

The settlement of soldiers and their families in and around Lincoln was Roman, but the racial mix must have been diverse, and we know of an episode in the history of the Brigantes denoting racial tension. In 155, Pausanias records the punishment of the Brigantes for an attack on the 'Genounian district' which turned into a major rebellion with serious consequences for the Brigantes. The 'Genounian district', a territory of Roman subjects, is unidentified, but it must have been adjacent to the Brigantes territory.

There are two candidates:

Roman Castleford (Lagentium) on the south bank of the River Aire was a comparatively busy fort and town. It was excavated between 1974 and 2005 and yielded evidence of spoon, pottery and glass flask manufacturing. The fort was guarded by the Fourth Cohort of the Gauls until about 100, after which it remained a commercial centre until it was abandoned circa 180. An excavated building, described as a pottery shop, had been destroyed by fire but the cause is unknown. Castleford may well have been considered protected or outside Brigantes territory. Perhaps these were river people such as Frisian Gauls who had settled with the troops and remained. The town's demise could easily have been a pogrom inflicted by their troublesome neighbours.

The other candidate is located in Lincolnshire along the Trent at Gainsborough, home of a tribe called the Gaini, who we will discuss later.

Modern Lincolnshire formed the largest part of Flavia Caesariensis. Lindum Colonia (Lincoln), we are told, derived its name from the lake, in Welsh 'Lynn', that was overlooked by the legionary fortress. The Celtic name 'Lindon' was then Latinised to 'Lindum' and the region became known as 'Lindes'. But I have always thought this seemed far too narrow an explanation, and I have an alternative suggestion.

The region associated with the name 'Lindes' is vast and covers not just North Lincolnshire but extends across the Trent to Thorne Waste and Hatfield Moor and includes the Isle of Axholme. The 1903 Ordnance Survey map of the region shows an isolated settlement called Lindholme, but not only is this far away, near Doncaster, it is also across the Trent, some thirty-five miles from Lincoln. Also, this vast region is known collectively as Lindsey and must surely have derived its name from something other than a small lake!

In the aftermath of the last ice age, the area was covered by Lake Humber, and while, over thousands of years, the waters receded, no significant drainage was undertaken until the Middle Ages. Many homesteads in this remote area were abandoned in the late fourth century because of flooding in the Humber estuary as a result of rising sea levels. It is difficult to picture how the area would have looked in Roman times, but it must have been a wild and dangerous marshland. Two plants grow naturally and thrive in these conditions – flax and hemp. Linen production is thousands of years old. The Welsh word for flax is, unsurprisingly, 'llin'. In Latin, flax is 'et linum meum' and linseed is 'lins semen'. I just wonder if an ancient linen trade existed, or perhaps the local tribe were 'people of the flax' or the 'linen people'. It is perhaps no coincidence that, by the Middle Ages, linen produced from flax was a significant cottage industry in the area. Just a guess, but it better explains why this vast area, stretching far out from a small lake, would have been known to the Romans as 'Lindes'. The Romans used linen for sails and hemp for rope. However, there is no archaeological evidence of any such trade in the region in the fourth century.

I suggested earlier that either Theodosius or Maximus may have engaged seafaring Angles as *foederati* to patrol the Humber and Trent. I also suggested they were deployed to protect Danum (Doncaster) because that area south of the Humber was vulnerable to barbarian landfall. In Roman times, there was a huge forest south of Danum and west of the Trent which stretched from South Yorkshire past Nottingham and almost to Leicester. This area is today known by the names of the famous forests

Sherwood and Charnwood. Much like in the legend of Robin Hood, I propose that this whole forested area was full of brigands and barbarians, making it impossible to patrol without a large army. It is no wonder the Saxons and Picts could strike at will then disappear – they were most probably hiding in the forest close by British territory but with excellent lines of communication to their settlements via the River Trent. Intriguingly, Geoffrey of Monmouth makes a reference to the diverse inhabitants who lived by the Humber, in 'Arthurs time'. So this is probably how the Saxons came to dominate such a vast area so quickly and were capable of raiding as far inland as Watling Street.

Prior to 410, the Humber Angles were working hand in glove with the Romans, but sometime later in the fifth century, they appear to have consolidated lands to the south of the Humber to the east of the Trent. This area included the Roman ferry across the Humber to Brough, a key crossing point. It seems likely that their settlement had the full support of the local British elite in exchange for services and perhaps protection. This settlement of Angles later became known as the kingdom of Lindsey.

The kingdom of Lindsey

Lindsey was never a powerful kingdom, and for all of its known history was under the domination of more powerful neighbours, constantly changing hands between Northumbria and Mercia. Great battles occurred on its margins, ultimately deciding its fate.

One such battle at Hatfield Chase (632) was fought between Edwin of Northumbria and Penda of Mercia. Edwin had been recognised as overlord of all Britain and had himself conquered Elmet, driving out Cerdic, the last ever king. Both Edwin and his son Ostrid lost their lives at Hatfield Chase, and according to Bede, there followed the most appalling slaughter of men, women and children. A later battle called the Battle of Trent (679) was fought between Ecgfrith of Northumbria and Aethelred of Mercia when Lindsey was lost to Mercia. In his account, Bede mentions a defeated Northumbrian *thegn* from Lindsey called Imma (perhaps giving his name to Immingham) who was captured and sold into slavery. A Frisian merchant discovered his identity, and he was ransomed to the King of Kent.

Little is known about the kings of Lindsey, although the names of many of them are recorded in the genealogy of Aldfrith, the last king. This list is remarkable in that, unlike most Anglo-Saxon royal genealogies, it does not trace Aldfrith's lineage back to the god Woden. The Lindsey genealogy lacks the evidence of surviving chronicles, but more so than any other genealogy, the names echo in the landscape within the boundaries of the Angles' territory:

c.740 Aldfrith Eatting
Eatta Eanferthing
Eanferth Biscoping
Biscop Beding (Benedict Biscop 628–690)
Beda Bubbing
Bubba Caebaeding (Bubwith, Humberside village)
Caedbaed Cueldgilsing (Welsh name, perhaps Caenby, North Lincolnshire village)
Cueldgils Cretting
Cretta Winting

c.470 Winta Wodning (Winteringham, Winterton, north Lincolnshire villages)
Woden Frealafing

Frealaf Friothulfing
Friothulf Finning

c.380 Finn Goduulfing (Finningley, south Yorkshire village)
Godulf
Goeting

The name Caedbaed in the list is thought to be Welsh, which suggests that the royal family of Lindsey had links with the native Britons.

This collection of Anglian genealogies was created in the last years of Offa of Mercia in the 780s. To establish estimated dates for these kings of Lindsey, we need first to identify someone from history. Dating King Aldfrith is tricky. One might tend to think that the Lindsey line came to an end at the Battle of Trent in 679, but then there would be no reason to record a list in the late eighth century unless, perhaps, important or dispossessed *thegns* were still alive. It may be possible to identify one of the names on the list because Biscop Beding looks very much like Benedict Biscop (aka Biscop Baducing) who lived circa 628–690. It is generally accepted that an average generation is thirty years, and this seems to work with the Lindsey king list. So, if we count generations, we can estimate Aldfrith's floruit in the 740s, which seems reasonable. If we count generations backwards, we arrive at Winta consolidating his kingdom in the 470s, but perhaps more importantly, Finn operating as *foederati* in the 380s. Lots of guesswork, but this indicates that the Angles were appointed as *foederati* by either Magnus Maximus or Coel Hen.

Anglo-Saxon king lists are, to say the least, unreliable. The concept of the divine right of kings (appointment by God) was important to most cultures, not just Christianity, so it was essential to lay claim to the right forebears. All Anglo-Saxon king lists are euhemerised and the genealogy of the kings of Lindsey is no different.

One hero stands out: a certain Finn. There is an Old English poem known as the 'Finnesburg Fragment' which is incomplete, being about fifty lines long, and which mentions 'Finns stronghold' (Finsburuh), which could correlate to the place name 'Finningley'. This village is just south of Doncaster (Danum) on the old A1, a good location for an early contingent of *foederati* to be stationed if they were there to protect Danum from the south and east. This would seem to be an indication that the threat to Danum was not actually from sea raiders using the river but from bands coming north out of Sherwood Forest.

Finn and the Angles of Lindsey may rank as the earliest *foederati*, arriving some forty-five years before the *Adventus Saxonum*, and this rather explains their established position and perhaps the respect with which later chronicles refer to the kings of the Angles. RAF Finningley was the home of a squadron of the mighty Vulcan bombers following the Second World War but was decommissioned in 1996. Thereafter, the aerodrome was opened to commercial traffic in 2005, and despite its crucial role in the Cold War, it was renamed Robin Hood Airport, a classic example of modern-day euhemerism I believe!

I have read a paper by Caitlin Green, titled 'The British Kingdom of Lindsey', originally published in 2008 but now available on the internet. Dr Green displays an excellent knowledge of Lindsey and more than adequately justifies her claim that Lindsey, post-Rome, was at first a Romano-British kingdom that later coalesced with the Angles.

It even seems that Christianity survived within the Roman walls of Lincoln, and a recently excavated apsidal timber church, known as St. Paul in the Bail, is now confirmed as fifth to sixth century. Sited in what was the Roman forum, there is still some debate as to whether this is the church mentioned by Bede – he apparently thought it was stone, not timber, but Bede did not travel much further than York so much of his information was hearsay. When I visited the church site and city museum in 1999, nobody was then sure how long the church had survived post-Rome, and claims about the discovery were coy. It was a weekday morning, so I had the place to myself and I was able to chat with the curator who was a retired archaeologist. Displayed on the wall was one of those section diagrams showing the depth of each period. The fifth and sixth centuries were wafer-thin, denoting little activity other than perhaps horticulture. We arrived at the conclusion that the Christians were purposefully cloistered within the walls, probably as defence against raiders.

I have always been fascinated by the scribal gloss to the version of the *Historia* from Sawley Abbey denoting that Vortimer, son of Vortigern, was buried at Lincoln (circa 465), particularly since he was supposed to be battling in Kent. This could well have been at St. Paul in the Bail and perhaps derives from similar northern bardic sources to Arthur's battles, since Sawley is on the western tip of Craven which remained principally Cumbric (British) right up to the Norman Conquest. You will read in the following chapters that I believe Vortimer actually died in Lincolnshire, making the Sawley gloss particularly relevant.

More settlements

It will be obvious by now that I am not an etymologist, but despite my weaknesses, I do hope it is becoming apparent that Britain was subject to ongoing settlement from the fourth century onwards. We have yet to reach the *Adventus Saxonum* of Gildas, Bede and the *Historia*, but we already suspect the presence of Saxons, Angles, Frisians and perhaps even Picts in Britain. Flavia Caesariensis had become host to them all. The distribution of Saxon place names across this region not only outlines the extent of early control but also defines where it was halted by partition following the Battle of Mount Badon. It therefore appears that Saxon place names in this northern area are mostly attributable to the fifth and sixth century.

Another significant place, and name, is Gainsborough which is believed to come from a tribe called the Gaini. In 868, King Alfred married Ealswitha, daughter of the chief of the Gaini which was already a 'very old tribe'. An entry in the *Anglo-Saxon Chronicle* in 1013 shows the name as *Gegnesburh* which means 'Gegne's fortified place'. Gainsborough became a strategic river port and increasingly important over the centuries. The early stronghold and port developed on the east bank of the Trent but south of the Anglian settlements. It is possible that this tribe were Frisian river people or settled families of Germanic soldiers, and perhaps this is the 'Genounian district' that the Brigantes attacked in 155.

There are also a lot of 'Gun' place names along the Vale of the Trent. The oldest clan in Scotland with Pictish roots is called 'Gunn', which translates as 'war', and for about fifteen exciting minutes I wondered if these were remnants of a Pictish settlement. However, I quickly discovered that 'Guni' in Old English, Danish, German and Dutch means 'sack'. So, we are back to hemp, flax and trade which is much more mundane but no less relevant.

XI

Adventus Saxonum

When the accounts of the arrival of the Saxons are compared it becomes apparent that they all rely on Gildas as their source. Both Bede and the *Anglo-Saxon Chronicle* recount that the landing site of Hengist and Horsa was in Kent; the *Historia* follows suit. But the place names recounted in these sources may actually indicate a landing on the Humber, a much more appropriate location if they were brought in to counter the Picts. Peter Hunter Blair, writing in 1956, cautioned that, although Bede gave locality, definition and chronological rigidity to the tradition, he was nonetheless writing two hundred years after Gildas who merely said they landed in the east.

We now step back into the fifth century to try to establish who arrived in Britain, when they arrived and perhaps where they landed. There are differing opinions about when Vortigern decided to take charge of Britain and when the Saxons were first invited. §66 of the *Historia* gives the best indication of the dates, but in a rather convoluted way:

> *From the reign of Vortigern to the quarrel between Vitalinus and Ambrosius are 12 years, that is Guoloppum, or Catguoloph. Vortigern, however, held the empire in Britain in the consulship of Theodosius and Valentian, and in the fourth year of his reign the English came to Britain, in the consulship of Felix and Taurus, in the 400th year from the incarnation of our Lord Jesus Christ.*

This dating information is from a section describing the *Discordia* between Vitalinus and Ambrosius, known as the Battle of Wallop; it also helpfully provides the information we need. Theodosius and Valentinian held joint consulship in 425. Felix and Taurus held the consulship in 428 which was the fourth year after 425. The Saxons therefore first arrived in 428 and the *Discordia* occurred in 437, twelve years after Vortigern came to power. This battle is important, and I will outline why later, but first we need to study in detail what all the sources say about the arrival of the Saxons. In *De Excidio*, Gildas first records an incidence of plague which must have made the Britons feel even more vulnerable:

> *§22. a deadly plague swooped brutally on the stupid people and in a short period laid low so many, with no sword, that the living could not bury all the dead. But not even this taught them their lesson...*

He emphasises the hopelessness of the Britons with the kind of detail that can only have come from someone who witnessed the brutality and terror, quite possibly his parents.

> *§22. And they convened a Council to decide the best and soundest way to counter the brutal and repeated invasions and plunderings by the people I have mentioned.*

> *§23. Then all the members of the Council, together with the* superbo tyranno *(proud tyrant), were struck blind. As protection for our country, they sealed its doom by inviting in among them, like wolves into a sheep-fold, the ferocious Saxons, hated by man and*

God, to beat back the peoples of the North. Nothing more destructive, nothing more bitter has ever befallen the land. How utter the blindness of their minds. How desperate and crass the stupidity. Of their own free will they invited under the same roof a people whom they feared worse than death even in their absence.

Then a pack of cubs burst forth from the lair of the barbarian lioness, coming in three keels, as they call warships in their language. The winds were favourable; favourable too the omens and auguries which prophesied, according to a sure portent among them, that they would live for three hundred years in the land towards which their prows were directed and that for half that time, a hundred and fifty years, they would repeatedly lay it waste. On the orders of the ill-fated tyrant they first of all fixed their dreadful claws on the east side of the island, ostensibly to fight for our country, in fact to fight against it. The mother lioness learned that her first contingent had prospered and she sent a second and larger troop of satellite dogs. It arrived by ship and joined up with the false units. The barbarians who had been admitted to the island asked to be given supplies, falsely representing themselves as soldiers ready to undergo extreme dangers for their excellent hosts. The supplies were granted and, for a long time, 'shut the dog's mouth'. Then they again complained that their monthly allowance was insufficient, purposely giving a false colour to individual incidents, and swore that they would break their agreement and plunder the whole island unless more lavish payment was heaped upon them. There was no delay: they put their threats into immediate effect.

§24. In just punishment for the crimes that had gone before, a fire heaped up and, nurtured by the hand of the impious easterners, spread from sea to sea. It devastated town and country round about and, once it was alight, it did not die down until it had burned almost the whole surface of the island and was licking the western ocean with its fierce red tongue. All the major towns were laid low by the repeated battering of enemy rams, laid low too all the inhabitants – church leaders, priests and people alike – as the swords glinted all around and the flames crackled. It was a sad sight. In the middle of the squares the foundation-stones of high walls and towers that had been torn from their lofty base, holy altars, fragments of corpses covered with a purple crust of congealed blood, looked as though they had been mixed up in some dreadful wine press. There was no burial to be had except in the ruins of houses or the bellies of beasts and birds

§25. So a number of the wretched survivors were caught in the mountains and butchered wholesale. Others, their spirit broken by hunger, went to surrender to the enemy; they were fated to be slaves forever, if indeed they were not killed straight away, the highest boon. Others made for lands beyond the sea. Others held out, though not without fear, in their own land, trusting their lives with constant

foreboding to the high hills... To the densest forests and to the cliffs of the sea coast.

After a time, when the cruel plunderers had gone home, God gave strength to the survivors. Wretched people fled to them from all directions, as eagerly as bees to the beehive when a storm threatens, and begged whole-heartedly that they should not be altogether destroyed. Their leader was Ambrosius Aurelianus, a gentleman who, perhaps alone of the Romans, had survived the shock of this notable storm; his parents, who had certainly worn the purple, were slain in it. His descendants in our day have become greatly inferior to their grandfather's excellence. Under him our people regained their strength, and challenged the victors to battle. The Lord assented and the battle went their way.

§26. From then on, victory went now to our countrymen, now to their enemies, so that in this people the Lord could make trial of his latter-day Israel to see whether it loved him or not. This lasted right up to the year of the siege of Badon Hill, pretty well the last defeat of the villians, and certainly not the least. That was the year of my birth; as I know, one month of the forty-fourth year since then has already passed.

While it is often pointed out that *De Excidio* is a powerful sermon, there is no disguising the bitterness Gildas felt for the tragedy that befell his parents' generation. Later chroniclers focused on the detail of Gildas, perhaps failing to appreciate that the rebellion had greater breadth and that there must have been not only Saxons but also elements of *bacaudae*. Loyalties may have been confused, and clearly, some areas fared better than others, but there is no doubting the shock and brutality of this incursion. By the time the *Historia* was written, the Saxons had been given an identity and more information was known about their background:

> *§31. In the meantime, three ships, exiled from Germany, arrived in Britain. They were commanded by the brothers Horsa and Hengist, sons of Wihtgils... Vortigern received them as friends, and delivered up to them the island which is in their language called Tanet and, by the Britons, Ruoihm. Gratianus Æquantius at that time reigned in Rome. The Saxons were received by Vortigern three hundred and forty-seven years after the passion of Christ*

Bede provides more origin detail:

> *Then the nation of Angles, or Saxons, being invited by the aforesaid king, arrived in Britain with three ships of war and had a place in which to settle assigned to them by the same king, in the eastern part of the island, on the pretext of fighting in defence of their country, while their real intentions were to conquer it. Accordingly they engaged with the enemy, who were to come from the north to give battle, and the Saxons obtained the victory. When the news of their success and of the fertility of the country, and the cowardice of the Britons, reached their own home, a more considerable fleet was*

quickly sent over, bringing a greater number of men, and these, being added to the former army, made up an invincible force. The newcomers received of the Britons a place to inhabit among them, upon condition that they should wage war against their enemies for the peace and security of the country, while the Britons agreed to furnish them with pay. Those who came over were of the three most powerful nations of Germany – Saxons, Angles and Jutes. From the Jutes are descended the people of Kent, and of the Isle of Wight, including those in the province of the West-Saxons who are to this day called Jutes, seated opposite to the Isle of Wight. From the Saxons, that is, the country which is now called Old Saxony, came the East-Saxons, the South-Saxons, and the West-Saxons. From the Angles, that is, the country which is called Angulus, and which is said, from that time, to have remained desert to this day, between the provinces of the Jutes and the Saxons, are descended the East-Angles, the Midland-Angles, the Mercians, all the race of the Northumbrians, that is, of those nations that dwell on the north side of the River Humber, and the other nations of the Angles. The first commanders are said to have been the two brothers Hengist and Horsa. Of these Horsa was afterwards slain in battle by the Britons, and a monument, bearing his name, is still in existence in the eastern parts of Kent. They were the sons of Victgilsus, whose father was Vitta, son of Vecta, son of Woden; from whose stock the royal race of many provinces trace their descent. In a short time, swarms of the aforesaid nations came over into the island, and the foreigners began to increase so much, that they became a source of terror to the natives themselves who had invited them. Then, having on a sudden entered into league with the Picts, whom they had by this time repelled by force of arms, they began to turn their weapons against their allies.

The constant reference to the three Saxon boats, known as 'three keels', is intriguing and clearly shows there is one key source, Gildas. This can only be a tradition arising from the memory of a ceremony or official event where the Saxons were given their territory. While warfare scaled back considerably in the Dark Ages and recorded battles may have looked more like skirmishes compared to Roman encounters, it is unlikely that three keels of Saxons was even slightly representative of the initial *Adventus*. There is plenty of evidence on the Continent for tribes, such as Goths, Huns and Alemanni, forming into large ethnic groups on the move, and there was surely an element of this to the *Adventus*. The *Anglo-Saxon Chronicle* (the Peterborough Manuscript) provides further detail in the following entries, noting the name of the place the Saxons landed:

443. Here the Britons sent across the sea to Rome and asked them for help against the Picts, but they had none there because they were campaigning against Attila, king of the Huns; and then they sent to the Angles and made the same request to the princes of the Angle race.

449. In their days Vortigern invited the Angle race here and they then came here to Britain in three ships at the place Ypwines Fleot. The king Vortigern gave them land in the south-east of this land on condition that they fought against the Picts. They then fought against the Picts and had victory wheresoever they came. Then they sent to Angeln. Ordered (them) to send more help and ordered them to tell of the worthlessness of the Britons and of the excellence of the land. They then at once sent here a larger troop to help the other. These men came from three tribes of Germany: the Old Saxons, from the Angles, from the Jutes. From the Jutes came the Cantware and the Wihtware – that is the tribe which now lives on Wight – and that race in Wessex which they still call the race of Jutes. From the Old Saxons came the East Saxons and South Saxons and West Saxons. From the Angeln, which has stood waste ever since between the Jutes and the Saxons, came the East Angles, Middle Angles, Mercians, and all the Northumbrians. Their commanders were two brothers, Hengest and Horsa, that were sons of Wihtgils. Wihtgils was Witta's offspring, Witta Wecta's offspring. Wecta Woden's offspring. From that Woden originated all our royal family, and (that) of the Southumbrians also.

The above excerpts from four important sources form the sum total we know about the arrival of Hengist and Horsa, and more or less, it all crosschecks. It is now fashionable to make the point that the names Hengist and Horsa are known to be horse gods, making them even more myth than they were already. There is no reason for us to be concerned about this since they are universally accepted as the nominal leaders of the Saxon rebellion and the protagonists in respect of the war. I will show later how they became the specific target of British campaigns.

That it was necessary for Vortigern to call a council to sanction federate troops is significant. In many respects it is surprising that he stepped up to take full control – after all, his own region had its own specific raiders, the Irish and the Scotti. While there are no further reports of these western raids, we should not forget Patrick's abduction from the west coast about this time. Vortigern, it seems, was taking his role as Protector seriously, and I suspect the council's purpose was to agree how to share the cost for the federate troops.

The actions of the man do not fit the legend, and almost all the close-quarter information about Vortigern and Hengist in the *Historia* seems to be more fable than myth. Gildas never blames Vortigern for the *Adventus* but considers him to have been unlucky. Federates had been sought from far and wide by the Britons, and their deployment was very similar to the Late Roman way of managing defence on the Continent. There is no doubt that professional *foederati* were deployed in Kent and up the Thames. This is evident from the belt buckles and weapons found buried with them. But the Jutes that are known to have occupied Kent appeared later and are said to be descendants of Octha, Hengist's son or grandson.

However, the mythical landing of Hengist and Horsa in Kent is one of the great red herrings of the fifth century.

The *Historia* contradicts its own earlier reports when noting the following:

> *§51. At that time the Saxons were becoming strong in numbers and growing in power in Britain. When Hengist died, his son Ochta crossed from the Northern part of Britain to the kingdom of the men of Kent. And from him the Kings of the men of Kent were sprung.*

This statement is strangely inserted after the section on Patrick but before Arthur's battles. It suggests Hengist was never in Kent and, much like the references to Arthur, it is out of historical sequence, suggesting a different source.

So how did all this confusion arise? It seems likely that place name traditions became mixed up with origin myth. Kent became a mighty kingdom in the sixth century. Aethelberht (King of Kent 584–616) is the first reliably attested Anglo-Saxon monarch, and Bede states he was *Bretwalda*, which means 'high king', and he controlled all his people's territories south of the Humber. The Christianisation of Anglo-Saxon England by the Roman Church began in Aethelberht's reign when Augustine arrived with the Gregorian mission in 596. This was an extraordinarily important event, particularly to Bede. So, perhaps this powerful kingdom was given an even more glorious origin by the bards of this time, which was picked up later by the chroniclers and never questioned, or perhaps Kent being noted as the original landing site was simply a result of the assumed genealogical connection to Hengist and Horsa, which is noted in the *Anglo-Saxon Chronicle*.

Bede is not the only chronicler to mention Kent (Cantiae), but he was the first to reference the monument to Horsa which has, of course, never been found. This is probably why modern historians dismiss Hengist and Horsa as myth – the evidence simply isn't reliable. This is no big surprise if we have been looking in the wrong place all this time. I propose that the place names, locations, topography and historical relevance all fit much better in the north. In many ways this reassessment counters their mythical status and adds weight to their historicity, lending more credence to their role in the recorded events. After years of research, in which I have attempted to reconcile all the sources, this is the conclusion I have reached.

Along the south bank of the Humber, past the confluence with the Trent, and therefore beyond the Anglian settlements and the Roman ferry, are four villages side by side: Swinefleet, Reedness, Whitgift and Ousefleet. This area could well represent the place referred to in the *Anglo-Saxon Chronicle* as the first landing site, because Swinefleet looks a dead ringer for *Ypwinesfleot*. Whitgift may well refer to the gift of the land to Wihtgils, father of Hengist and Horsa. The land behind the landing point was very much an island bounded by rivers that flooded, making it inaccessible by land. In Roman times, the land was poor quality and completely isolated. To this day, it is known as Goole Moor, Thorne Waste and the Isle of Axholme. The ground around Thorne Waste is black from peat, the result of it being a marsh for thousands of years.

Tanet (the name of the land given to the Jutes), rather than being Thanet in Kent, more likely derives from *terram tennerit* which means 'land holding' in Latin and is the origin of the word 'tenant'. Bearing in mind all this information comes to us via 400-year-old oral tradition, the closest parallel in Welsh to the alternative place name claimed as the landing place by the *Historia* is *Ruoihm* (*Ruym*) from 'rhwymo' which means 'to bind' or 'a bond'. So, the descriptions in both languages show that the granting of the land came with some kind of obligation. Mike Ashley, in *A Brief History of King Arthur*,[14] broadly agrees with this but also says that a spelling in a different manuscript, *Ruoichin*, could be translated as 'river island' which certainly could be used to describe Thorne Waste and the neighbouring Isle of Axholme. If we were looking for epithets then, by adding two letters to an otherwise medieval name, we arrive at the Isle of Se-axholme! This would certainly confirm this area as a Saxon territory, as the seax was a short sword or large knife that was the favoured weapon of the Saxons, and Essex derives its name from it.

The confusion with Kent is odd but perhaps not without due cause. There exists a list of all place names in the Roman Empire, known as the Ravenna Cosmography, originally compiled in the seventh century. Rivet and Smith have utilised this information in their book *The Place-Names of Roman Britain*. They confirm Cantium as Kent and Cantiaci as the people of Kent, but they also list another town called Cantia. Research into the British section of the Cosmography is relatively recent and Rivet and Smith describe it as 'most baffling'. Cantia is thought to be in the far south-west, on the edge of Roman territory.

[14] Mike Ashley, *A Brief History of King Arthur: The Man and the Legend Revealed* (London: Robinson, 2010).

The similarity between these names is interesting and will certainly have proved confusing for early chroniclers.

The reference to Kent in the *Historia* appears in the mythical section where Vortigern covets Hengist's daughter and gives him land in exchange for her hand in marriage:

> *And when Hengist took counsel with his elders as to what they should seek in return for the girl, they all had one suggestion that they should ask for the district which is called in their language Cantwaraland but in ours Caint. And he (Vortigern) gave it to him while Gwyranfon was ruling in Cantia.*

This demonstrates the confusion. The compiler clearly believes that Cantwaraland and Caint are in fact Cantia. The *Historia* was compiled three hundred years after these events and suffers from interpretive hindsight bias. There are further possible translations: *kante* in German is 'edge' and *kant* in Dutch translates as 'side'. There are two villages in Britain called Cantley and both have topographically comparable locations. One is in Norfolk, positioned on the edge of the Norfolk Broads and the other is Cantley by Doncaster, positioned at the side of the watersheds of the Rivers Don, Went and Torne into the Ouse and Trent. Alternatively, *caeint* in Welsh means 'fall', and where the Trent meets the Ouse just around from Whitgift is known as 'Trent Falls'. None of this proves very much except that chroniclers were often guessing locations. Professor D. P. Kirby in *The Earliest English Kings* notes:

> *The preservation of later traditions about the events of the conquest of Britain by the Anglo-Saxons in the fifth and sixth centuries in the* Anglo-Saxon Chronicle, *first compiled at the court of Alfred, king of the West Saxons, in the 890s, and even more the wealth of information concerning the conversion of the Anglo-Saxons to Christianity in the seventh century in Bede's* Historia Ecclesiastica Gentis Anglorum, *completed c. 731, can easily obscure the lack of contemporary evidence for much of the history of the Germanic regions of Britain during these post-Roman centuries. It is more appreciated now than ever before that just as the Chronicle preserves essentially a late ninth-century view of the Anglo-Saxon Conquest, so the Ecclesiastical History provides an early eighth-century view of the conversion of the Anglo-Saxons. Both are some distance removed in time from the events in question, and their materials have been shaped by the interests of their own age. In the absence of any considerable body of earlier evidence it is generally difficult to verify or qualify these later accounts.*[15]

Geoffrey of Monmouth, in particular, preferred the main power centres of his own times as the background to his *History of the Kings of Britain*, somewhat misleading everyone for centuries.

Since many of these place names came to the *Historia*, Bede and the *Anglo-Saxon Chronicle* through oral

[15] Kirby, *The Earliest English Kings*, p 30.

tradition, it is understandable how hindsight will have played its part in their placement. However, repositioning the *Adventus* to Humberside allows for a complete rethink of locations for recorded battles and produces astonishing results, not only bringing the campaigns of Vortimer, Arthur and Ambrosius into sharp focus but also providing a sensible location for, and a better chance of dating, the Battle of Mount Badon.

While the sources appear to focus almost entirely upon the Jutes, Hengist and Horsa, we should not forget that there is much evidence in Lincolnshire for existing *foederati* already deployed in defence of Roman towns, most probably as a follow-on from the Theodosian restoration. This evidence comes from the study of late military buckles, some of which were made on the Continent and others which were British copies. There have been finds of these at Saltersford, Sleaford, Dragonby, Osgodby and Lincoln, and many Saxon cemeteries attest to their occupants being *foederati* as they are close by Roman towns such as Ancaster Caistor, Great Casterton and Sleaford. J. B. Whitwell in *Roman Lincolnshire* makes the following comment about a discovery in the Fens at Horncastle north of the Wash:

> *Little is known of any Anglo-Saxon settlement in the area of Horncastle, but one piece of evidence is tantalizing. A burial of the period is recorded, without a precise location, in the vicinity of Horncastle. It was accompanied by an iron sword and two spearheads. The possession of a sword may have marked the individual buried as an important local leader, for swords are not commonly found as*

grave goods, even on sites where excavations have been extensive. If he was, in fact, a local leader, this implies that there was at least a group to be led in the vicinity of Horncastle. It would be of greatest interest to know the provenance of this burial, for there is the possibility that some of the numerous other burials recorded to the south of Horncastle belong to this period. Not all of these by any means are certainly Roman, for the majority have been discovered by chance finds and no details are recorded.[16]

Just south of Horncastle are the havens of the Wash where the rivers Witham, Welland and Glen meet the sea. From this area, there runs an ancient pre-Roman path known as the Salt Way which can be traced as far as the Midlands. It crosses both Ermine Street and the Fosse Way, eventually seeming to terminate in Charnwood Forest by Bardon Hill. This route appears to have become important in the fifth century not just for salt but also for Anglo-Saxons moving inland. In a lot of respects, it looks like a southern boundary to early Saxon annexation leading to the western limit of their territories: Bardon Hill, the place where I propose the Battle of Mount Badon actually occurred.

By 430, Britons must have felt beleaguered by raids on every coast. It had been twenty years since the Romans had left and there was no indication they would return soon. The career of the great Roman general, Aetius, was

[16] J. B. Whitwell, *Roman Lincolnshire* (Lincoln: History of Lincolnshire Committee, 1970), p 139. © History of Lincolnshire Committee and J. B. Whitwell, 1970, permission to quote kindly granted.

not yet secure on the Continent. In fact, in 432, he was stripped of his military command and was on the point of starting a civil war with a rival general, Bonifacius. High volumes of contact between Britons and the Continent will have continued. The Church, the Armorican settlements and perhaps even some Gallic nobles will have kept their lines of communication open.

Knowing no help would be coming from Rome, the decision by Vortigern, and perhaps a council, to employ and deploy *foederati* must have seemed the only quick solution to the raiding and was likely a genuine attempt to counter the problem. Both Gildas and the *Historia* criticise this decision because of its outcome, but the treaties that were put into effect lasted for almost ten years, and they appear to have had a significant impact on reducing Pictish raiding. We will never know the detailed arrangements for all the professional *foederati* that were deployed, but it is likely that if the Jutes were based on the Humber, their mission was to defend against and seek and destroy the Picts in exchange for their *tenat* and *epimenia* (land and monthly supplies). Gildas, Bede and the *Historia* all agree that Hengist and Horsa went on to increase the size of their force and, in consequence, sought increased supplies. In justification for this demand, they reported fantastic successes against the Picts. The *Historia* records:

> *... and Hengist summoned Octha and Ebissa with fourty ships. And when they sailed around the Picts, they devastated the Orkney. And they came and seized very many districts beyond the Frisian Sea all the way to the boundary of the Picts.*

This does sound far-fetched and a rather obvious cover for the subsequent arrival of forty ships. It is also likely that the Jutes reached accord with the *bacaudae* in Sherwood Forest, perhaps recruiting them and other settlers to their ranks. Ad hoc raiding was not so lucrative post-420 as the vulnerable regions were generally more prepared and resilient, their portable wealth dwindling. The bottom had fallen out of old-style raiding! The Picts, as enigmatic as ever, seemed to be focusing their aggression elsewhere, perhaps at their immediate neighbours. The Strathclyde Britons, the Votadini/Gododdin and the Scots were all forming into nascent kingdoms about this time, posing new threats. Territory was becoming more desirable than the ever-diminishing Roman treasure.

At the same time as the Saxons were bolstering their forces, the *Historia* records an incident, or what could have been civil war, between the Britons, known as the *Discordia.* It seems Ambrosius and a Vitalinus clashed at the Battle of Wallop (circa 437), but no victor is recorded. This matter is mentioned in §66 of the *Historia*, but earlier in §31 the following entry perhaps describes the politics at play:

> *the Britons went in fear for 40 years following the usurpation of Maximus. Vortigern then reigned in Britain. He had cause for dread not only from the Scots and Picts but also from the Romans and a dread of Ambrosius.*

It is always assumed that Ambrosius and Vortigern were rivals and that the Vitalinus at Wallop was the personal name of Vortigern. There is a view that

Ambrosius, being a Roman, might benefit at the expense of Vortigern from a return of the Romans. This is a simplistic assumption and may be incorrect. Vortigern had 'assumed overlordship' while Ambrosius was a very young man, and this encounter comes too soon to be a challenge by Ambrosius, so it must have been something else.

Nether Wallop, the presumed location for the battle, is less than 12 miles from Winchester, the main *civitas* of the area where Ambrosius is thought to have held property. The Battle of Wallop was therefore deep inside Belgae territory and looks very much like a surprise visit by Vortigern who may well have been debt-collecting to pay for *foederati*. It is not known the extent to which blows were exchanged, and given that both families subsequently cooperated in the Saxon wars, a parley was the most likely outcome. Perhaps, Ambrosius was refusing to contribute to the cost of the Jutes – this is likely, given that unpaid *epimenia* was a cause of the rebellion that would shortly commence.

I have read it suggested that this was the battle at which Ambrosius' father was killed, but I think that Gildas or the *Historia* would have likely noted this. The two leaders were perhaps rivals but probably not enemies. However, this clash rather demonstrates the immense pressure Vortigern was under to fulfil his obligations to the Jutes, and he may have been aware that rebellion was imminent.

The arrangements with the Thames and other Saxon *foederati* are not known, and there is no evidence that they joined the Jutes in rebellion. So, by 440, we know there are Jutes, Angles, Saxons and indeterminate *bacaudae* in substantial numbers concentrated in Lincolnshire and

Nottinghamshire – surely amounting to the 'invincible force' described by Bede.

XII

The Saxon rebellion and wars

Unlike the battles of Arthur, which have been studied and reviewed time and again, the battles of the Saxon wars are rarely given much more than superficial analysis. Locating these battles closer to where Gildas inferred the Saxons first landed gives them a shape that not only better fits elements of the legend in the *Historia* but also connects them directly to Arthur's first battle. This suggests there was no significant break in the hostilities between Vortimer's last battle and the start of Ambrosius' campaign, as described by Gildas, which culminated in the Battle of Mount Badon. If this was the pattern of events, Arthur's battles should be considered central to the Ambrosian fightback, thus changing the traditional view of the chronology of the fifth century.

I hope the analysis in this chapter and the next will significantly improve our understanding of the mid-fifth century. I mentioned in chapter I how misleading the myriad of published theories and synthetic history about the period, particularly relating to Arthur, can be. Historians generally refer to these authors as 'Arthurian experts'. Guy Halsall summarises his view in *Worlds of Arthur*:

> *The old quest for King Arthur is fruitless. The documentary evidence cannot respond to those sorts of questions. More seriously, to pretend to have provided the answers sought by that romantic quest from the surviving written sources is downright dishonest. In this and the previous chapters I have*

argued that we can find new questions to ask, ones for which the evidence to hand might be able to provide plausible responses, even if ones always susceptible to refinement and correction. Many people will be unsatisfied by this but – in my view – it must be more interesting and exciting than chasing answers to unanswerable questions. Fact, after all, is stranger than fiction.[17]

While this may be so, I believe we can identify Arthur's known deeds as part of a logical historical framework, which, for genuine history, would be a major step forward. My research indicates it is possible to profile the polities on all sides and analyse where and at which point known events occurred, ensuring that the lead-up to the Battle of Mount Badon and its outcome justifiably fit a historical framework. It would seem it is possible to solve a large proportion of the mystery with little more than a shift in perspective.

But dating exactly when and where the Saxon rebellion commenced has always been problematic. In 441, a Gallic chronicler claimed the British were 'reduced to the power of the Saxons', although this may not mean 'at war' or 'defeated'; it could just be an observation in respect of the Saxons' strength in numbers relative to the Britons. If this entry had been dated later, I think we might more readily accept the 'at war' or 'defeated' interpretations, but we know it is dated too early in the decade to refer to even the rebellion.

---

[17] Guy Halsall, *Worlds of Arthur: Facts and Fictions of the Dark Ages* (Oxford: Oxford University Press, 2013), p 307.

During the 440s, the Roman general, Aetius, having defeated his rivals, was settling barbarians in Gaul under treaty – sometimes to the detriment of Gallo-Roman owners. Alans were settled in the Loire, and Burgundians in Savoy. *Bacaudae* rebellions in Armorica were a constant problem for Aetius, though the kind of relationship that existed between the settled British émigrés and the Armorican *bacaudae* is not known, despite there already being a significant colony which was about to increase further as a result of the Saxon rebellion.

At this time, Gildas reports a famous appeal to the Romans; the '*Gemitus Britannorum Agito Ter Consuli*' or 'Groans of the Britons to Agitius Thrice Consul'. Agitius is assumed to be Aetius, and the date of the missive must be sometime after his third consulship in 446. In it, the Britons lamented that:

> *... the barbarians drive us to the sea and the sea drives us back to the barbarians; death comes by one means or another; we are either slain or drowned.*

It is sometimes thought that this may allude to Saxon expansion and rising sea levels, but it is more likely meant to imply the Britons were embattled by enemies on both land and sea. Perhaps the Britons were hoping that publicising the appeal might improve morale or go some way to discouraging their enemies. The *Anglo-Saxon Chronicle* records:

> *443. Here the Britons sent across the sea to Rome and asked them for help against the Picts, but they had none there because they were campaigning*

against Attila, king of the Huns; and then they sent to the Angles and made the same request to the princes of the Angles race.

This entry is a summary report and attests in hindsight to the general awareness of the appeals and plight of the Britons. Curiously, about this time, Constantius reports the return of St. Germanus to Britain where he meets a senior ranking Briton called Elafius of whom nothing further is known. The *Historia* recounts a disproportionately extensive myth in respect of the downfall of Vortigern at the hands of the saint which tells us only that Germanus became subject to apocryphal stories out of veneration. In fact, it is widely held that Germanus educated one of Vortigern's sons, Faustus, who became an abbot of Lérins Abbey, but evidence for the connection to Vortigern comes mainly from the *Historia* itself. It is intriguing that Germanus seems to pop up at key moments, and there is no reason to doubt Constantius of Lyon who wrote *Vita Germani* in about 480. This would seem to indicate that Germanus may well have acted as a special envoy to the Britons, especially as he later travelled to Rome to represent a case on behalf of Armorica which was under threat of invasion by Alans sponsored by Aetius.

All this suggests that the Saxon rebellion commenced at about the same time as the appeal and that Germanus may well have coordinated the wave of émigrés to Armorica to which Gildas refers.

There are several references to the strength of the Saxons. Bede in particular refers to an 'invincible force', and the *Historia* refers to Hengist as a 'shrewd, clever, cunning man'. All sources recognise in hindsight that it was always the plan of Hengist to make war with the Britons and invade their territories. For there is no doubt that is what it effectively became – an invasion. With only one eyewitness account and some random archaeological finds with varied interpretations, it is an immense challenge to try to give any shape to the Saxon rebellion and wars.

It is tempting to picture scenes similar to those described in the aftermath of the Barbarian Conspiracy, with raiders and brigands roaming the countryside at will. However, the Saxon rebellion was no temporary change, and the territory taken over by the Saxons was in large part never recovered. Similar land invasions on the Continent eventually saw Childeric establish the Merovingian Dynasty which conquered most of Gaul in the sixth century, but these were Romanised Franks who understood the value of retaining the centralised Roman administration. The Saxons showed no interest in continuity – many towns were violently depopulated and destroyed, as described in Gildas' eyewitness account.

There is a great deal of debate about the fate of Roman towns in England. Pestilence, plague and famine seem to have played their part in the decline, and in disease-ridden antiquity, the record of a contemporary chronicler describing *mortalitas magna* (the great death) most certainly meant exactly that. John Wacher in *The Towns of Roman Britain* summarises the questions:

> *Among the things that we have to explain are: instances of unburied bodies lying beside streets in some of the towns; the apparent decay and desertion of many towns for reasons not connected with*

warfare, sometimes in favour of other nearby, fortifiable sites such as Iron Age hill-forts, or even ampitheatres, and this despite the fact that walled towns must have been among the safest refuges, so long as the walls could be manned; the general manpower shortage in the Empire from the fourth century onwards; the rebellion of the foederati; the reluctance of Germanic peoples to settle in 'captured' towns of the Rhineland even as early as the late fourth century; the description of towns as 'tombs' surrounded by nets; and, if we exclude the early foederati, the same reluctance on the part of the first genuine Anglo-Saxon immigrants in Britain. Nearly forty years ago, Myres drew attention to the striking non-urban pattern of the settlement. As he then observed, urban traditions in some other western provinces were often preserved by the Church, whereas in lowland Britain even the Church collapsed, requiring later missionaries from the west and from Rome to re-establish it... We have also to explain the flight of low-land Britons to Wales and possibly even to Brittany, and the migration of tribal peoples within the country. We must also account for the fact that the main periods of Anglo-Saxon aggression almost immediately followed our suggested two most serious epidemics in Britain, when confusion would have been at its worst.[18]

[18] John Wacher, *The Towns of Roman Britain* (London: Book Club Associates/B. T. Batsford Ltd, 1976), pp 416–417.

We know from Gildas that the Saxons devastated town and country and that the 'fire' once alight 'did not die down until it had burned almost the whole surface of the island and was licking the western ocean with its fierce red tongue'. Only archaeology will ever be able to tell us more about the rebellion, though we can review what is known about the destruction of towns such as Leicester and Wroxeter.

But first, it would be worthwhile to consider how the rebellion proceeded and was conducted, bearing in mind both the Saxons' starting point and the later fightback by Vortimer and Ambrosius.

The Saxons had assembled a powerful army that initially met no opposition in the lowlands. It would be wrong to surmise that the key leaders of the Britons were not expecting an attack. However, it does appear they were unprepared. It is likely the north, the west and the south will have raised some militia to engage the rising Saxon threat. Even so, we know their coastlines remained vulnerable to raiding, though it is difficult to establish if the raids in the west were Saxon or Irish Scotti, who were particularly active at this time.

After twenty years as *foederati*, the Saxons will have known a great deal about the geography and strongholds of Britain, so there was likely a strategy behind the choice of targets for attack. However, there were many physical barriers to the movement of a large army around Britain. Mountains, hills, rivers and estuaries not only made movement a challenge but also presented opportunities for the opposition to ambush and harry an army on foot. The Saxons were solely foot soldiers, and it is often assumed, rightly or wrongly, that the Britons had cavalry. Certainly, the northern Britons were expert cavalry soldiers. The Saxons will have avoided the Pennines, the Cambrian Mountains and the Cotswolds. Natural defensive positions such as the Marlborough Downs, the Chiltern Hills and the Northamptonshire Uplands will have been patrolled by Britons and presented too great a risk for an army to traverse. However, in the lowlands and on the plains, the Saxon army will have roamed at will and doubtless seemed the 'invincible force' described by Bede.

It is not known if there were competing Saxon leaders in Norfolk or Kent or even separate rebellions – it is possible, but the major engagements described by the sources appear to have been with Hengist and Horsa.

It would be very interesting to discover the source of the apparent eyewitness account mentioned in Gildas. The information could have come from his parents, although there must have been many cleric refugees from the previous generation who could have provided the account. Gildas probably wrote *De Excidio* somewhere in the south-west. His detailed knowledge of Welsh kings and Ambrosius Aurelianus might place him in Cirencester, Bath or Dorchester. These are not towns that show evidence of attack by the Saxons, so his vivid descriptions will have been hearsay from a source who came from further afield. Tradition places his birth in the north-west, but there is no evidence for why that should be so.

I have, however, good reason to suggest that, in the course of the rebellion, the Saxons advanced into the north-west along the Vale of Trent to the Cheshire Plain, and that this is where they reached the western ocean. Bodies discovered and dated to the period found near the baths at Wroxeter should be taken as evidence of this sack and slaughter. It appears that an old man with some companions had crawled under the floor into a hypocaust to hide with their life savings. They were not found by the Saxons but sadly perished, probably from asphyxiation. Such attacks will have been unexpected by the Welsh kings, and this audacious Saxon advance will have caused grave concern.

There can be no doubt that the east of England had already been ravaged probably as far south as Cambridge, but London, St. Albans and Colchester, while possibly attacked, appear to have survived and remained sub-Roman. Leicester was right on the frontier of Saxon-claimed territory, and its forum was apparently destroyed by fire and sacked.

For what length of time the Britons endured the Saxon onslaught is difficult to estimate. In §25 of *De Excidio*, Gildas comments that 'after a time… the cruel plunderers had gone home'. By 'home' I presume Gildas meant to their settlements in Lincolnshire rather than their countries of origin. However, there is another possibility behind this withdrawal and subsequent quiet from the Saxons. If the rebellion had commenced in 446, about the time of the appeal to Aetius, then the Britons must have begun to engage the Saxon army sometime before 450.

On the Continent in 451, Aetius faced Attila the Hun. This confrontation resulted from the new ruler in the Eastern Empire, Marcian (450–57), refusing to pay the subsidies to the Hun that had been agreed by treaty. Attila turned against the western provinces in order to replace these sums with plunder. He was given a pretext when the sister of Valentian III, Honoria, sent her signet ring to him, urging him to rescue her from an imperial order to marry a Roman she disliked. Attila interpreted this as an offer of marriage and demanded half the Western Empire as a dowry. This was turned down, so he marched towards Gaul. He was confronted by the combined force of Aetius' Roman army and the Visigoths, together with other federate Germans. Edward Gibbon, who published *The History of the Decline and Fall of the Roman Empire* between 1776 and 1789, wrote 'the nations from the Volga to the Atlantic were assembled' [19]. The battle that followed on the Catalaunian Plains, west of Troyes in Champagne, was included by Sir Edward Creasy among the fifteen decisive battles of the world. The Visigoth king, Theodoric I, was one of the many who fell. Attila was defeated and withdrew from Gaul. This was the one and only defeat of his lifetime and the greatest success of Aetius' career.

Jordanes, who is the chief source for the battle, says that Aetius had assembled warriors from everywhere. His troops included 'Franks, Samaritans, Armoricans, Liticians, Burgundians, Saxons, Riparians and Olibriones (once Roman soldiers and now the flower of the armed forces)'. It is even possible that the adventurers Hengist and Horsa withdrew from Britain at this time to fight for Aetius alongside the greatest array of mercenaries ever assembled. Jordanes mentioned Saxons, and this may explain the pause in their British campaign and the break between the rebellion and subsequent war. Gildas reports they had 'returned home'. Aetius was friend only to his own ambitions, and had he engaged Hengist and Horsa for

---

[19] Edward Gibbon, *The Decline and Fall of the Roman Empire.* Abridged by D. M. Lowe. (London: Book Club Associates/Chatto and Windus Ltd, 1972).

his campaign, it would certainly put a different complexion on the appeal by the Britons in 448. Aetius moved barbarian tribes around the Continent like gaming pieces on a board. He may well have recruited the Saxons to relieve pressure on the Britons, but he was assassinated in 454, hence their return to Britain. By this time, the Britons were better organised and as the *Historia* claims:

> *Meanwhile Vortimer son of Vortigern was fighting impudently (bravely) against Hengist and Horsa and their people; and he drove them forth as far as the aforementioned Island of Tenat and three times he confined, blockaded, struck, crushed and terrified them there.*

This indicates Vortimer driving the Saxons out of the west, perhaps after their campaign on the Cheshire Plain, and confining them back in Lincolnshire. It does appear that the Britons held the defensive line along Watling Street with some forward positions, certainly at Derby and perhaps Leicester. The village of Ambrosden (Ambrosius) in Oxfordshire is particularly relevant as it is close by the Roman fort of Bicester which sits on the crossroads of the Cirencester to St. Albans road and between Dorchester and Towcester, which is located on Watling Street. Whether this represents cooperation between Vortigern and Ambrosius cannot be proven, but it would make sense in the circumstances. The *Historia* continues:

> *And then they fought against the kings of the people sometimes they were victorious and extended their frontiers at other times they were defeated and driven out. And Vortimer eagerly fought four battles*

against them the first battle was on the river Derguentid.

The River Derguentid is traditionally taken as the Darent in Kent, but this would not fit this reinterpretation. However, the Derwent at Derby certainly does. The Roman fort of Derventio was sited at Little Chester on the east bank of the River Derwent which flows into the Trent near Cavendish Bridge.

This area was of immense strategic importance. Derby is at the southern tip of the Pennines which gives way to the Vale of Trent in advance of the sharp climb up to Bardon Hill. This was likely the corridor followed by the Saxon advance into the west and the route provides access to the western Roman road system. Patrolling and controlling this area was key. It is approximately fifteen miles wide and hosts the confluence of the rivers Trent, Derwent, Dove and Soar. Closing the gate here would have frustrated the Saxon advance westwards, and it would be no wonder if this was the location of Vortimer's first battle.

The Britons maintained a strong presence here, perhaps even a garrison, throughout the Saxon wars, and I am confident that the nearby village of Ambaston, the medieval Ambro Mill and Ambro Hill by East Midlands Airport all attest to that continued presence. There is no mention in the *Anglo-Saxon Chronicle* of the battle at Derguentid or the Saxon containment, so we have no date for it, but it may have occurred anytime between 450 and 454.

The *Historia* continues to list Vortigern's battles and records:

... the second battle was at the ford which is called Episford in their language but Rither Gabail in ours and Horsa fell there with the son of Gwrtheyrn whose name was Cateyrn.

The *Anglo-Saxon Chronicle* dates the battle to 455:

Here Hengest and then Horsa fought against Vortigern the King in the place which is called Aegaelestrep [some other versions of the Chronicle list Agelsford] and his brother Horsa was killed. And after that Hengest and Aesc his son succeeded to the Kingdom.

I believe this was the most significant battle of the early part of the Saxon wars and a major setback for the Britons. For whatever reason, the Britons mounted an attack in the heart of claimed Saxon territory. Perhaps this was the legendary meeting mentioned in §45 and §46 of the *Historia* where Hengist invited Vortigern to ratify a treaty. When the Britons had been wined and dined, Hengist's men drew their knives and murdered 300 of Vortigern's noblemen. Here, again under the assumption the Saxons were settled in Kent, the battle is considered to have taken place at Aylesford on the River Medway. However, there are three other place names which pinpoint the location.

Rithergabail in Welsh means 'ford of the horses'. Mike Ashley, in *A Brief History of King Arthur*,[20] draws our attention to an alternative but similar sounding word: Sathnefabal, meaning 'the station of the ferry boat'. In Yorkshire, close by Sherburn-in-Elmet, there is a village

[20] Ashley, *A Brief History of King Arthur*

called Ryther by the River Wharfe just before it joins the Ouse, and there was a ferry here from ancient times. This was within the kingdom of Elmet, which remained Welsh-speaking until the seventh century, and helps confirm a correct interpretation for the battle taking place at the site of a ferry.

Perhaps the Saxons had returned to their *tenat*, or Hengist and Horsa had indeed been abroad and the Britons were aware of their return. Whatever the reason, this battle would seem to have taken place on the Isle of Axholme. Aegaelestrep can be taken as Althorpe on the Trent where a ferry boat was sited even in recent times, hence Rithergabail. Episford is most likely Epworth, the high ground on the Isle of Axholme. Both places are no more than five miles apart and were, in antiquity, surrounded by rivers and fords. The death of both Horsa and Catigern (Vortigern's son: Cateyrn in the *Historia* extract) suggests a vicious battle which did not dislodge Hengist, and this is the last time we hear of Vortigern. On that basis, I suggest this was a significant defeat.

The Britons may have retreated to either Lincoln or Derby, but retribution quickly followed. The *Anglo-Saxon Chronicle* tells us in 456 that:

> *Here Hengest and Aesc fought against the Britons at a place which is called Crecganford and there killed four thousand troops and the Britons then abandoned the land of Centland in great terror to the stronghold of Lundenbyrg.*

The tradition for this battle is that it took place at Crayford, but we have already discussed and set aside the confusion with Kent. Instead, following our revised location for the Saxon territories and the battle at Rithergabail, the Britons are likely to have retreated down Ermine Street to form a defensive line, taking a position no further south than Stamford, parallel to Leicester. The Roman fortified town at Great Casterton lay to the north of the ford over the River Welland, and this is, I believe, the site of the Battle of Crecganford.

Arthur Mee, in his book *The King's England: Lincolnshire*,[21] tells us that Stamford's name 'was originally Stane-ford, the stone paved ford and the word stone is significant for close by at Barnack, Ketton and Chipsham are famous stone quarries'. Modern Welsh for stone is 'creigiau' so Stoneford becomes Creigianfford. And a battle at Stamford is more in keeping with the shape of the Saxon wars, particularly since we can identify the next battle occurring less than twenty-five miles to the east, albeit some years later.

We detect that the Britons begin to surround Lincolnshire and Nottinghamshire not long after this, so if they had fled in terror to London (if Lundenbyrg is indeed London), they returned in due course. The Saxons did not seem interested in garrisoning towns or patrolling their acquired territory, and their settlements were random and agrarian. The Roman Empire had turned the peoples living outside its boundaries into military states, like the Picts, whose martial skills became their sole purpose, or raiders, pirates and mercenaries like the Saxons and Franks, who lost purpose without an enemy to fight or treasure to steal.

---

[21] Arthur Mee ed. *The King's England: Lincolnshire – a County of Infinite Charm* (London: Hodder and Stoughton, 1949).

After Rithergabail and Crecganford there was a significant break in hostilities, and the *Anglo-Saxon Chronicle* records the next battle as nine years later in 465. Vortigern may well have died shortly after 456. His son Vortimer looks to have remained in command of the army, and by 465, he will have been about forty-five years old. Ambrosius would have been about sixty-five, whereas Arthwys and Riothamus would both have been about thirty-five. Hengist had come to Britain with his father and was likely a similar age to Ambrosius. After Vortigern, we may assume that Ambrosius became the High King of the Britons, as we read of him granting the towns of Builth and Guorthegirnaim to Vortigern's third son, Pascent. Ambrosius is described as 'the great king among the Kings of Britain'. This statement makes him appear a Briton, when in fact, we know him to be a Roman, having more in common with his contemporaries on the Continent, such as the Roman warlords Aegidius and Syagrius in their kingdom of Soissons in Gaul. This is perhaps why tradition remembers and records the Britons Vortigern and Arthur but says little of Ambrosius and why finding evidence for him requires scrutiny of the landscape and place names.

Whether or not 465 is the correct date for the next battle is impossible to say, but by then, Ambrosius had consolidated his control and the fightback had commenced. As Gildas describes:

> *... under him our people regained their strength, and challenged the victors to battle. The Lord assented and the battle went their way.*

The *Anglo-Saxon Chronicle* states in 465:

Here Hengest and Aesc fought against the welsh near Wippedsfleot and one of their thegns whose name was Wipped was killed there.

The *Historia* tells us that Vortimer:

... initiated the third battle in the plain near Lapis Tituli [inscribed stone] which is on the shore of the Gaulish Sea and the barbarians were defeated and he was the victor and they were put to flight as far as their ships and they drowned like women as they tried to get into them. [Vortimer] however died after a short space of time.

This is most likely the battle where Arthwys took command from Vortimer who was perhaps fatally wounded in the fighting. The compiler of the *Historia* had not made the link, but this was also the first battle in the famous Arthurian battle list:

Then in those days Arthur fought against them with the kings of the Britons, but he was commander in the battles. The first battle was at the mouth of the river which is called Glein.

In effect, we have three different sources confirming a single battle, most notably a victory for the Britons. This conclusion is incredibly exciting for fans of Arthur because it provides better evidence for his historicity than is usual.

Holbeach is about six miles from the Wash, and in Roman times, prior to drainage, was much closer. Either side of the town are two villages: Whaplode and Fleet. This looks similar to Wippedsfleot, particularly since

Wipped, who died at the battle, is described as being a very rich man within Hengist's party. An extensive area, Whaplode Fens and Whaplode Drove, is potentially named for him. The 'Gaulish Sea' is doubtless the Wash, but the plain near *Lapis Tituli* is probably the area around Whaplode. There are not many inscribed stones around this area – I know because I have scoured Arthur Mee's notes on every village and parish church in the region to find the relevant *Lapis Tituli*.

In fact, I believe the inscribed stone to which the *Historia* refers is the Elloe Stone, originally sited two fields north-west of Whaplode and now mounted on a base by the roadside. The Elloe Stone is claimed as early Saxon and has been used as a meeting place marking the site where the men of Elloe Wapentake held their Hundred Court. It is clearly very old and may even be the memorial stone Bede assumed was raised in Horsa's memory. Wipped (or Whaplode) seems to have been an important Saxon *thegn*.

Five miles north-west from Whaplode we reach the River Glen at Surfleet Seas End. This is the point where the river used to meet the sea and was perhaps a haven for Saxon boats. We have already mentioned the Horncastle Saxons and also the ancient track, the Salt Way, which led to the Midlands from this area. The strategic importance to the Saxons of this landing place is therefore obvious, and the outcome of the battle to break their hold on it seems to have been a resounding victory for the Britons.

Most importantly, we have reasonable evidence that the first of Arthur's battles forms part of the Ambrosian fightback, and we may assume our candidate for Arthur,

Arthwys, took command of the campaign at this crucial time, possibly because Vortimer was severely wounded.

The next chapter seeks to show that the entirety of Arthur's battle list should be considered part of the Ambrosian fightback. The *Historia* reports that Hengist dies and Octha transfers to Kent immediately before the compiler begins to recount the famous but displaced battle list of Arthur. Certainly, Octha does not appear to have been involved in the battles that followed. The later battle of 473, involving Hengist and recorded by the *Anglo-Saxon Chronicle*, is surely erroneous, or it is recorded out of sequence. I estimate Hengist to have reached his mid-seventies in 473, making this an unlikely time for him to be fighting his final battle. Apart from this, we do not hear of Hengist again, except in *The History of the Kings of Britain* by Geoffrey of Monmouth where he is defeated by 'Aurelius' at the Battle of Maisbeli (perhaps Maltby) then retreats to Conisbrough where he is captured then beheaded. While it is wise to remain at arm's length from claims made by Geoffrey of Monmouth, this location is interesting with respect to Arthur's later battles. He notes:

> *... the saxons dreaded him (Aurelius) and they now retreated across the Humber. They fortified the towns and castles in those parts, for the region had always been a refuge towards which they could retreat. The nearness of Scotland afforded them protection, for that country had never missed an opportunity of making matters worse whenever the Britons were in distress. It was a land frightful to live in, more or less uninhabited, and it offered a safe lurking place to foreigners. Indeed, by its*

geographical position, it lay open to the Picts, the Scots, the Danes, the Norwegians and anyone else who came ashore to ravage the island.[22]

This is a striking observation and rather agrees with my conjectured location for the Jutes and the theatre for the Saxon wars but is of course complete fiction.

Reassigning the battles to Lincolnshire and Nottinghamshire allows for a different interpretation of the legends which perhaps now make a little more sense. Hengist and Horsa were probably seeking to establish a homeland for the disparate groups of Saxons, but terms could not be agreed. There does appear to have been some legal structure to the initial arrangement with a later attempt at a parley. Why else would Vortigern travel to Axholme? Perhaps the element of the legend in the *Historia*, where Vortigern requests Hengist's daughter, was actually a proposed hostage exchange which was common practice to guarantee treaties. It does look as if Hengist and Horsa were either unable to accept Vortigern's terms or perhaps were unable to control all the elements of their own party. Lincolnshire is an enormous area, being 75 miles long and 45 miles wide. The Isle of Axholme and surrounding area alone is 50,000 acres. Much of the countryside was wetland, but even so, there was still more than sufficient territory to go around.

It was clearly the Britons who recommenced the war in 465. Perhaps raiding had continued and the need for constant vigilance along a long border had become

---

[22] Geoffrey, of Monmouth, *The History of the Kings of Britain,* trans. Lewis Thorpe (London: The Folio Society, 1969), pp 165–166.

frustrating and expensive. That Ambrosius, Vortimer and Arthur should campaign in concert is fascinating and indicative of an earlier date for the Badon campaign.

Following Wippedsfleot, Vortimer had requested to be buried on the coast where he fell, but a scribal gloss in the Sawley version of the *Historia* tells us he was buried at Lincoln. If this is true, Arthur will have likely taken his body up the River Witham which will have proved a solemn but imposing procession that sent a clear message of impending change as this Christian army of Britons passed across Saxon territory unchallenged for the first time in ten years.

The next battles followed quickly as the Britons pressed home their advantage, and Arthur's battle list should be read as an immediate and ferocious campaign.

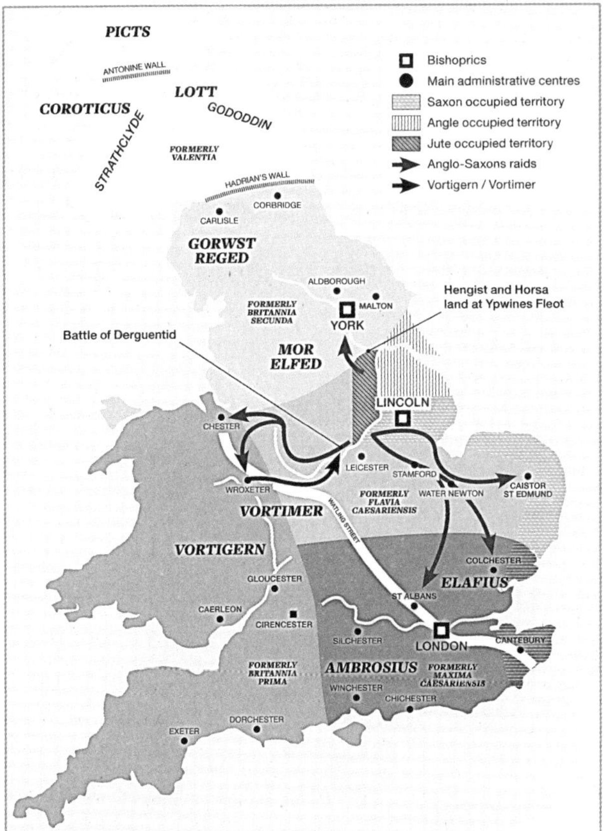

Map 3: The Saxon rebellion and war prior to 464
Gildas, a monk writing circa 512, graphically describes the Saxon rebellion and notes in § 24 of *De Excidio* how 'a fire heaped up and, nurtured by the hand of the impious easterners, spread from sea to sea. It devastated town and country round about and, once it was alight, it did not die down until it had burned almost the whole surface of the island and was licking the western ocean with its fierce red tongue'.

XIII
The Badon campaign

Before going on to analyse it, I quote the translation of Arthur's battle list from *The Celtic Heroic Age* by Pamela S. M. Hopkins and John T. Koch [23] for your reference:

> *Then Arthur fought against them in those days, together with the kings of the Britons, but he was their battle leader [dux bellorum].*
>
> *The first battle was at the mouth of the river called Glein [ostium Glein]. The second, the third, the fourth and the fifth were on another river, called Dubglas, which is in the country of Lindsey [Lïnnûïs]. The sixth battle was on a river called Bassas. The seventh battle was in the Caledonian Forest, that is, the Battle of the Calendonian Forest [Cat Coït Celïdon]. The eighth battle was in Guinnion castle, and in it Arthur carried the image of the Holy Mary, ever Virgin, on his [shield (MSS says humeros 'shoulders'),] and the heathen were routed on that day, and there was a great slaughter of them, through the intercession of Our Lord Jesus Christ and the power of the holy Virgin Mary, his mother. The ninth battle was fought in the city of the Legion. The tenth battle was fought on the bank of the river called Tribruit. The eleventh was on the hill called Agned [aka Bregomion]. The twelfth battle*

---

[23] John T. Koch and John Carey, eds., *The Celtic Heroic Age: Literary Sources for Ancient Celtic Europe (Andover & Aberystwyth Celtic Studies Publications, 2000)*, pp 285 - 286.

was on Badon's Heights and in it nine hundred and sixty men fell in one day, from a single charge of Arthur's, and no one killed them but he alone; and he was victorious in all his battles.[24]

If we look at Arthur's battles in Lincolnshire and Nottinghamshire as a single campaign targeting the Jutes and other Germanic people settled throughout the region, it becomes clear why the ultimate battle at Bardon Hill was seen as such a momentous victory.

All warfare is violent, but the slaughter that followed early medieval battles was horrific. If a battle was lost on home turf, mass murder would follow, and no quarter would be given. Germanus, Gildas and Bede all showed their repugnance for war, but they lived at a time when life was less valued and the Church had not yet established the moral influence that would reform medieval warfare through the code of chivalry. The Saxons were particularly vicious as their gods demanded slaughter and sacrifice; Gildas described them as the 'ferocious Saxons hated by man and God'. It is little wonder, then, that there are few loan words between the Welsh and Anglo-Saxon languages. In Saxon-dominated areas, Britons had mostly fled or been slaughtered, and it is perhaps no surprise to learn that these battles were followed up with a high degree of revenge and the taint of genocide.

The pattern of the proposed Badon campaign suggests that the Britons were targeting specific groupings of Saxons. It was the Jutes who started the rebellion, and

---

[24] Koch and Carey, eds., *The Celtic Heroic Age: Literary Sources for Ancient Celtic Europe and Early Ireland and Wales*, pp 285-286

there will have been tribes that coalesced and fought alongside them. I have suggested that there were *bacaudae* in Sherwood who opportunistically joined the Jutes, but it is difficult to establish whether or not the Angles got involved. However, there is no evidence that the Angles suffered any kind of suppression during the Badon campaign, so it would seem that, while they may have aided and abetted the Jutes, they did not get involved in the rebellion and wars.

Following the Battle of Wippedsfleot/Glein, we can surmise that all the above groups and tribes were hemmed into Lincolnshire and Nottinghamshire. To the north, Arthwys' home kingdom of Elmet stood guard; to the west and south-west, the armies of Ambrosius and his son Riothamus were likely stationed at the strategic points of Derby and Bicester. Vortimer's field army, now led by Arthwys after Vortimer's death, will have just pushed up from the south and crossed Saxon territory to Lincoln.

Here we see further evidence that the Britons were not hostile towards the Angles, who ultimately became the kings of Lindsey, as it is likely that the army passed through Angle territory to the north of Lincoln. This would seem to suggest some kind of formal cooperation or compliance, and if terms were indeed agreed with the Angles, it was quite possibly an Angle leader called Vinta (470) who did the negotiating, as it is his name we see reflected in the landscape at Winterton and Winteringham. Professor Caitlin Green has argued that the Angles not only acculturated with the Britons, but they also later intermarried with the British elite, thereby beginning a tradition that the kings of Lindsey had British forebears.

However, an entirely different fate awaited the Jutes and other Germanic inhabitants on the other side of the Trent. I believe that events hereafter escalated, and the battles occurred in quick succession. I cannot guess if Arthwys crossed the Trent or if he returned to Elmet, but the Jute scouts will have been watching his every move, and preparing to counter and engage him. Whichever way it happened, it seems Arthwys ultimately positioned an army behind the Jutes on the north-western edge of their territory, perhaps at the crossing point at Boothferry. From here, we return to the battle list from the *Historia*:

> *The second, third, fourth and fifth [battles] on another river which is called Dubglas and is in the region of Linnius.*

The year is likely 466 or 467. Dubglas is the original form of the name Douglas and translates as 'black water'. Running across a large area of peat, known as Thorne Waste, is Blackwater Dyke, and parallel to the River Don on Inkle Moor is a cut known as Black Drain. The 1400s map of Inclesmoor, which was created during a dispute over peat and pasture between St. Mary's Abbey, York and the Duchy of Lancaster, may well show the River Dubglas before drainage changed the courses of the rivers thereabouts. In fact, this map is, by coincidence, an early record of the area that was likely the *tenat* of Hengist and Horsa. Swinefleet, mentioned as the place they first landed, is not far beyond the confluence of the rivers Aire and Ouse.

All of this seems less like mere conjecture when we consider the number of battles Arthwys fought thereabouts. He seems to have encountered fierce resistance since it required four battles to subdue the Saxons. Elmet neighboured this region, and his troops would have been able to follow the north bank of the River Aire all the way to the village of Airmyn, the most likely crossing point where Boothferry Bridge is now located, making this area Arthwys' bridgehead. Once assembled, his army will have been well placed to embark on its mission to slaughter every living being associated with the Jutes and their allies. Arthwys' warriors will have swept away all elements of settlement in this area and around Axholme, creating a wave of fleeing refugees.

And so, the battle list continues:

The sixth battle on the river that is called Bassas.

There are a multitude of rivers that flow into the Trent and Ouse from South and West Yorkshire, most of which had their courses altered in the seventeenth century when Cornelius Vermuyden set about draining Hatfield Chase. I suspect that the River Bassas was one of these, perhaps situated due east of Doncaster. In Welsh, 'bassa' means 'low' and 'bas' can mean 'shallows'. There are 'bas' place names throughout Nottinghamshire and Lincolnshire, such as Basford, Bassingfield and Basingthorpe, proving the name description was in common use in the immediate region.

One river in particular has been completely redirected and this is the River Torne. The name Torne, or Thorne, translates into Welsh as *draeneu* which also means drain and that is certainly what it became when Cornelius Vermuyden drained Hatfield Chase in 1626. Many rivers were rerouted and renamed over the next two hundred years, so which one is the River Bassas? On the eastern side of Doncaster, there is a profusion of 'carr' place names, which is Old English for fen woodland typically dominated by alder or willow. For example: Carr House, Doncaster Carr, Black Carr, Loversall Carr. Just at the point where the River Torne passes under the main East Coast railway line it is joined by another river simply called Mother Drain. Here is an area of higher ground known as Bessacarr and, close by, Bessacarr Grange. It is an odd name, which I suggest incorporates the Welsh 'bassa' with the English 'carr'. If the name is strangely familiar, it is probably because this area has given its name to a whole family of caravans, and like me, you have probably been stuck behind a Bessacarr caravan on a narrow road at some point. It is also the hometown of a member of the former band One Direction: Louis Tomlinson – a well-known bard!

Following this logic, six out of Arthur's first seven battles were fought in territory adjacent to Elmet. He will have been a leader who knew where the Saxon settlements were, and doubtless, his scouts will have observed the activities of the region's various inhabitants over a period of years. As I have shown, none would have been better placed for this role than Elmet's leader, Arthwys.

It is often said that Arthur's battle list originally formed part of an ancient Celtic praise poem. If so (and I can see no other purpose to it), it is safe to say the bard was someone who had a detailed knowledge of this remote area, suggesting that he was actually involved – much like Aneirin who fought at and recorded the Battle of Catraeth.

If we look at these battles as one extended military campaign, it is easy to comprehend the strategic motivation for the location of these encounters. The battles on the Humber and near Doncaster served to attack and remove the enemy from their safe haven, while also expanding Elmet's domination of the region, effectively removing the problem from its own borders. This is not King Arthur charging around the countryside; it is a northern king consolidating his own position. I doubt this element of the campaign formed part of Ambrosius' detailed plan, but more likely, it was Arthwys taking advantage of a weakened enemy. As we shall see, however, the impetus created by this move was what turned the tide and created the decisive pincer movement.

The seventh battle was in the forest of Celyddon, that is the battle of Coed Celyddon.

It is interesting that the compiler of the *Historia* chose to re-emphasise in Celtic what he had already written in Latin. Perhaps he was suggesting that there was more than one Celyddon, or alternatively, he was simply quoting his source for the avoidance of doubt. Just about all the books I have ever read on Arthur claim this to be a battle in a Caledonian forest. Caledonia was the Roman name for all of Scotland, but to my knowledge, there is no evidence for Saxons north of Hadrian's Wall in the fifth century. However, there is a much simpler translation, much closer to Elmet and completely relevant to the course of the campaign. Celyddon simply means 'the forest with the River Don at its centre', which points to the northern edge of Sherwood Forest on Elmet's southern border. 'Cell' means woodland grove and 'Don' is, of course, the River Don that flows past Conisbrough and Doncaster. Arthwys and the Britons from Elmet were, I propose, systematically clearing out all the Saxon/*bacaudae* settlements in the immediate region.

There is a striking similarity between this battle location and the site of the Battle of Maisbeli (perhaps Maltby) near Conisbrough, as noted in Geoffrey of Monmouth's *History of the Kings of Britain*. While I am associating all Arthur's battles with the Ambrosian fightback described by Gildas, Geoffrey separates the campaigns, giving Arthur's glorious career a later date. Ambrosius, who is named Aurelius in Geoffrey of Monmouth's book, defeats Hengist at this battle then captures him at Conisbrough where he is beheaded and buried. Conisbrough is a magnificent medieval castle where there is some evidence of earlier Saxon settlement, particularly in St. Peter's Church in the town.

Quite why Geoffrey places these events here is a mystery, other than, perhaps, the tradition of Hengist's burial mound. In fact, John Warburton's map of Yorkshire (1720) actually shows the location of Hengist's grave, now lost, to the north-west of the castle. When I spoke with the castle curator, he said he'd been in the job ten years, and this was the first time, in 2019, he'd heard it mentioned! William Camden (1551–1623), an antiquarian, historian and topographer, who, like many of us, searched for evidence of King Arthur, mentions the event but not the burial mound in his work *Britannia*. Geoffrey's version of events has pervaded throughout history and has misled readers for centuries, but Conisbrough was a Saxon settlement, and perhaps the tradition of Hengist's grave genuinely predated Geoffrey's book. I confess I had a good look around to see if I could pinpoint the location, but the entire area is now built up in every direction. It is, nonetheless, an interesting coincidence and adds further weight to my proposed location for the battle of Celyddon.

The next battle listing highlights the Christian purpose of fighting the Saxons:

> *The eighth battle was at the Castellum Guinnion, where Arthur carried the portrait of St Mary, ever virgin, on his shoulders; and the pagans were routed on that day, and there was a great slaughter of them through the power of our Lord Jesus Christ and the strength of the holy Virgin Mary, his mother.*

It is often pointed out that 'shoulders' and 'shield' are similar sounding words in Welsh, and since the battle list will have started out as oral tradition, both translations are possible. The 'shoulders' translation is interesting since the cloak was a recognised insignia of authority. Cunedda's grandfather is believed to have been called Padarn Pesrut, which means 'Paternus of the Red Robe', indicating some devolved imperial authority. Both the Lindisfarne Gospels and the Book of Kells show an array of magnificent cloaks. Clothing was a far more important measure of position and message, whereas shield devices were mostly abstract, denoting a legion or a division of soldiers.

However, there should be no doubt about this army's Christian purpose. As previously mentioned, there are *eccles* place names throughout the north denoting churches, and the Britons will have been devout Christians at this time. They had suffered at the hands of heathens for two decades, and the Church must have been the vehicle that sustained hope throughout this dark period.

Christianity, as the shared religion of all Britons, was a unifying force, lending greater purpose to their campaign.

'Castellum Guinnion' suggests a fortress, and there were not many in Lincolnshire. The Roman road between Bawtry and Lincoln crosses the Trent at Littleborough (Segelocum), and there is a recently identified Roman settlement on the east bank of the Trent at Marton. Arthwys will probably have crossed the Trent here to pursue his campaign. Five miles to the north is Gainsborough or Gegnesburh, meaning 'Gegn's fortified place', the home of the tribe known as the Gaini. I suggested earlier that these Saxons or Frisians may have been adversaries of the Brigantes, and I propose Gainsborough for the location of the fortress of Guinnon.

We can only speculate as to why the Gaini were singled out for the eighth battle, but it is likely they were allies of the Jutes in the Saxon wars, or that they were harbouring high-ranking Jutes and/or refugees from the conflict on the western bank of the Trent. Either way, it looks as though Arthwys' purpose was subjugation rather than annihilation in this instance, because we know the Gaini survived, even though there was 'great slaughter'.

The ninth battle was fought in the Urbs Legionis.

Most historians propose one of the three main legionary towns for this battle: Caerleon, Chester or York. However, Lincoln more obviously fits the progression of this conjectured campaign and was itself, initially, a legionary town. It is often overlooked how Lincoln dominates the region, being atop a hill and eminently defensible. In many ways, this city inside its Roman walls compares to later medieval fortresses, which may have assisted its survival as a Christian centre – a reasonable assumption for, had the heathen Saxons sacked Lincoln, the wooden church known as St. Paul in the Bail would surely not have survived. We know from Bede that there was a church there in his day and that an Anglian *Praefectus Lindocolinae Civitatis* was present, suggesting there had been a return to ordered life. We have also already noted that Vortimer may have been buried at Lincoln in the midst of the Saxon wars, so why, then, was it necessary for Arthwys to fight a battle there?

I assume the Saxons, whom the Britons had already engaged, were fleeing south, and perhaps those settled around Lincoln at places such as Saxelby decided their best course of action was defence, which may not have been within the city walls. It appears Arthwys' army was becoming feared, even by the warlike Saxons, and they were retreating or digging in to defend themselves wherever possible. The *Historia* notes, before these battles, that Octha, Hengist's grandson, relocated to Kent, suggesting retreat, although we are not told the reason. It is hard to assess how much time elapsed between battles – this was an army on the move and, much like the Allied campaign on the Continent in the Second World War, delays would only give the enemy opportunity to regroup and fight back. There does not seem to have been a siege at Lincoln, only a battle, which suggests it occurred outside the city walls. The Saxons were now surrounded and completely cut off from the sea. The net was closing in.

> *The tenth battle was fought on the shore of the river which is called Tribruit.*

I mentioned earlier that it has always been assumed that the Britons chiefly used cavalry in their battles. However, the amphibious nature of the enemy in this campaign suggests the increasing need for the Britons to form a navy of their own, and it is quite likely that boats were deployed, whether captured or British, to sail up the Trent, assist with river crossings and engage the enemy as required – we will note later how Riothamus likely used a similar tactic. Presumably, the Saxons retreated up the Trent in the face of this building onslaught, while the Britons advanced both down the Fosse Way from Lincoln and up the Trent, driving the enemy towards the waiting army of Ambrosius/Riothamus at Ambaston where, doubtless, the river was blockaded.

The final two battles of the Badon campaign look very much like last stands by the Saxons. Tribruit, by contrast, looks more like a battle in open country, where their boats were moored and defended. For a river to be described as having a 'shore' means that it must be a large one, pointing to this being the Trent. 'Tribruit' could be a name for the Trent, although John T. Koch, one of the country's most eminent Celtic experts, suggests the river's name actually derived from 'trisantona' meaning 'great thoroughfare', which it certainly is. Perhaps 'tri' or 'tre' suggests the number 'three', similar to 'tributary'. Three rivers become one where the Derwent and Soar join the Trent above Thrumpton.

There was certainly a Roman settlement thereabouts as a tessellated pavement was discovered at Parsons Barn a mile away, and just to the north-east of Barton-in-Fabis, there are 'ancient fortifications' noted on the 1836 Ordnance Survey map, although I can find nothing more about them. Behind Thrumpton is an area of high ground, formerly known as Wrights Hill, which now accommodates the recently closed Ratcliffe-on-Soar Power Station.

With all of this in mind, I suggest the Battle of Tribruit occurred near Barton-in-Fabis. As well as being an important shore and junction point, this was the nearest river port to Bardon Hill. The Britons would have been proceeding towards the Derwent to link up with the army of Ambrosius/Riothamus. They would have left the Fossway at Saxondale to take the Roman road that followed the Trent past Nottingham to Barton-in-Fabis. This route leads directly to the next battle at Breedon on the Hill.

> *The eleventh battle was fought on the mountain which is called Agned.*

Throughout this book, I have mostly referred to and quoted from the 1975 translation of the 'Harleian' recension of the *Historia* by the late Professor David Dumville.[25] However, where I have quoted other authors, I have used their interpretations which may vary slightly. Later versions of the *Historia* call this battle site Breguoin, and I believe this is because later scribes knew where it had actually occurred. Breguoin is likely to be Breedon on the Hill, between Derby and Bardon Hill, and there are many reasons why I believe this.

I have considered why the most reliable recension of the *Historia* called this battle 'Agned' and have reached

[25] David N. Dumville, 'The Textual History of the Welsh-Latin Historia Brittonum', (PhD diss. University of Edinburgh, 1975). https://era.ed.ac.uk/handle/1842/8972.

the following conclusion. Breedon is a remarkable and prominent hill about which there is much to tell. It may well have been a religious site before this battle and certainly became so afterwards. Given the highly charged Christian mission of the Britons, I wonder if Agned refers to Agnus Dei, the Lamb of God, the epithet applied to Christ by John the Baptist. In other words, Agned is the name for 'the battle of Christ', whereas Breguoin correlates to the location. Battles were sometimes given names rather than locations, such as the Battle of the Standard at Northallerton in 1138. In my opinion, Breedon and Breguoin are sufficiently similar when spoken. The hill was a formidable Iron Age fort, and a battle here fits the shape of the campaign and my proposed historical framework for the entirety of the Saxon wars.

One mile to the north-east of this stronghold is Ambro Hill, and we perhaps begin to see that this could well have been the front line of the western defence against the Saxons. It appears that Bardon Hill and Breedon had been colonised by the Saxons, initially to launch raids from and then to retreat to. These were forest locations capable of sheltering the many different groups that had coalesced into the Saxon invasion force that Vortimer had harried from the west. The local 'Ambro' place names suggest there was an army of Ambrosius' Britons patrolling this frontier, and this Saxon frontline position was threatening enough, with their imposing strongholds and the extent of the territory they controlled behind the boundary, to require this level of military presence.

Prior to the Badon campaign, the Saxons had been in control of the coastline from the Humber all the way down the east coast and round to the Wash. An assault on this extended front line would have been impossible without a huge army, and Vortigern's former attempted attack on the Saxon leaders at the centre on Axholme had dismally failed. The Saxons had always been able to fall back and then later recolonise. With this in mind, we can begin to understand why Arthwys' campaign was so remarkable. Under his strategy, the Saxon armies had been pressed into the Midlands and cut off, unable to fall back. The scene was set for siege and slaughter.

If you should be driving along the M42 close by the M1 at any time, cast a glance northwards, and you will see the parish church of St. Mary and St. Hardulph sitting atop a huge quarry cliff. This is Breedon on the Hill. A visit is more than worthwhile, not just for the extensive views, but to see the Iron Age fort known as the Bulwarks. The location provides a commanding position.

The church is medieval but houses some of the best Saxon sculptures in the country, remnants of a Saxon priory founded here in the seventh century by Friduricus and central to the Christian development of Mercia. The priory even produced an Archbishop of Canterbury: Tatwin, in 731. The wall sculptures, known as the Breedon Angel, the Three Saints and the Byzantine Blessing, are particularly famous. The inhabited vine scrollwork is intriguing and includes three warriors, two mounted with spears and an infantry soldier kneeling with a spear as if to defend himself.

It is easy to picture why this battle would be referred to as a siege. The hillfort was originally a stronghold of the Midlands tribe, the Corieltauvi, in the late Iron Age. The Saxons may have already resisted earlier attacks by the Britons, and as I noted in the previous chapter, this area formed the western front where Vortimer had fought a battle on the River Derwent at the start of the Saxon wars. On this occasion, however, there were at least two armies attacking the stronghold, which will have quickly overwhelmed the now isolated Saxons.

The Britons' victory at the Battle of Agned may actually have been more significant than that of the Battle of Mount Badon. It seems unlikely that there were two fortified locations so close to each other. Breedon itself is only 8 miles from Bardon Hill which may have only been the location of a large Saxon settlement, somewhere the remaining Saxon forces escaped to for their last stand, and this might explain why the Welsh Annals seem to confuse the Battle of Badon described by the *Historia* with the siege of Agned/Breguoin.

> *The twelfth battle was on mons Badonis where in one day nine hundred and sixty men were killed by one attack of Arthur, and no one laid them low save he himself.*

Following their defeat at Agned, the Badon Saxons will have realised that the Britons not only had a large army but also that genocide was their clear intent. Sieges can last a very long time where the defences are strong. However, Bardon Hill's only real defensive advantages were its forest and high ground. I suspect it became known as a siege because the armies of Arthwys and Riothamus had surrounded what was more likely to be a large hillside settlement than a fortress.

I noted at the beginning of this book some of the reasons why I initially suspected this location to be the Mount Badon mentioned by Gildas. Firstly, it is unquestionably a *mons*, the remains of a volcano, and the highest point in Leicestershire. It has been quarried since 1622 and produces high quality granite. Much of this hill is now quarried away and the site hosts the headquarters of Aggregate Industries which is currently owned by the Swiss cement maker Holcim. Their tipper trucks display a mountain logo with 'Bardon' in blue and can be seen working throughout the UK. The similarity of the name to Mount Badon always struck me, and I could never work out why historians had not spotted this. It is interesting to note that other rocky outcrops in Leicestershire are described as 'mons', for example Mountsorrel, which is also the site of a quarry. From the summit of Bardon, it is possible to see Lincoln Cathedral in one direction and the Shropshire Hills in the other. The area known as Battle Flat just below the summit may actually be the location of this final battle.

The battle itself was clearly one-sided from the report of the casualties, and while I'm sure that the translation of the battle list is accurate, I doubt that Arthwys killed 960 Saxons all by himself. Saying that, this number is an interesting inclusion and rather precise. My own view is that the battle-experienced army led the charge and, in one attack, killed a significant number of the enemy who, by this stage of the campaign, may have only been defenceless settlers. As Gildas describes:

> *The Britons slaughtered no small number of their foes about forty four years after their arrival in Britain.*

I have said from the outset that this battle occurred no later than 469, so forty-four years earlier was 425. This is only three years shy of the date given in the *Historia* for the arrival of the Saxons. Although there is a battle dated to 473 in the *Anglo-Saxon Chronicle* which mentions Aesc and Hengist, I believe this is recorded out of sequence as both had already perished in the course of the war. It is unlikely that it took the Britons more than one to two years to complete this entire campaign because it owed its success to the brutal momentum that never gave the Saxons a chance to regroup or retreat to safe ground or waters. The war was over, and the Britons' relief must have been immense.

I doubt that archaeology will ever be able to confirm the locations of these battles. Identifying battlefields is notoriously difficult, even for much later sites or larger encounters. The Battle of Bosworth keeps moving from field to field, and Hastings has moved inland. Even the mass graves of Marston Moor are lost.

My summation may prove disappointing for Arthur enthusiasts who are inspired more by the romantic mystery and traditional locations, but I'm sure Bardon Hill was equally as mystical prior to the Industrial Revolution! Personally, I believe Arthwys' achievements were outstanding, if brutal, and he deserves his place in history. The military threat of the Saxons was stemmed for a generation by his strategic campaign, but in many ways the victory proved Pyrrhic – no significant territory was subsequently recovered and the Britons, who had fallen back to Watling Street, made no attempt to recolonise the regions. By contrast, the Anglo-Saxons seem to have made a vigorous recovery as Professor D. P. Kirby notes in *The Earliest English Kings*:

> *The Angles and Saxons did not lose their association with their continental homelands following settlement in Britain. Maritime communications remained of great importance. ... Anglian communities in northern or midland England may have participated along with the Eastern Angles in their probably long-established contacts with north-European commerce which are revealed by the range of goods from the famous East Anglian boat-burial of the early seventh century in the Sutton Hoo barrow cemetery.*[26]

By contrast, the Britons were to become increasingly isolated with the fall of the Western Roman Empire, the damage from which should not be understated. Gildas clearly describes how the optimism following Mount Badon was dashed within his lifetime. This brief military success could no longer secure borders or guarantee the continuity the Western Empire had for so long enjoyed, and the continental Romans were enduring the same experience as their barbarian enemies swept away the old order. If my proposed timing of this final battle is correct, then the events that followed the year 469 start to make more sense.

[26] Kirby, *The Earliest English Kings*, p 61.

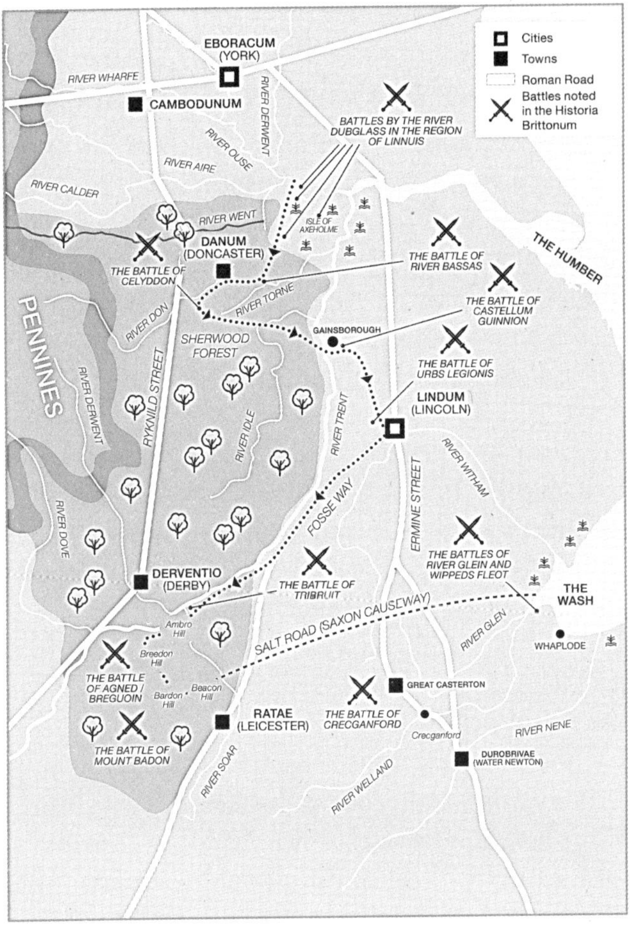

Map 4: The Badon Campaign, circa 460–468

The twelve battles of Arthur as described in the *Historia Brittonum* were probably a campaign against the Jutes and Saxons who had become established in Lincolnshire and Nottinghamshire. This campaign culminated in two final battles at their strongholds at Breedon on the Hill (Bregouin) and Bardon Hill (Mons Badonicus). The troops of Ambrosius Aurelianus were likely present at the final two battles and were possibly led by his son, who I believe was Riothamus. Ambrosius must have died around this time because Riothamus became 'King of the Brittones' and shortly afterwards led his army into Gaul (471).

XIV

The end of the Western Roman Empire

One of the datable events that followed on from our revised date for the successful defeat of the Saxons at the Battle of Mount Badon was the expedition of a British king called Riothamus with an army of twelve thousand men to the Loire region in support of the Western Emperor Anthemius. Geoffrey Ashe, in his book *The Discovery of King Arthur*, was convinced that this king was Arthur, not least because elements of Geoffrey of Monmouth's narrative incorporated Roman names that have proved contemporary to this optimistic adventure. There is little question that Riothamus contributed to the myth of Arthur, but the outcome of this very real expedition was a serious defeat from which the Britons would never recover. Euric and his Visigoth forces were simply too powerful by then, and the Western Roman Empire itself was only six years away from its demise.

It is difficult to write about the second half of the fifth century without introducing some sense of foreboding. But describing how event after event added crisis to the chaos, leading to the eventual end of imperial control over the Western Empire may be misleading. To fully understand the developments of this time, it is necessary to suspend hindsight. Key leaders, such as Majorian, Ricimer and Anthemius, could not predict the future; these powerful men were still optimistic, pressing on with their ambitions, oblivious to how close to the end it all was.

The defeat of Attila at the Battle of the Catalaunian Plains in 451 should have been sufficient to re-establish Roman control on the Continent, but Rome's vulnerability continued. The steady hand of Aetius was removed from the tiller when he was murdered by Valentinian III in 454, and in the following year, Valentinian was himself assassinated by followers of Aetius, encouraged by the ambitious Petronius Maximus. He proclaimed himself Emperor only to be stoned to death by a mob in Rome after eleven weeks. A few days later, King Gaiseric and his Vandals took advantage of the chaos, captured Rome and sacked it for two weeks. During his brief reign, Maximus had appointed Avitus to *magister militum*. Avitus was a Gallo-Roman noble who was closely associated with Theodoric of the Goths, and upon the death of Maximus, he was proclaimed Emperor by the Gothic king. Avitus decided the Western Empire's future would be best run from Gaul and this garnered him many enemies in Rome. Ricimer and Majorian were two outstanding generals, both of whom had served under Aetius. They rebelled and overturned Avitus in 457. Ricimer, a German, had assisted Majorian, a Roman, who became Emperor.

By this point, the Western Empire consisted only of the Italian Peninsula and portions of southern Gaul. Ricimer, the senior of the two, had expected to control Majorian, but Majorian proved vigorous in recovering both Gaul and portions of Hispania. Despite this success, Ricimer plotted against Majorian and deposed him in 461. This did not sit well with the military establishment, in particular two generals, Aegidius in Gaul and Marcellinus in Dalmatia. They both broke with imperial authority, becoming warlords of their territories and, in this respect, were similar, and contemporary, to Ambrosius Aurelianus in Britannia.

The next Emperor, Libius Severus, was Ricimer's puppet and reigned until 465. He was allegedly poisoned by Ricimer who was seeking a reconciliation with the Eastern Emperor, Leo I, who had refused to accept Severus as his Western counterpart. But Leo responded by appointing the commanding general of the Illyrian army, Anthemius, as Western Emperor. The new Emperor arrived in Rome with a now compliant Marcellinus whom he appointed patrician in an attempt to balance Ricimer's power. Anthemius was a capable politician and, for a while, was able to cooperate with the Eastern Empire and calm rivalries in the west. Ricimer even married Anthemius' daughter, Alypia. However, this amical accord soon changed when the Emperor's foreign policy was undermined by military failure.

In 468, Leo, Anthemius and Marcellinus organised a planned invasion of the Vandal kingdom of Africa. Under the command of Basiliscus, a fleet of one thousand ships was defeated at the Battle of Cape Bon. Marcellinus who had been impeded from joining the campaign by Ricimer was later murdered in Sicily, quite probably on Ricimer's orders. After this disastrous campaign, Anthemius turned to the reconquest of Gaul.

Although southern Gaul was still governed from the Western Court, the Visigoths, under King Euric, had isolated Auvergne (Clermont-Ferrand) which was governed by Ecdicius, the son of the former Emperor Avitus. Ecdicius later valorously defended Auvergne from the Goths with only a small force. It is at this point that Anthemius invited Riothamus with his army of Britons to enter Gaul to hold a position to the north of the Visigoths. Anthemius' plan seems to have been to attack the

Visigoths on two fronts, dividing Euric's forces. Penny MacGeorge in *Late Roman Warlords* summarises the outcome:

> *Anthemius did not wish to abandon the last Roman possessions in southern Gaul. In AD 471 an army was sent from Italy to attack the Visigoths; one of the four leaders was his son Anthemiolus. Shortly before this Anthemius had made an alliance with the British, or Breton, leader Riothamus with the intention, presumably, of attacking Euric on two fronts. Riothamus, however, was defeated by Euric north of the Loire, 'before the Romans could join him', and fled to the Burgundians. According to the Gallic chronicle, the army sent by Anthemius was defeated and destroyed somewhere trans Rodanum. All the commanders, including Anthemius' son, were killed making this a personal tragedy, as well as yet another military and political reverse. Euric went on to begin the conquest of Auvergne, and within five years had obtained all the remaining Roman possessions in southern Gaul. By this time the relationship between Ricimer and Anthemius (probably one of distrust from the outset) had developed into a struggle for power, and was ultimately to become, in effect, civil war.*[27]

I have always thought it unlikely that Riothamus' army came from Armorica, as is sometimes suggested. It would have been a large commitment to gather a force totalling

---

[27] Penny MacGeorge, *Late Roman Warlords* (Oxford: Oxford University Press/Oxford Classical Monographs, 2007), pp 242–243.

twelve thousand, but if we look at it in the context of the Badon campaign having been successfully concluded by 469, then this number could well have been available in the form of the large standing army raised originally by Ambrosius Aurelianus, but now under the control of his son, Riothamus, in Britain for the Badon campaign. Jordanes' description of Riothamus as 'King of the Brittones' implies that Ambrosius was dead by this time. Christopher A. Snyder, in his book *An Age of Tyrants: Britain and the Britons A.D. 400–600*, makes the point that Riothamus is the first British king to be mentioned in written sources since Tacitus!

Jordanes, in Getica XLV 237–238, tells us:

> *Now Euric, king of the Visigoths, perceived the frequent change of Roman Emperors and strove to hold Gaul by his own right. The Emperor Anthemius heard of it and asked the Brittones for aid. Their King Riotimus came with twelve thousand men into the state of the Bituriges by the way of Ocean, and was received as he disembarked from his ships. Euric, king of the Visgoths, came against them with an innumerable army, and after a long fight he routed Riothamus, king of the Britons, before the Romans could join him. So when he had lost a great part of his army, he fled with all the men he could gather together, and came to the Burgundians, a neighbouring tribe then allied to the Romans. But Euric, king of the Visigoths, seized the Gallic city of Arvernum; for the Emperor Anthemius was now dead.*

In one of his many letters to have survived, Sidonius Apollinaris, a Gallo-Roman noble who was a poet, diplomat and Bishop of Auvergne, wrote to 'his friend Riothamus' discouraging his recruitment of a fellow Gallic noble's slaves to fight alongside the Britons. Ecdicius, mentioned earlier, was brother-in-law to Sidonius, and both men took charge of the defence of Auvergne between 471 and 474. That Sidonius was acquainted with Riothamus helps to explain a few matters.

It appears that Riothamus was accorded the respect of a Roman noble, and as son of Ambrosius Aurelianus and perhaps the grandson of an emperor, he most certainly would have been considered as such. News of his military success against the Saxons must have reached the Roman elite, encouraging them to include him in their plans. For him to have answered Rome's call, Riothamus must have felt a commitment to the Western Empire, gauging the risk of the expedition worthwhile. We have no clues as to whether or not he held estates in Gaul or Armorica, but with his strong connections to the Western Empire, it is entirely possible. There is also a reasonable chance that his kingship extended to the colony in Armorica or that there was some form of hegemony. The earlier comings and goings of Germanus may indicate the latter. Gregory of Tours in the *Historia Francorum* tells us:

> *The Britanni were driven from Bourges by the Goths and many were slain at the village of Déols.*

Nothing more is known about Riothamus except that the failure of the expedition likely damaged the prestige of the family of Ambrosius, of whom Gildas says:

His descendants in our day have become greatly inferior to their grandfather's excellence.

It is easy to see how these events have become associated with the folklore of Arthur. The defeated Britons retreated in the direction of Avallon, a place name connected to Arthurian legend. My own interest was drawn by the use of boats on the Loire, similar to those used in the Badon campaign – many Saxon keels would have become available to the Britons following the Saxon defeat. It is likely the Britons sailed as far as Orléans (Civitas Aurelianorum). There is a chance that Arthwys accompanied Riothamus on this adventure, but I have reached the conclusion that this is unlikely. Breton folklore about Arthur bears a remarkable similarity to Welsh and Cornish tales, so it is more probable that continued contact between these areas is responsible for this rather than the memory of a Roman campaign.

Following the defeat of the Saxons, Arthwys' focus must surely have been on his own territories in northern Britain, which were still under threat from the Picts and civil war, and far away from the concerns of the Western Empire on the distant Continent.

We hear nothing more about Riothamus after the defeat of his army, whereas we do have more information in respect of Arthur. That said, establishing the revised date for the Battle of Mount Badon does provide a better framework from which to conjecture who these people might have been and what their motives were, and from there, have greater context to assess their impact on history.

The Western Roman Empire would shortly come to a tragic end. Anthemius was reduced to hiding as a beggar until captured. Ricimer had him beheaded in 472 but died himself eleven weeks later from natural causes – which some consider an injustice given the blood on his hands. In 476, the leader of the Goths, Odoacer, deposed the last Western Roman Emperor, Romulus Augustulus. From Romulus to Romulus, Rome had dominated the Western World for a thousand years. The political map of the Continent was about to be redrawn as, indeed, was the map of Britain.

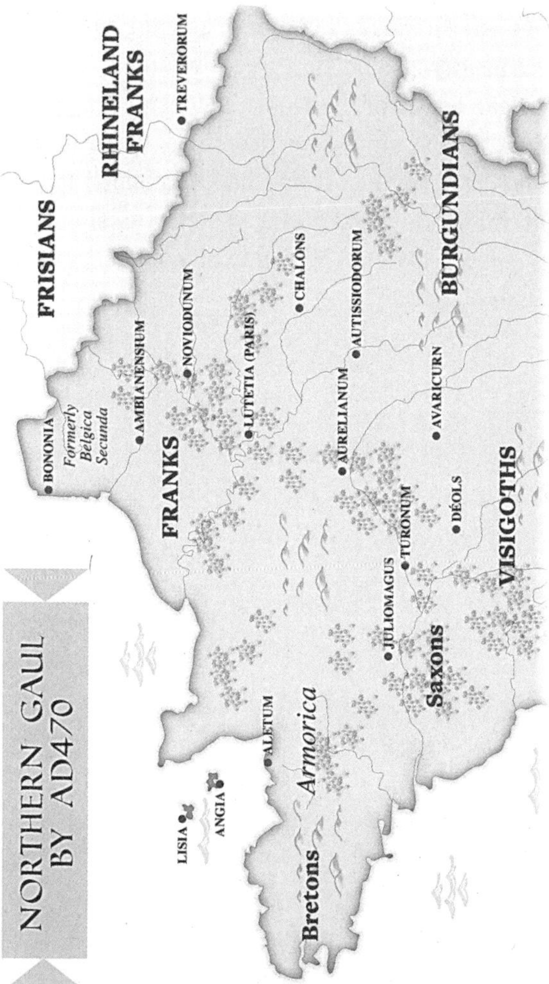
NORTHERN GAUL
BY AD470
FRISIANS
RHINELAND
FRANKS
TREVERORUM
BONONIA
Formerly
Belgica
Secunda
AMBIANENSIUM
NOVIODUNUM
FRANKS
LUTETIA (PARIS)
CHALONS
AUTISSIODORUM
AURELIANUM
BURGUNDIANS
AVARICURN
DÉOLS
TURONUM
VISIGOTHS
JULIOMAGUS
Saxons
ALETUM
Armorica
LISIA
ANGIA
Bretons

XV

The aftermath of Badon, and Britain in the early sixth century

Revising the date of the Battle of Badon to circa 469 allows for a re-examination of Gildas to see if what we know about the events of the late fifth century fits his narrative and observations. Similarly, a review of the *Anglo-Saxon Chronicle* and the *Annales Cambriae* may well present events in a different perspective.

It would seem there was a power vacuum following the defeat of Riothamus, and after 470, there was never again the political will for the kings of Britain to act together nor a big brother in the shape of Rome influencing the provinces. The Roman Church was reeling from events on the Continent, and while the shock of the outcomes did not diminish the mission, it certainly frustrated progress. Travel, in particular, presented a greater risk. There is a great deal of evidence that the Church became a refuge for the sons of the famous. Pious retirement was also an honourable end to the careers of the mighty and afforded a degree of protection under new regimes.

Sidonius Apollinaris, mentioned in the last chapter, is one of the few sources who casts light on the Church and society in the second half of the fifth century. Many of his letters to acquaintances, and much of his poetry, survive. As a wealthy Gallo-Roman noble, he was elected to Bishop of Auvergne (Clermont-Ferrand) in circa 470. When the Goths captured Clermont, he was imprisoned for helping to defend the city. However, he was released from captivity by Euric, King of the Goths, to continue to shepherd his flock.

Sidonius was acquainted not only with Riothamus but also two other Britons: Faustus, Bishop of Riez, and Riocatus. The *Historia* names a 'Faustus' as a son of Vortigern, born out of incest but baptised and reared by St. Germanus, and the existence of a 'Faustus' is upheld by the Pillar of Eliseg as well as the genealogies. Riocatus also features in the genealogies as a grandson of Vortigern. His name translates as 'Battle King', but he entered the Church at a young age and rose to the rank of bishop. It is therefore reasonable to see Faustus and Riocatus as two members of the Vortigern dynasty, and although the connection cannot be proved, they both had close Briton-Breton relations and belonged to the Gallo-British cultural nexus. Avitus, Bishop of Vienne, referred to Faustus as 'Britannus', and when writing to him, Sidonius refers to 'your Britons'.

In this letter, written about 475–478, Sidonius tells how Riocatus, after visiting Faustus at Riez, called on him during the return journey to Britain, having been forced to stay at Clermont as a result of the Goth-disturbed state of the roads. Sidonius mentions to Faustus that 'I had read those works of yours which Riocatus, bishop and monk (thus twice a stranger and pilgrim in this world), was taking back from you to your Britons'. Riocatus had remained at Clermont two months, keeping secret that he had some special work by Faustus with him. We may muse that the British-born cleric Faustus requested secrecy since all Britons were suspected of Pelagianism at this time. Word, however, got about, and Riocatus hastily left. Sidonius followed, caught him up and implored him to reveal the precious text; Riocatus duly obliged. In his letter, Sidonius proceeds to outline the book's contents, which apparently concerned philosophy. This event shows there was clearly a good level of communication between the British and continental churches in the latter half of the fifth century, despite the many shifts in power and the dangers of travel.

Gildas also gives a clear indication of the impediments to travel experienced in his day. He refers to Britain's martyrs:

> *St. Alban of Verulam, Aaron and Julius, citizens of the City of the Legions, and the others of both sexes who, in different places, displayed the highest spirit in the battle-line of Christ.*

But in respect of their shrines, Gildas says, in §10:

> *Their graves and the places where they suffered would now have the greatest effect in instilling the blaze of divine charity in the minds of beholders, were it not that our citizens, thanks to our sins, have been deprived of many of them by the unhappy partition with the barbarians.*

Whether this was politically or self-imposed is not known. Much is made of this partition, which is generally seen as definite British control following Mount Badon, although it may also suggest the opposite. The distribution of Saxon place names shows that westward expansion came to a dead stop at the eastern base of the Pennines and roughly along the line of the A1 trunk road. Gildas was therefore likely referring to Lincoln or perhaps York, but his statement implies that the Britons had ceded a huge amount of territory to the Angles and Saxons in the east and perhaps he was simply observing this was now heathen territory. Furthermore, when Part II of *De Excidio* is considered, it appears that British territory may well have shrunk, despite the success of Mount Badon, and that in the absence of combined political will, a power vacuum existed – albeit peaceful. As Gildas observes:

> *But the cities of our land are not populated even now as they once were; right to the present they were deserted, in ruins and unkempt. External wars may have stopped, but not civil ones. For the rememberance of so desperate a blow to the island and of such unlooked for recovery stuck in the minds of those who witnessed both wonders. That was why kings, public and private persons, priests and churchmen, kept to their own stations. But they died; an age succeeded them that is ignorant of that storm and has experience only of the calm of the present.*

Gildas supplies a surprising amount of detail about five contemporary Welsh kings, but before their time, it appears that Arthur had been killed. The *Annales Cambriae* contain two entries in relation to Arthur as follows:

> *Year 72 (c. AD 516) The Battle of Badon in which Arthur carried the cross of our Lord Jesus Christ on his shoulders for three days and three nights and the Britons were victors*

Year 93 (c. AD 537) The Strife of Camlann in which Arthur and Medraut (Mordred) fell and there was death in Britain and in Ireland.

There is a great deal of debate about the 'years' of the *Annales* which are not standard dating. This is because the entries are sequential, and Year 1 is generally thought to run from AD 444. Year 72 is therefore usually taken as 516. But the *Annales* are the least reliable of all the sources, and some say they are influenced by Geoffrey of Monmouth's pseudo-history, *The History of the Kings of Britain*. Christopher Gidlow, in *The Reign of Arthur: From History to Legend*,[28] mounts a case in their defence, but the dating remains difficult to interpret.

Regardless, I am interested in the time lapse between the two entries which, combined with my conjectured dates, would suggest Arthwys may have been killed twenty-one years after Badon, in 490, aged about sixty. This seems to accord with the statement by Gildas that civil wars continued to be waged. 'Strife' suggests civil war, and there is no better candidate for the location of Camlann than Camboglanna on Hadrian's Wall. It is impossible to conjecture this battle – tradition has Mordred as an enemy, but no one can really say. Camboglanna, however, was on the north-west frontier of Coeling territory which is known to have fragmented in the sixth century. It is also tempting to place this battle in the context of the defence of northern territories because battles with Picts and Scots surely continued, although they are unrecorded.

[28] Christopher Gidlow, *The Reign of Arthur: From History to Legend* (Stroud: Sutton Publishing, 2004).

There is always debate, and it is a thorny issue for specialist commentators to explain, about why Gildas never mentioned Arthur, particularly in light of the detail he presents for the five Welsh kings. The *Annales*, therefore, assist in a very important way. We may assume, following Mount Badon, Arthwys was campaigning in the northern territories, making it less likely that he accompanied Riothamus on his continental adventure. It is also clear that he was dead twenty years before Gildas was writing and was therefore not a contemporary of the five kings.

Gildas had very little to say about northern Britain, which rather undermines both histories written about the saint. The Rhuys *Life* and the Llancarfan *Life* both claim he was the son of a northern king. The Rhuys *Life* was written by a ninth-century monk in Brittany at the Abbey of Saint-Gildas-de-Rhuys, founded by St. Gildas. The Llancarfan *Life* was written in the twelfth century by Caradoc of Llancarfan who was a friend of Geoffrey of Monmouth. Both are difficult to substantiate. If there were older and more genuine sources for the *Annales Cambriae*, they were most likely similar to those of the *Historia*, initially northern and only subsequently considered to originate in Wales.

While the entry in the *Annales* regarding Camlann looks synthetic and perhaps influenced by Geoffrey of Monmouth, the added comment to Year 93, that there was 'death in Britain and in Ireland', could be genuine for 537 and may refer to an unrecorded plague or pestilence or more likely relate to poisoning and famine following the now identified cataclysmic Icelandic volcanic eruption in 536, which was followed by two more in 540 and 547. The

Plague of Justinian is recorded as starting in 541 and is perhaps too late for this entry, although it is difficult to be precise with pandemics.

These corroborated events, nevertheless, help to provide an outer limit to the date of the writings of Gildas. He did not write *De Excidio* after 536, because such portents of divine judgement would certainly have been mentioned – they were on a biblical scale. Aside from my own assessment, there is a developing view among historians that Gildas wrote much earlier than is previously thought, and this accords with the case for an earlier Battle of Mount Badon. Whether or not *De Exidio* was written as a single work or on separate occasions is not known. It is usually read as a single treatise, but there seems to be a second section which commences at §27 and begins 'Britain has Kings but they are tyrants'. It is thought this could have been written later, because it is a curious condemnation of five western British kings, all broadly within Wales or perhaps the former territory of Vortigern, known in Roman times as *Britannia Prima*. This rather suggests that Gildas was expressing the views of a remnant of the Romano-British elite that was still clinging to the old ways, making it also relevant to those scholars seeking to measure the boundaries of Late Antiquity.

It rather explains why Gildas did not concern himself to the same extent with the other provinces and provides further clues to both where and when he wrote. His familiarity with the five kings suggests proximity, and he viciously derides them. It is sometimes suggested that he levelled his criticism from a safe distance, perhaps Brittany. However, his more remote handling of both the north and the successors of Ambrosius Aurelianus suggests a close location to the five kings. There must have been an audience for, and sympathisers with, Gildas' views. It is important to understand that Christianity had been the declared religion of the Roman state, facilitating the development of the Church and granting power and position to prelates. This was a status that will have transcended kings and warlords, so Gildas clearly would have felt sufficiently secure to deride and criticise, even at close quarters.

He wrote at a time that was confusing for the Church and citizens alike. Christopher Snyder, in *An Age of Tyrants*, explains the divided loyalties of the period:

> *More than one commentator has suggested that in Gildas's day Romani and Britanni were 'antipathetic parties' that divided the loyalties of independent Britain. Such division is undoubtedly an oversimplification, for there were other loyalties competing in Britain. Christianus must certainly have been a strong identifier, though we do not know the precise relation (or ratio) between Christians and pagans in Britain. Tribal loyalties – sentimental or real – were undoubtedly strong at his time, as indeed they had been even under Roman rule. Gildas denounces 'Constantine, tyrant of Dumnonia (Damnoniae tyrannicus)', and 'Vortipor, tyrant of the Demetae (Demetarum tyrannae).' Such tribal names, many of which predate the Roman conquest, appear as well in post-Roman inscriptions. Three early inscribed stones from Wales (dating from the fifth to the early sixth centuries) commemorate an 'Elmetian' (Elmetiacos*

i.e. a native of the kingdom of Elmet in Yorkshire), an 'Ordovician' (Ordous i.e. a native of north-central Wales) and a 'citizen of Gwynedd' (Venedotis cives). The Llandaff Charters and Welsh vernacular literature as well show that such territorial associations were quite common among the Britons in Wales especially.[29]

There is no question that Gildas was thoroughly disappointed with the regional kings he criticised, and the following passage leaves no doubt about this:

Britain has kings (reges), but they are tyrants (tyrannos); she has judges (iudices), but they are wicked. They often plunder and terrorize the innocent; they defend and protect the guilty and thieving; they have many wives, whores and adultresses; they constantly swear false oaths; they make vows, but almost at once tell lies; they wage wars, civil and unjust; they chase thieves energetically all over the country (patriam), but love and even reward the thieves who sit with them at table; they distribute alms profusely, but pile up an immense mountain of crime for all to see; they take their seats as judges (arbitraturi), but rarely seek out the rules of right judgement (indicia regulam); they despise the harmless and humble, but exalt to the stars, so far as they can, their military companions (commanipulares), bloody,

[29] Christopher A. Snyder. *An Age of Tyrants: Britain and the Britons A.D. 400–600* (Stroud: Sutton Publishing, 1998), pp 69–70.

> *proud and murderous men, adulterers and enemies of God – if chance, as they say, so allows: men who should have been rooted out vigorously, name and all; they keep many prisoners in their jails (in carceribus), who are more often loaded with chafing chains because of intrigue than because they deserve punishment. They hang around the altars swearing oaths, then shortly afterwards scorn them as though they were dirty stones.*[30]

Snyder compares Gildas' style and tone to two other moralising clerics of the fifth century:

> *The Old Testament reges were warleaders, but they were instruments of God, and their successes and failures depended upon their behaviour off the battlefield. Apolocalyptic undertones made this model attractive to many ecclesiastical writers in the fifth century, as imperator steadily gave ground to rex in the West. The best example is the moralist Salvian of Marseilles, who attributed fifth-century disasters to the sins of wicked judges. Patrick also subscribes to this model, even though his purpose is not political reform. He is dismissive of the milites of Coroticus, who fight and plunder 'for the sake of a miserable temporal kingdom (miserum regnum temporale) which will in any case pass away in a moment,' concerning himself instead with 'the righteous... (who) shall judge the nations (nationes) and hold sway over wicked kings (regibus iniquis)'.*

---

[30] Snyder. *An Age of Tyrants*, p 84.

Gildas, however, does not just want restitution from the reges iniquis; he wants them to change their ways. His critique of British rulers, running some forty chapters, is an impassioned sermon aimed at exposing all the public and private sins of five ruling dynasties (family members are not spared). More than one scholar has commented that Gildas's moralising is modeled after the Old Testament book of Jeremiah and parallels the tone of Salvian's writing. Like many Old testament kings, Gildas's reges are 'anointed' (ungebantur), but they do not live up to their vows to God. Patrick and Gildas both show concern about rulers swearing false oaths. For Gildas, Christian kingship – to which his reges at least give lip service – means that the ruler is responsible both to God and to his people. Because these British reges have lied to God and are behaving immorally, their irresponsible sins are bringing punishment – plague, famine, civil wars, and barbarian raids – upon the Britons. This idea is not far removed from those of Salvian, and it will have a great impact on the moralizing histories of Bede, 'Nennius,' and Geoffrey of Monmouth.[31]

By 512, then, or shortly thereafter, we can register a perceived decline in justice, education, morality and central control in the former province of *Britannia Prima*, as regional warlords seized control and began to fight among themselves. A similar pattern had begun to develop in *Britannia Secunda*, as the powerful Coeling dynasty

---

[31] Snyder. *An Age of Tyrants*, p 86.

shared out the territory among descendants. The strife at Camlann could easily have resulted from dynastic squabbling as much as from external attack.

Camboglanna (Castlesteads), near Hadrian's Wall, was the next settlement west from Banna (Birdoswald) where a significant post-Roman occupation has been proven. Archaeological excavations are ongoing, but two large timber halls have been located that were built over the Roman granaries. These are dated to at least 500. The whole site is highly defensive, and it is tempting to view the location as strategically important to the Coeling dynasty. The strife at Camlann, therefore, may be considered to have taken place close by Coeling headquarters, rather confirming, as inferred by 'strife', that the clash was a result of dynastic friction or civil war.

In the region previously the domain of Ambrosius Aurelianus, it appears from the *Anglo-Saxon Chronicle* that Saxon and Jute raiding and settlement gathered momentum during the early part of the sixth century. But while the *Chronicle* reports a number of engagements starting around 491, they nevertheless seem minor. Octha had established himself in Kent and Aelle in East Sussex. The Weald (named after the Welsh) and the South Downs represented substantial physical barriers to Saxon expansion westwards. However, there are two entries in the *Anglo-Saxon Chronicle* of significance. For the year 501, we read:

> *Here Port and his two sons Bieda and Maegla came with two ships to Britain at the place which is called Portsmouth and immediately seized land and killed a certain young British man – very noble.*

There is an early Welsh poem called the 'Elegy for Geraint' that records a battle at Llongborth which is considered by some to be Portsmouth. The poem is found in the *Black Book of Carmarthen*, a collection of medieval manuscripts, and is a stirring tale of a brave cavalry engagement that includes the following lines:

In Llongborth I saw Arthurs heroes cut with steel.
The Emperor, ruler of our labour.

Geraint, the son of a Dumnonian king, is slain. 'Dumnonia' was the name for Devon and Cornwall, and quite why Arthur's troops were apparently involved is intriguing. Perhaps this reference applies to soldiers known to have fought at Mount Badon? After all, Llongborth would seem to be in the region associated with Ambrosius Aurelianus. It may be nothing more than fiction, although as an 'elegy', this might suggest the work of an early bard writing about the death of a prince and may contain elements of known encounter.

By contrast, another entry in the *Anglo-Saxon Chronicle*, for the year 508, provides some real history:

Here Cerdic and Cynric killed a certain British king whose name was Natanleod and five thousand men with him – and after whom the land all the way to Cerdicesford was named Netley.

Cerdicesford is usually taken as Charford in Hampshire which is central to the former territory of Ambrosius. The name 'Natanleod' used to be considered folk etymology, deriving perhaps from Netley Marsh near Totton, but there are, however, other clues to Natanleod. In 1623, a mosaic was discovered at Thruxton Roman Villa, close by

Amesbury, which displayed the name 'Quintus Natalius Natalinus et Bodeni'. I suggest Natanleod was an ancestor of this landed Romano Briton family who had lived in the area since the 300s and were perhaps allied to the family of Ambrosius Aurelianus.

This incursion mentioning Natanleod does not seem to have been on Gildas' radar, and his silence on this may indicate a later date, or it could otherwise support his disappointment with the descendants of Ambrosius. However, its location was of huge significance, being six miles south of Salisbury and twenty-four miles west of Winchester, right in the centre of the former territory of Ambrosius. This attack and subsequent settlement were the tide-turning event that saw the Wessex-area Britons reoccupying their former hillforts, such as Cadbury Hill and Old Sarum out of fear. I believe this was the beginning of the south Saxon war that King Arthur is so often associated with in legend.

Named correctly or not, Natanleod, if not a grandson of Ambrosius, was certainly a regional successor. In August 2001, Saxon burials were excavated at Breamore, in Hampshire, which is on the River Avon, one mile south of the North Charford crossing. The archaeologists in charge were with the much-missed TV show *Time Team*. It was Season Nine, episode thirteen and can still be viewed on YouTube. The grave goods discovered were remarkable. There was a great deal of focus on a Byzantine tin bucket manufactured in Antioch which had become a prized possession of its owners and had been replicated as a result. The Saxons had been buried with spears and shields denoting leaders, possibly even royalty. There had been a considerable period before the Saxons closed these graves, suggesting that they had remained open for homage purposes.

This is an important burial site and may yet prove to be the graves of the legendary Cerdic or Cynric or both. The ornate tin bucket is on display at Rockbourne Roman Villa, two miles from where it was found. This Saxon foothold became a huge challenge for the Britons, yet Gildas mentions nothing. Perhaps he had already left for Brittany.

Another key consideration for dating *De Excidio* is the floruit of Maglocunus, otherwise known as Maelgwn, King of Gwynedd. Gildas describes him as 'dragon of the island' and 'the king of all kings' who was 'higher than almost all the generals of Britain' – apparently in both his kingdom and his stature. Maelgwn is criticised ferociously by Gildas who describes him as 'first in evil', having murdered his uncle then his wife followed by his nephew. The *Annales Cambriae* record his death in a 'great mortality' at the estimated date of 547, and tradition holds that he died of the yellow plague which is often associated with the Plague of Justinian.

The confirmed Icelandic volcanic eruptions of 536, 540 and 547 caused famine and, combined with the Plague of Justinian, must have been dreadful to endure. Nearly all chronicles and records of the time register an impact on or a pause in events. I noted earlier that we cannot be so precise about the dates of recorded pandemics, so it would be imprecise to rely on a specific outbreak to date Maelgwn's death, and I suspect that his reign was earlier than the estimated date, as indeed was the date when Gildas wrote about him.

The north seems to have abandoned Roman influence more readily than the west and defaulted to tribal militarism. It is difficult to assess if this part of the country was any less Christian, but these northern areas came to confront a greater degree of warfare and dynastic friction. Maelgwn had more in common with his northern allies than the sub-Roman Britons around Cirencester, which did not sit well with Gildas.

Christianity continued to flourish in the British west and in Ireland, with missionaries from Ireland and south-west Wales travelling extensively along the Atlantic seaways, establishing churches in south-west Britain and Brittany. It is thought that Britons continued to emigrate to Armorica where monasteries were founded by Britons in Gaul and beyond. Atlantic trade hosted these journeys; Irish traders were noted for leather exports, and imports of Mediterranean pottery and amphorae continued to arrive until the middle of the sixth century. Perhaps it was these traders who brought the plague that devastated Ireland and western Britain, weakening its resistance to renewed Saxon aggression?

By the 570s, two entries in the *Anglo-Saxon Chronicle* note a significant collapse in the British resistance showing that the south Saxon war was well underway:

> *571. Here Cutha fought against the Britons at Biedcanford and took four settlements: Limbury and Aylesbury and Benson and Eynsham; and in the same year he passed away. That Cutha was Ceawlin's brother.*

> *577. Here Cuthwine and Ceawlin fought against the Britons and they killed 3 kings, Coinmagil and Candidan and Farinmagil, in the place which is*

called Dyrham; and took 3 cities: Gloucester and Cirencester and Bath.

The Anglo-Saxon age had truly arrived.

XVI

The heroic Old North

As I bring our search for Arthur to a close, I should take a bit more time to talk about the dynasty and area from which I claim he came. By examining the Old North's proud history and enduring legacy as defender of Britannia, you will see why the region has generated heroes throughout history, and why it is so credible that Arthur would have been a northern king.

By the end of the fourth century, the province of *Britannia Secunda*, with the addition of *Valentia*, covered a huge area, with Roman influence apparent as far north as the Clyde–Firth isthmus to the line from the Mersey in the west, to the Humber in the east. Under the Roman occupation, this entire region eventually came under the control of the *Dux Britanniarum*, the most senior Roman general resident in Britain. The troops under his command were extensive and the *Notitia Dignitarum* lists fourteen units with three *vexilationes* of cavalry. Troop levels and fort locations do seem to have varied though, particularly since the tenure of this office encountered crisis after crisis, culminating in the withdrawal of all remaining Roman troops.

I suggested in chapter V that Coel Hen may have been appointed the last *Dux Britanniarum*, but even if this were not the case, we know he was made 'Protector' – an appointment that seems to have given military control of threatened areas to tribal leaders. He appears to have awarded equivalent roles to his allies – the Strathclyde Britons and the Votadini of Lothian and was also likely responsible for the transfer of Cunedda to Gwynedd in Wales to resist Irish infringement. All of these men left in control of this vast region of some 19,000 square miles became known as kings, in particular Coel Hen, though it is not known when the area acquired the name of Rheged or the extent to which hegemony was claimed by or attributed to the Coeling dynasty.

So much of what we know about this entire area has become legend, legend which must surely contain some history, so it is important that readers seeking to understand the post-Roman period of British history fully appreciate the scale, topography and archaeology of the region we know as the Old North.

There is a reasonable quantity of medieval Welsh (Brittonic) literature that has survived and contains the earliest prose stories of the literature of Britain, in particular relating to the Old North. This includes the *Mabinogion*, the *Book of Taliesin* and the *Book of Aneirin*. The *Mabinogion* is a nineteenth-century collection of Welsh poetry and tales known to originate from the *White Book of Rhydderch* and the *Red Book of Hergest*. There are many references to Arthur which are both pre- and post-Galfridian (literature written before and after Geoffrey of Monmouth's account of King Arthur), but one in particular is thought to have been composed in Scotland in the late sixth century – *Y Gododdin*.

It is a medieval Welsh poem consisting of a series of elegies to the men of the Brittonic kingdom of Gododdin (known to the Romans as the Votadini) who, according to conventional interpretation, died fighting the Angles of Deira at a place named Catraeth in about 600. The source is traditionally ascribed to the bard Aneirin, and the battle is considered to have been fought near Catterick in North Yorkshire. Only one manuscript from the thirteenth century survives, and the poem has been variously dated from the seventh to the tenth century. Crucially, the poem references Arthur as well as Coel Hen and his descendants.

Authors writing in support of Arthur's historicity always contend that it is early written evidence of both his existence and reputation. In the first chapter, I mentioned that in the 1980s I spent a great deal of time in the South West, and for a time in the 1990s, I was a regular work visitor to Wincanton. I remember standing on Cadbury Hill, looking towards Glastonbury Tor, feeling completely flummoxed by how a regional sub-Roman warlord's reputation might resurface in a Brittonic heroic poem composed in Scotland. Catterick, the scene of the battle, was at the other end of the country, so it didn't seem to make sense. Now, of course, I see clearly that Arthur's region, family and achievements were not to be found near Glastonbury, and Arthwys would have been well-known in both Rheged and Din Eidyn.

I am particularly familiar with the area around Catterick and Richmond and have walked and explored Wensleydale and Swaledale extensively. Even before I had considered challenging the conventional date for the battle, I could not quite see how Angles and Deirans had so quickly colonised the North Riding or had somehow acquired the political will to respond to a remote border challenge from a small force of elite warriors. This battle was more likely regional, most probably personal and, in consequence, must have been earlier than previously posited.

The Ridings of Yorkshire are not just civil administration areas; they are distinctly separate geographical regions which, across the centuries, have been home to different tribes and peoples. The North and West Ridings are primarily difficult Pennine terrain, whereas the East Riding is mostly flat and bounded by rivers. Deira, with its first Saxon king, Aelle, only began to emerge towards the end of the sixth century and still faced a powerful Elmet at that time. Bernicia, the Borders kingdom that developed under Ida and Aethelfrith into Northumbria, similarly faced the Votadini and Rheged until the early seventh century. Much is made of the later link-up of these two kingdoms, and while Catterick appears, from a map, to dominate the passage between the Pennines and the North York Moors, it actually backs up against the hills and would not have posed a specific threat to unification.

In 1997, John T. Koch published a new study on *Y Gododdin* which links the battle with another: *Gweith Gwen Ystrat* (the *Battle of Gwen Ystrat*), a poem by Taliesin sometimes called the *Battle of Wensleydale*. He believes both were originally composed in the sixth century. It commences:

> *The men of Catraeth arise with the day around a battle victorius, cattle rich sovereign this Uryen by name, the most senior leader*

Koch draws attention to the mention of the sons of Godebog in *Y Gododdin*, these being the descendants of Coel Hen, as well as other names that cross reference. Eighty warriors are eulogised in the poem, and there is one reference to Arthur:

He fed black ravens on the rampart of a fortress
Though he was no Arthur
Among the powerful ones in battle
In the front rank Gwawrddur was a palisade

The poem tells how a force of three hundred picked warriors were assembled and, after a year feasting at Din Eidyn, attacked Catraeth. After several days and overwhelming odds, almost all the warriors were killed. Koch's view brings the date of the battle forward to circa 570.

Heroic poems are immensely important for the study of the development of language and literature. Wales has one of the earliest literary traditions in northern Europe, stretching back to Aneirin and Taliesin. Welsh poetry is connected directly to bardic tradition, that which predates 1100, known as 'the old poetry'. Interpolations and additions are, however, common, as bards and scribes 'improved' their versions. It is therefore likely that the addition of 'Arthur' to *Y Gododdin* is a later interpolation.

I tend to agree with Koch's view that the battles were one and the same. I have diligently stuck to the dating formula used throughout this book which suggests that Urien was active after 550, if the generations of the *Bonedd Gwŷr y Gogledd* are followed. I am not at all certain that the battle had much to do with Elmet, although Gwallog ap Lleenog, mentioned in the poem, was known as 'Judge of Elmet' and was an ally of Urien. It is difficult to establish which Coelings were where and who inherited what, but Eliffer 'of the great Host' appears to have acquired Arthwys' army, and his sons, Gwrgi and Peredur, became renowned as brave warriors.

Urien will have had many allies as he was a popular, wealthy and brave king, as indicated by the many praise poems composed about him. It is likely that diverse settlers aligned themselves to him in the face of a northern incursion. *Y Gododdin* implies overwhelming odds in favour of the enemy, and *Gweith Gwen Ystrat* refers to 'the men of Prydein' and 'the throng of three regions dead'. These could be references to the Picts but more likely the Britons of South Caledonia, otherwise known as the Votadini/Gododdin.

In the *Historia*, Urien is noted as fighting bravely against the Angles, but this was in fact referring to Ida and his sons of the early Bernician kingdom. Urien was apparently murdered 'out of envy' by Morcant, another of his allies, on a campaign at Lindisfarne. Morcant may have been a prince of the Votadini, and this might indicate that there were still tensions between neighbours. The Gododdin claimed territory as far south as the Wall and perhaps beyond, yet we are told Urien was campaigning in Lindisfarne almost on the doorstep of their tribal centre at Din Eidyn. This suggests the Gododdin were weak after the Battle of Catraeth, and this may have been a motive for Urien's murder.

It is interesting to contrast the two poems in which both describe a battle fought to a standstill. *Gweith Gwen Ystrat* translates as the 'White Valley' and may refer to the limestone relief of either Wensleydale or Swaledale. Personally, I prefer the latter because there are limestone cliffs close upstream to Catterick. Both dales are ideal to safely corral and protect large herds of cattle, but Swaledale is the more defensible and the more relevant. There is an Iron Age rampart known as Scots Dyke that runs from the Swale to the Tees which may be mentioned in both poems.

In respect of the reference to Arthur, praise poems about Arthwys may well have been sung at both Catraeth and Din Eidyn. Most authors quoting *Y Gododdin* point out that Aneirin was citing Arthur as a martial exemplar, as Professor Kenneth Jackson describes: 'a paragon that no hero can quite equal'. This may be so, but I am suspicious because the use of the name Arthur instead of the northern name Arthwys suggests a late interpolation courtesy of the *Historia Brittonum.*

For readers who are interested in, but unfamiliar with, the Roman archaeology of the north, there is a treat in prospect should they visit the region. While lacking the lavish villas of the south, the military zone north of Chester in the west and York in the east bristles with military installations all along the roads built to expand the Empire. The frontier witnessed a great deal of activity and much has been carefully excavated particularly along Hadrian's Wall. York similarly abounds with Roman archaeology but holds little of relevance to the early fifth century. As the Roman army's northern headquarters, it is often suggested that there was continuity with the likes of Coel Hen and Mor stepping in following the departure of the Romans, but this is unlikely. The River Ouse, once a significant advantage to the Empire, made the city vulnerable to Saxon attack, and the bridge over the river was likely swept away in the early fifth century. All the evidence suggests the Brittonic kingdom of Elmet extended only to the River Wharfe in the east and Rheged was administered initially from Carlisle and did not extend its territories into the Vale of York or the Vale of Mowbray.

Rather better evidence for regional activity in the fifth century can be seen at the National Museum of Scotland in Edinburgh in the form of the Traprain Law treasure discovered during excavations on a hill fort in Lothian in 1919. The contents of the hoard are hack silver, which is Roman silver plate and vessels cut into fragments or crushed. At 23 kg, it is the largest Roman hoard of its type and was initially thought to be loot from raiding. More recent examination has determined that much of the silver was cut carefully to standard Roman weights and converted to bullion for use as diplomatic gifts or perhaps payment to *foederati*. It is now believed the hoard remained buried from 450, but prior to that, it was regularly added to and used in the production of jewellery.

Traprain Law itself is a hillfort that attracts much speculation and was a fortress of the Votadini who were considered allies of the Romans. For centuries, this hillfort has been associated with King Lott (or Loth or Lleu) of whom many legends are told. What is clear is that the hoard was not recovered at the time and the knowledge of its whereabouts lost. This indicates a shift in power to Edinburgh perhaps to the court of Mynydogg or his predecessors who became the kings of the Gododdin and were perhaps less favourably disposed to the Romano-Britons.

XVII

The case for Arthwys of the North

Ever since Geoffrey of Monmouth fired up the imagination of his contemporaries by writing *The History of the Kings of Britain* there has been speculation about Arthur's historicity. With the passing of the centuries, the popularity of the legends and myths has grown, enjoying a significant resurgence in the nineteenth century which has continued to this day. As with all such mythical mysteries, the debate about whether the figure at its centre ever truly existed and, if so, who he might have been has become increasingly technical and rather misleading. For example, it would have been possible for me to write pages about the root of the name *Arthur* and discuss whether it derives from the Roman name *Artorius*, or *Arth*, the Welsh name for bear, or whether it is somehow associated with *Arcturus*, a bright star near Ursa Major, otherwise known as the Great Bear. But while this kind of analysis lends mystery to so-called Arthuriana, it helps not a jot with identification of the man himself.

We know him as Arthur simply because that is what he is called in his first mention in the *Historia Brittonum*. However, this spelling is in no way set in stone as it will have come from phonetic memory and not been written down until the ninth century, some four hundred years after his birth. We simply cannot know the spelling, the pronunciation or the derivation. All we can say is that it sounded like *Arthur* to the first scribe responsible for writing his name.

While I hope I have covered every aspect of my argument for suggesting that Arthwys, great-grandson of

Coel Hen, is the most likely Arthur in the *Historia Brittonum*, I realise that the detail supporting this case is complex even for a regular history reader. The clarity of the argument is further muddied by the many books written on the subject that revel in the confusion of the sources and purposefully arrive at open-ended conclusions. There are shelf-loads of such books, and I have read many of them. I regret to say that much Arthuriana is misleading, albeit thoroughly enjoyable. For the purposes of this argument, I therefore consider simplicity as key. I think it is reasonable to suggest that one recension or another of the *Historia Brittonum* is the 'old book' that Geoffrey of Monmouth claimed for his sources, so perhaps, for our sources, we should concentrate purely on Gildas, Bede, the *Historia Brittonum*, the *Anglo-Saxon Chronicle*, early Brittonic poetry and near contemporary Empire-wide chronicles. For the reasons I have outlined in this book, I will not be considering candidates for Arthur after AD 470, so all Arthuriana, non-contemporary hagiography, the *Annales Cambriae*, Geoffrey of Monmouth and associated myths and legends – in particular Merlin – fall out of contention.

There are several key elements that support a case for Arthwys, and the first is the chronology for the period in question.

When I started researching this subject, I began by attempting some synchronisation. I tracked everything forward from the usurpation by Magnus Maximus in 383 to as far as Gildas and Maelgwn in the early sixth century. This was no small task, and you will see from the bibliography that it entailed years of reading. It became apparent from early on that there was something amiss with the accepted chronology for the period. Gildas' description of the Saxon rebellion seemed more recent to his lifetime. He writes about it in the present perfect tense, which would not have been the case if a century had passed. The important leaders of the Britons facing the combined threat from both Picts and Saxons were surely the third generation following the departure of Maximus and as I slotted the key leaders into my table of fifth-century events a gap of some thirty years seemed to develop.

I should note here that none of this mis-chronology was apparent from a reading of the *Historia*, only from its interpretation. Gildas mentions the grandchildren of Ambrosius 'in his day', but to be the son of an emperor, Ambrosius must have been born before 414. So Gildas could only have known his grandchildren if he was writing circa 500. From the outset, it was apparent the sources did not agree, but as I added more detail to my table of events, it became clear that there was a difference of a generation in most other dating templates. I am still a little baffled by this, but it works in both directions. For example, how could Gildas give credit to Ambrosius Aurelianus for the ultimate victory at Badon if it was fought in the last decade of the fifth century? Ambrosius would have been at least ninety years old!

This misdating is insidious throughout the sixth century with assumed dates for Coel Hen, Cunedda, Arthwys, even Urien, often miscast. Arthwys' lifetime is not 455 to 499 as is sometimes suggested but more likely 429 to 479. Bede appears responsible for the confusion through his interpretation of Gildas, and consequently, benchmarked dates using this source are usually wide of the mark. It is interesting to muse upon how much misinformation emanated from that small cell in Jarrow, particularly in respect of the arrival of the Saxons.

I hope I have adequately proved that Lincolnshire hosted an *Adventus Saxonum*, probably since the fourth century, and that the Jutes, Hengist and Horsa, joined their throng through a landing on the Humber in the 420s. Those readers who are familiar with the Humber estuary and the River Trent will readily understand why the seafaring Anglo-Saxons would have thrived in this region already colonised over centuries by multi-ethnic retired Roman soldiers. Rivers flow into the Humber from every direction, and the River Trent, in particular, enabled the Saxons to row their keels almost to the centre of Britain. I remain convinced that a great many historians fail to comprehend the full geographical extent of the Saxon threat, even though there should be no doubts, because Gildas is extremely graphic.

It is apparent the Roman Empire, towards the middle of the fifth century, cared little about former provinces and was fraught with its own lost causes right across the Continent. Aetius and his generals were short of manpower and sought strong allies wherever the need arose, and it must have seemed to the high command in Gaul that the Saxons had gained the upper hand through their amphibious superiority. It was only after the containment, first led by Vortimer then the following campaign led by Ambrosius and Arthwys, that this superiority was seen to have been countered.

I have wondered if the '*Superbus Tyrranus*' mentioned by Gildas was neither Maximus nor Vortigern but Aetius rewarding the Saxons for services rendered. For similar reasons, Goar and his tribe of Alans were given territory centred upon Orléans in Gaul in 442. When displaced peoples became *foederati*, they were considered legions in waiting.

The key to defeating the Saxons was a sustained campaign in an area where knowledge of the location of their settlements and connecting waterways could be utilised to outmanoeuvre their amphibious superiority. The planning of the campaign may have taken years and looks as if it was hatched in the north.

I began to realise when researching my first book that I had truly stumbled upon something important when I tried to find two of the battles of the Saxon war where I believe they actually occurred on the southern border of Lincolnshire. I had already reached the conclusion that eleven of Arthur's battles followed a campaign running north-east to south through Lindsey to Doncaster and, thereafter, following the Trent to its furthest navigable point at the foot of Bardon Hill. This list of seemingly separate battles is actually in keeping with a rather obvious, in hindsight, sustained military campaign. But I remained puzzled by how Arthur's initial battle did not appear to fit with this north-east to south progression.

It was only when I realised that Arthur's first battle at the River Glen was in precisely the same location as Vortimer's last battle by the Gaulish Sea that I grasped the significance of it all. Vortimer and Arthur had been attacking the havens of the Wash together to curtail the supply of warriors from the east by sea. In other words, they were shutting the back door before beginning their strategic campaign. Vortimer is reported as dying shortly thereafter, which rather suggests that this is the point where Arthur assumed command and continued the campaign.

While the *Historia Brittonum* contains obvious myth, many sections read differently, as you might expect from a miscellany, and determining a likely original source for each section is key. When I studied Professor Dumville's translation of Arthur's battle list from the *Historia Brittonum*, I considered a most important question. Did Arthur's battles immediately follow Vortimer's death? In which case, the dates usually postulated for the Battle of Mount Badon would be inaccurate to the extent of an entire generation. This certainly agreed with my earlier conclusions.

Professor Dumville's thesis on the *Historia Brittonum* agrees that the annals were assembled by a synchronising cleric, whether this was the monk called Nennius remains a mystery, but from a read of the translation of the Harleian recension, it is clear that the ordered entries he numbers from 29 to 42 all concern the Saxon rebellion and wars in association with Vortigern, St. Germanus, Hengist and Horsa, and include the deaths of both Vortimer and Vortigern. Entry numbers 43 to 50 then switch to St. Patrick and his mission to Ireland. Entry 51 records that, when Hengist died, his son Octha crossed from the northern part of Britain to Kent (so Hengist was definitely not in Kent), then Dumville's entry 52 is the famous Arthurian battle list, which does not end with the victory at Badon as is often quoted but on a reflection that the Saxons were reinforced many times over without interruption and that they brought kings from Germany to rule over them in Britain up to the time when Ida ruled as the first King of Bernicia.

Entry 52 is broad-ranging both in time and geography, incorporating Arthur (460) through to Ida (550), and it seems likely this is what has misled later readers to believe that Arthur's battles were later, even though they appeared to culminate at the Battle of Mount Badon. There is, however, an altered style and tone for this entire entry, suggesting that the source of this information was entirely different to that of Vortigern and St. Patrick, and entry 59 helpfully tells us why:

> *Then at that time Eudeyrn (Urien) struggled bravely against the race of the English. Then Talhaern 'Father of Muse' was renowned in poetry; and Aneirin and Taliesin and Blwchfardd and Cian (who is called 'wheat of song') were illustrious all at the same time in British poetry.*

The sources of the information that follow entry 59 are certainly northern and were perhaps gleaned originally from these northern Britons. I suspect it was one of these bards who recounted the battles of Arthur and quite possibly, as with Aneirin and Taliesin, may actually have been present throughout the campaign. The detailed knowledge of the regional places and names would suggest this.

So, the *Historia* seems to tell us a lot more about the northern origins of Arthur than is usually claimed particularly when the grouping and tone of the entries is considered.

Perhaps it is time for a progressive review of the *Historia Brittonum*. There is no doubt that the compiler knew that he was adding mythic tales to the *Historia* to provide added context rather than to undermine the veracity of actual events.

I hope I have, at the very least, done justice to the *Historia* through the thorough analysis of both Vortimer's and Arthur's battles. We know that Gildas considered the Battle of Mount Badon and the defeat of the Saxons as the culmination of a fightback he attributes to Ambrosius Aurelianus, but Ambrosius was probably dead before the end of the campaign in 469 because, by 470, we know Riothamus had succeeded his father and was considered 'King of the Brittones' for, with the Saxons defeated, he seems to have taken his standing army to Gaul. Sidonius Apollinaris addressed Riothamus in their correspondence as a Roman noble, which of course he was. Gildas implies Ambrosius Aurelianus was the son of an emperor, and given his likely floruit, I have suggested either Jovinus or Sebastianus as his father. So, Riothamus was probably the grandson of an emperor.

It certainly seems that the Roman Empire knew a lot more about what was occurring in Britain than regional Britons, such as Gildas, truly appreciated. The Roman army sought manpower wherever it was available, and victorious armies were a boon. Just as I suspect Aetius was aware of the Saxon army's success and recruited it to fight the Huns (at the time, Gildas thought they had returned home), I'm sure that Anthemius was aware of the Britons' victory at Mons Badonicus and similarly recruited Riothamus to fight the Visigoths. However, neither the Romans nor these warrior lords were aware how close the Western Empire was to its collapse.

It is unlikely that Riothamus was the proto-Arthur as Geoffrey Ashe suggested, and as I have outlined, I rather suspect the success of the campaign against the Saxons actually belonged to the strategy of the northern Arthwys. The expedition of Riothamus does however give us a firm date of before 470 for the defeat of the Saxons at Mount Badon, thus eliminating numerous later candidates for the proto-Arthur.

This is perhaps a disappointing conclusion for those who immerse themselves in the mystery of Arthuriana, but realistically, Arthwys of the north is the most obvious proto-Arthur. Gildas tells us about the powerful families in Britain at the time of the Saxon rebellion, these being Vortigern in the west and Ambrosius Aurelianus in the south, but he says nothing about the north. The *Historia Brittonum* only gives us a sketchy view of Arthur and Urien clumped together with the list of their bards. However, we know from Brittonic poetry that many of the kings of the vast area known as the Old North traced their lineage back to Coel Hen, and even though Aneirin and Taliesin were perhaps on opposing sides one hundred years later, they still both reference the Coelings and Godebog – another name for Coel Hen.

In summary, only one prince or king contemporary to the Saxon wars and the Battle of Mount Badon has a phonetically comparable name to Arthur and that is Arthwys, son of Mor. We do not know if he claimed hegemony over Rheged or Elmet or both, but as great-grandson of Coel Hen, he would have been a trained cavalry warrior with his own militia. It is generally held that Coel Hen became responsible for the defence of the north following the departure of Magnus Maximus in 385. Gildas reports the Picts were defeated sometime around 412, although this did not stop Pictish raids by sea. This suggests a formidable military presence in the north, and Rheged, the kingdom that developed from the Roman province of *Brittania Secunda*, was certainly powerful, enduring alongside its sister states of Elmet and Strathclyde for almost two hundred years. It should not be surprising that a military leader of Arthur's calibre would have come from the region where the Romans had concentrated their elite cavalry forces for nearly three hundred years.

It seems unlikely that he departed for Gaul with Riothamus, who never returned, and it is therefore quite possible that, during the twenty years following the Battle of Mount Badon, he was considered High King of Prydein, until he died in an apparent civil war. Hegemony, thereafter, was continually challenged everywhere. We have examined how Gildas writes about both the strife and his gloomy view of his regional contemporaries with their lack of morals – probably encouraging his own move to Brittany (if Gildas of Rhuys is the same cleric).

So-called Late Antiquity was, it seems, a brief experience in the former Roman provinces, or was it? We know so little about Rheged and the royal house of Coel Hen, except that it endured. During Roman times, Luguvalium (Carlisle) was an important city visited by at least two Emperors, and coin finds dating right to the end of the fourth century have been discovered there. Certainly, the House of Rheged will have been Christian, the close proximity to the *Candida Casa* of St. Ninian surely indicating this, and perhaps Palladius passed through the city on his mission to convert the Picts. It is apparent from contemporary Empire-wide Christian writings that there was a profound belief that the second coming of Christ was imminent, and perhaps this explains the Christian intensity conveyed by the *Historia* in Arthur's battle list.

I realise history needs something more than just circumstantial evidence, no matter how robust the arguments may appear. But archaeology bounds along, even if it is somewhat influenced more by property developers than by identifying sites with potential to yield progressive finds. That said, a more sensitive and scientific approach to the fifth and sixth centuries is yielding information that was perhaps unidentified on digs before the 1980s. There is yet much to come from excavations near Garforth and in Carlisle that may tell us more about both Elmet and Rheged, and while it is accepted that towns and defences declined in the fifth century, a trip to Vindolanda, a Roman town near Hadrian's Wall, perhaps followed by a visit to Castlesteads, Housesteads or Chester's fort near Hexham will dispel any thought that the north was any kind of backwater in the times of Arthwys.

So, is Arthwys of the north the proto-Arthur? I certainly believe so, and whosoever compiled the *Historia Brittonum* also knew his origins. There can be no doubt about the remarkable detail of the northern locations or indeed that the source was a Brittonic battle-listing poem. It is even possible to reconstruct the rhymes from which it is clear that the Battle of Mount Badon was always part of the lost original and attributed to the hero rather than subsequently added as is so often suggested:

... Bassas | ... Dubglas | ... Cat Coit Celidon | ... Castell Guinnion | ... Cair Legion | ... Tribuit abon | ... Bregomion | ... mynydd Badon |

Folklore is not history, but it is, nonetheless, a wonderful means by which to engage the young with the past. I recently met some Polish visitors to the Borders who recounted a tale they were told as children about the fabled knights of King Boleslaw the Brave who are asleep wearing golden armour upon their steeds in a deep cave below the Tatras mountain range. Boleslaw was the first king of united Poland (1025) and placed them there ready to spring to life to protect the Polish nation. Apparently, a lost young blacksmith discovered them and replaced their horses' shoes. This is obviously a myth, but the similarity of this tale to some of the tales of King Arthur is readily apparent – genuine historical characters mythologised... So, I shall end this book with my hero of the twentieth century citing his hero of the fifth century.

> *And wherever men are fighting against barbarism, tyranny, and massacre, for freedom, law, and honour, let them remember that the fame of their deeds, even though they themselves be exterminated, may perhaps be celebrated as long as the world rolls round. Let us then declare that King Arthur and his noble knights, guarding the Sacred Flame of Christianity and the theme of a world order, sustained by valour, physical strength, and good horses and armour, slaughtered innumerable*

hosts of foul barbarians and set decent folk an example for all time.[32]

[32] Winston Churchill, on King Arthur, *A History of the English-Speaking Peoples, Volume I: The Birth of Britain* (Weidenfeld Nicolson, 1956).

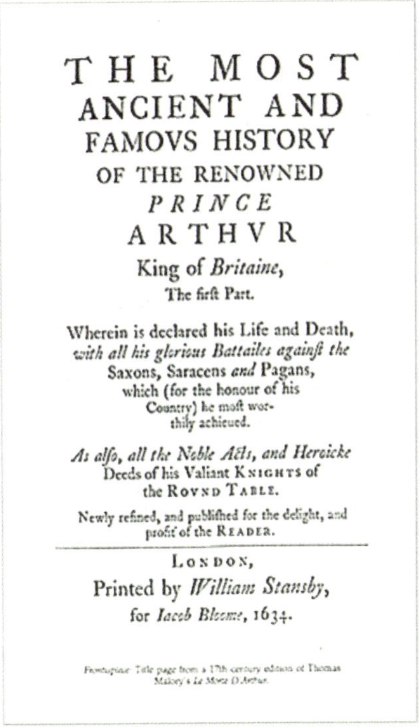

THE MOST
ANCIENT AND
FAMOVS HISTORY
OF THE RENOWNED
PRINCE
ARTHVR
King of *Britaine*,
The first Part.

Wherein is declared his Life and Death,
with all his glorious Battailes against the
Saxons, Saracens *and* Pagans,
which (for the honour of his
Country) he most wor-
thily achieued.

As also, all the Noble Acts, and Heroicke
Deeds of his Valiant KNIGHTS of
the ROVND TABLE.

Newly refined, and published for the delight, and
profit of the READER.

LONDON,
Printed by *William Stansby*,
for *Iacob Bloome*, 1634.

Title page from a seventeenth-century edition of Malory's Le Morte d'Arthur

The legends of King Arthur and his knights have stimulated poets, writers and artists for a thousand years, none more so than Sir Thomas Malory who is said to have written the first English version, 'the whole book of King Arthur and his noble knights of the Round Table', while in Newgate Prison. Malory is described in the Winchester manuscript, the only surviving manuscript copy of his work, as a 'knyght presoner' and he appears to have led a colourful life during the uncertain times of the Wars of the Roses. First published, and renamed *Le Morte d'Arthur*, by Caxton in 1485 there are only two original printed copies known to have survived. The Winchester manuscript was only discovered in 1934 and is thought to have been the copy worked on by Caxton.

The Death of King Arthur *by John Garrick, 1862 © Alamy*

One of four maps of Great Britain by the monk of St. Albans, Matthew Paris, showing the pilgrim route from Newcastle to Dover (and thence to Rome). A fascinating example of early cartography which was intended not just as a travel itinerary but also as a visual representation of the journey for monks to appreciate even if they never undertook the pilgrimage. It is thought Paris never completed the journey himself. The map includes Scotland and Wales which has led to speculation that it indicated England's claim to these countries at that time. It is also interesting to note the influence of Geoffrey of Monmouth to the notes on Wales. 'Karmerdin Civitas Merlini Vatis' means 'Carmarthen, the City of Merlin'. Both Hadrian's Wall and the Antonine Wall are clearly outlined but not intended to indicate a border with Scotland. The map gives a good idea of the medieval perception of the physical barrier presented by large rivers and estuaries and the itinerary itself follows a more central route where bridges or ferry crossings made the journey easier.

Matthew Paris Map of Britain, circa 1250. By permission of the British Library (Cotton MS Claudius D VI/1 f.12v) © Bridgeman Images

Genii Cucullati

The relief in the museum at Housesteads Fort, known as the Hooded Spirits or the Genii Cucullati, shows the need for substantial cloaks to brave the weather conditions of northern Britain.

Sesterce of Antoninus Pius showing a pensive Brigantia sitting on a rock
Image: The Portable Antiquities Scheme / British Museum © Derek Morton

Sesterce of Hadrian showing a saddened Brigantia, her head resting on her hand
Image: The Portable Antiquities Scheme / British Museum © Somerset County Council

Although the Roman historian Tacitus (56–120) claimed Britain was completely conquered following the defeat of the Caledonians at the Battle of Mons Graupius, there continued to be many rebellions. Following a period of serious warfare in Britain, the Emperor Hadrian (76–138) arrived in 122 accompanied by the sixth legion to replace IX Hispana, the fate of which remains a mystery. Combining with the other two legions in Britain, the second and the twentieth, they commenced the construction of Hadrian's Wall which was completed in about 128. Antoninus Pius, Hadrian's successor, authorised an advance into southern Scotland to the Forth–Clyde isthmus where the Antonine Wall was commenced in 142. Coins of both Hadrian and Antoninus symbolically show Brigantia, a goddess of victory associated with Britain, with her head bowed as if in defeat, but by 150 the Brigantes had again rebelled, causing the evacuation of the Antonine Wall so as to re-garrison Hadrian's Wall and the Pennine forts.

Hadrian's Wall
Hadrian's Wall, built from coast to coast to seal off the north and completed in 128, was Rome's great statement of power and control. It is a remote and often cold part of Britain.

Housesteads Fort
The north-west corner of Housesteads Fort with Sewingshields Crags beyond the trees. Arthur and his knights are said to sleep beneath the crags.

The Picts
The first Caledonian recorded in history was named Calgacus. He was chieftain of a confederacy that, according to Tacitus, fought with the Roman Agricola at the Battle of Mons Graupius in 84. Thereafter, there is not much evidence for the warriors that became known as the Picts until they harassed Britain in the fourth century. By the Dark Ages, they had evolved into a militarist tribe that has left an enigmatic record of their culture on carved stones across north-east Scotland. Some of their most famous memorials are the Aberlemno sculptured stones. The one pictured seems to record a

battle which occurred quite close by at Dun Nechtain in 685 and features both mounted warriors and infantry. The interpretation of Pictish symbols is much debated, but their meanings remain obscure.

Anglo-Saxon boats

Between 1859 and 1863 substantial remains of a clinker-built oak boat were found in a bog at Nydam in Denmark. Now known as the Nydam Boat, it has been dendro-dated to between 310 and 320 and is on display at Gottorf Castle in Schleswig. It is remarkable to think that boats such as this conveyed Anglo-Saxon raiders and settlers to Britain's shores. The boats were propelled by fifteen sets of oars, but it is not known if other boats used sails. Certainly, the Franks and Gauls used leather sails as described by Caesar.

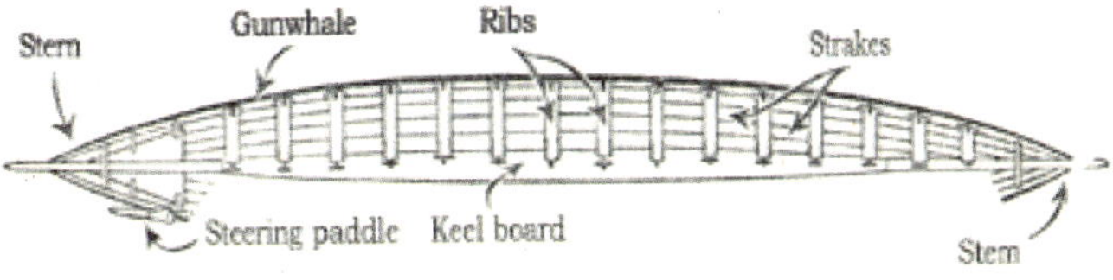

Looking down into the boat

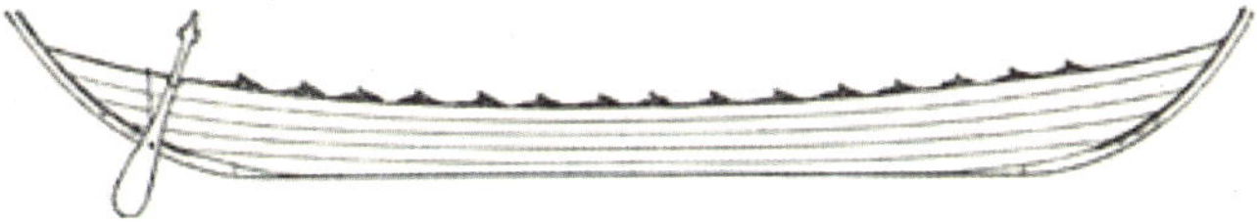

A clinker-built boat with a steering paddle and tholes (rests) for fifteen oars

The Notitia Dignitatum

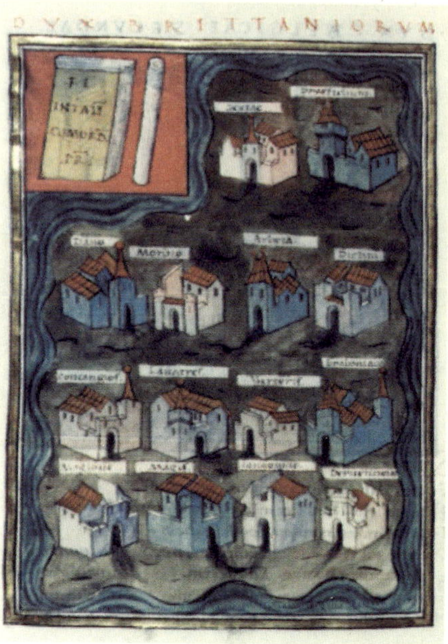

The Romans maintained a complete list of official posts, both civil and military, throughout the Empire. This list, entitled the *Notitia Dignitatum*, also gave the insignia of each of the high officers. None of the lists survive in original form and are copies made in the fifteenth and sixteenth centuries. A copy made for Otto Henry, Elector Palatine in 1542 is said to show illustrations faithful to the original. The *Notitia* is considered accurate for the Western Empire in the 420s (perhaps the 390s for Britain) and the Eastern Empire in the 390s and contains some data from as early as 379. However, there are problems with its interpretation, with Britain in particular. Some of the information has proved difficult to substantiate because of the sudden change in the course of events in 410. The insignia of the *Dux Britanniarum* outlines fourteen forts, and while some have been firmly identified others have not. This is surprising given the widespread interest in Roman history and Hadrian's Wall in particular.

A study known as *The Place-Names of Roman Britain* by Rivet and Smith is considered the bible for such matters, and reviews some of the information in the *Notitia*. The names of the forts along Hadrian's Wall have also recently been augmented by the Staffordshire Moorlands Pan, found in 2003, which bears an inscription listing the names of four forts at the western end of the Wall. Here is the list from the insignia of the *Dux Britanniarum* with some confirmed locations and some suggestions:

Fort	Rivet & Smith	Alternatives
Sextae		Location of VI Victrix Legion at York. Apparently still in situ in 390.
Praesidium		Close to the Latin word *praetorium*. Probably the army headquarters at York.
Dano	Doncaster (Danum)	
Morbio	Piercebridge, Durham or Greta Bridge	The prefect noted as responsible is Praefectus Equium Catafractariorum. Ammianus mentions *caterfractarii* which were heavily armed cavalry. The fort at Cataractonium is a similar name and is thought to refer to upstream rapids on the River Swale. Could Morbio be Catterick? Did this town acquire its name from this cavalry rather than its rapidly flowing river?
Arbeia	South Shields	
Dictim	Wearmouth	Rivet and Smith note this is based upon an assumed location as no such fort is known. Alternatives may be Hexham or Corbridge, towns which are surrounded by 'Di' place names such as Dipton Burn, Dipton Mill, Dipton Wood, Dilston Hall and Dilston Haugh.
Congangios	Chester le Street	
Lavatres	Bowes	
Verteris	Brough Castle	
Braboniaco	Kirby Thore	Casterton near Barbon is an interesting alternative.
Maglore	Old Carlisle	
Magis	Carvorum in Northumberland	
Longovicio	Lanchester in Durham	
Derventione	Malton	There is a fort on the River Derwent at Ebchester which is much closer to the Wall. It is known as Vindomora but could be a candidate. However, Malton was an important fort and most likely under the control of the *Dux*.

Place name etymology is notoriously unsafe ground for historians, but the clues it provides are often tantalising. For example, Uxelodunum, a fort on Hadrian's Wall attested by engravings on the recently discovered Staffordshire Moorlands Pan, is identified as Stanwix in Cumberland. The meaning of the name is perhaps 'high place' or 'noble place'. It is interesting to note that the large Brigantes *oppidum* on the eastern side of the Pennines at Aldborough St. John is also known as Stanwick Camp. The Brigantes retreated west over the Pennines in the direction of Carlisle and this may be something to consider in relation to the background of Coel Hen, the Romanised fourth-century warlord, who may have been appointed *Dux* by Magnus Maximus.

The insignia of the *Comes Britanniarum* from the *Notitia Dignitatum* refers to a military post held in Britain from the mid-fourth century onwards. This was the main field army. According to the *Notitia*, it consisted of six cavalry and three infantry units, probably a force of about 6,000 troops. It appears that this unit borrowed troops from both the Duke of Britain and the Count of the Saxon Shore as well as recruiting mercenaries. The office appears to have lapsed after 410, although cooperation later in the fifth century between Vortigern, Ambrosius and Arthwys may suggest the principal purpose of the Count of Britain – a mobile field force – was reintroduced in the face of intensified raiding and Saxon aggression.

Another section of the *Notitia Dignitatum* that refers to Britain is the *Comes Litoris Saxonici* (The Count of the Saxon Shore). This insignia shows the forts/ports under this Count's control. It is generally thought that it was the usurper Carausius (Emperor of the North 286–293) who planned and commenced the building work for the Saxon Shore forts. In 1924, Jessie Mothersole published her book *The Saxon Shore* which listed the nine forts as follows:

1. The Commander of the Fortensian band at Othona (Bradwell-juxta-Mare)
2. The Commander of the Tungrecanian foot soldiers at Dubrae (Dover)
3. The Commander of the Turnacensian band at Lemanae (Lympne)
4. The Commander of the Dalmatian horse at Branodunum (Brancaster)
5. The Commander of the Stablesian horse at Gariannonum (Burgh Castle)
6. The Tribune of the First Cohort of the Vetasii at Regulbium (Reculver)
7. The Commander of the Second Legion (Augusta) at Rutupiae (Richborough)
8. The Commander of the Abulcian band at Anderida (Pevensey)
9. The Commander of the band of Exploratores at Portus Adurni (Porchester

Jessie Mothersole was the first author to reproduce and publish a colour plate of the insignia of the Count of the Saxon Shore.

Walls of Isurium Brigantum (Aldborough, Yorkshire)

Pictured above is a section of the great walls of Isurium Brigantum (Aldborough, Yorkshire). This was the civitas capital of the Brigantes. The town was first given earthen defences but, by the middle of the third century, had been surrounded by massive walls 10 feet thick at the base. Isurium is one of the towns that had its fortifications reorganised, probably following the Barbarian Conspiracy in 367. Towers and bastions were added along with a new ditch 40 feet wide in front of these defences. A remarkable number of coins dated to the House of Valentian have been found in the town and vicinity. This rather suggests that a unit of the field army was quartered here, but a sharp decline in coinage from the House of Theodosius suggests the removal of this unit under Magnus Maximus.

The Multiangular tower, York

Late fourth century fortification forming part of the medieval walls of York, the lower layers are Roman.

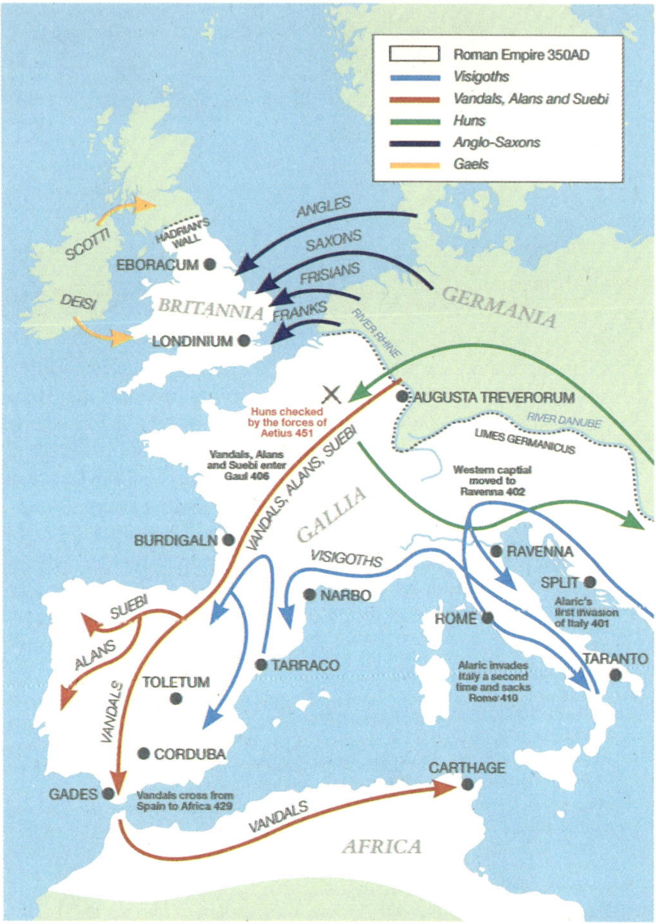

Barbarian invasions of the Western Empire in the late fourth and early fifth centuries

The eventual demise of the Western Roman Empire resulted from barbarian incursions and invasions that a weakened Roman army was unable to resist. It is often suggested that the rise of the Huns in the east pressured other Germanic tribes to move west and south and while this might be a significant factor, the power politics of the period are extremely complex and changed with each Emperor.

Coins of later Roman Britain

Roman coin of the Emperor Magnentius (350–353), a usurper whose bloody civil war with Constantius weakened Roman military might. His actions resulted in unparalleled retribution throughout the provinces of Britannia, Gaul and Hispania where his supporters suffered imperial confiscation and execution.

Image: The Portable Antiquities Scheme / British Museum

Gold solidus of Jovinus (411–413)

Siliqua of Sebastianus

Coins of the Belgic brothers Jovinus and Sebastianus who were usurpers between 411–413 following the demise of Constantine III. Their positions were dependent upon barbarian support from Burgundians, Alans and Goths. The Goths switched sides and assisted Honorius to defeat and execute both. Gildas mentions that the father of Ambrosius Aurelianus 'wore the purple', suggesting an emperor, and that his parents were slain in a 'notable storm'. Jovinus or Sebastianus may well be to whom Gildas was alluding, and it is interesting to note that the above rare coin featuring Jovinus was discovered in Kent in 2004.

Image: The Portable Antiquities Scheme/British Museum © Kent County Council

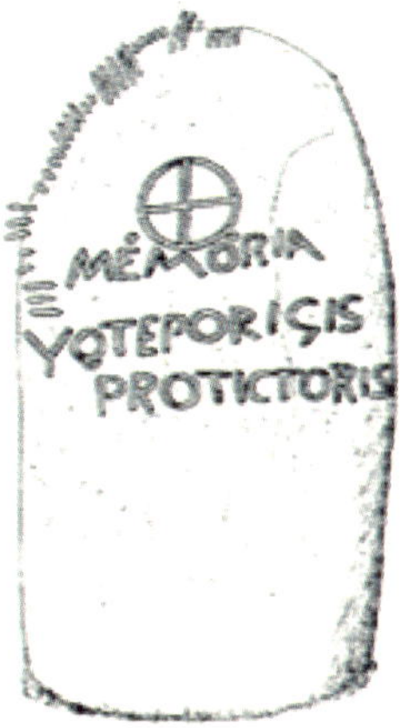

The Vortiporigis Stone

This memorial stone with inscriptions was first recognised by Miss Bowen Jones in 1895. Research by John Rhys determined that it had originally stood at Castell Dwyran, Dyfed, where it had been incorporated into the churchyard fence. It is now in the Carmarthenshire County Museum. It is one of 400 or so stones found throughout Ireland and western Britain that are inscribed with ogham, an ancient form of Irish writing. Most of these inscriptions are personal names. Outside of Ireland, the largest concentration of stones is in Pembrokeshire which is an area of Britain colonised by Irish settlers in Roman times. While evidence suggests ogham is ancient, all the stones identified relate to the fourth and fifth centuries. The location and age of the Vortiporigis Stone suggest a connection to the similarly named Vortiporius, or Vortipor, a king mentioned by Gildas in *De Excidio*. Using the beasts of the Christian Apocalypse to make allegorical condemnations of five British kings, he names Vortipor as 'the spotted leopard' and 'the tyrant of Demetia' (Dyfed). He declares him to be a bad son of a good father who had become grey with age. The memorial stone describes Vortiporigis as *Protictoris* (Protector). This suggests a Roman honorific title, and the genealogies suggest the great-grandfather of Vortipor was known as Triphun, which translates as 'tribune'. As well as this mention by Gildas, there is a similarly named person in the eighth-century work *The Expulsion of the Déisi*, a medieval Irish narrative that recounts a migration to Britain. Coel Hen, who features in medieval Welsh literature, is also named as Guotepac which means Protector. All considered, it seems likely that Vortipor's ancestors were given the task to defend the south-west Wales coast from raiders. Most probably an early Christian, Triphun may well have been appointed to this role by Magnus Maximus prior to the withdrawal of the Roman legions from Wales. I am not a linguist and cannot really comment about the different spellings of names for Vortipor. However, even in these literate times, my mail is sometimes addressed to Alasdair or Alister when my name is Alistair. It does not stop me opening the post and I can only hope my memorial stone will be spelled correctly.

Place names associated with the Belgae

There is a moderate concentration of 'Amb' place names throughout the West Sussex, Hampshire and Wiltshire regions. The farm name pictured is between Andover and Hungerford. Amberley village, to the north of Arundel, is close to Bignor Roman Villa, perhaps suggesting a connection with the family of Ambrosius Aurelianus. The entire region is associated with the pre-Roman settlers known as the Belgae whose chief tribe was the Ambiani. Their coins are found throughout the south and feature a horse as their motif.

Gold slater of the Ambiani
This gold slater of the Ambiani is dated to circa 50 BC and was discovered near Maidstone, Kent in August 2019. The Ambiani, who perhaps gave their name to Amiens in France and Amesbury in Wiltshire, were later Romanised. Their tribal centre in the south of England became Winchester which was known as Venta Belgarum, 'market of the Belgae'.
Image: The Portable Antiquities Scheme/British Museum © Kent County Council

The Ravenna Annals contain brief notes on events in the Western Empire from the fourth to the sixth centuries. They tell us that, on 8 August 412, the severed heads of Jovinus and Sebastianus were sent to Ravenna for display and that their brother Sallustius was killed. The cathedral library of Merseberg holds an eleventh-century parchment which contains this gruesome drawing from the sixth century illustrating events of the fifth century.

Hoard of silver siliquae
A hoard of clipped silver siliquae dated to 408 or later with coins of the Emperors Julian 360–363, Valens 364–367, Gratian 367–375, Valentian II 375–383, Magnus Maximus 383–388, Theodosius I 389–394, Arcadius 392–395, Eugenius 392–394, Honorius 395–402, House of Theodosius 388–408 and Constantine III 407–408. Discovered near Stokesley, North Yorkshire in 2012. This find demonstrates the scarcity of coinage in the early fifth century. Clipped siliquae are debased silver coins that fulfilled the role of currency in Late Antiquity Britain. It is fascinating that the hoarder collected coins spanning forty years which indicates not only the absence of trade but also a lack of means to pay for defence.
Image: The Portable Antiquities Scheme/British Museum © Durham County Council

Roman lead pig, or ingot, found on Hayshaw Moor
Pictured above is a Roman lead pig, or ingot, found on Hayshaw Moor south of Pateley Bridge, North Yorkshire in 1731. Nidderdale and Swaledale were mined for lead by the Romans as early as the first century. The pig is inscribed *Imperator Caesare Augusto Consule Septimum* referring to Emperor Domitian's Seventh Consulate and therefore dating it to 81. The word *BRIG* is inscribed on one side of the pig, presumably identifying its origin from a Brigantian mine. Whether this points to a partnership with the tribe is hard to say but it hints at some form of cooperation.
Reproduced by kind permission of Bonhams 1793 Ltd.

A.

B.

C.

D.

A–C: The ramparts around Stanwick
D: The church tower seen in the distance is the centre of the fort.

Stanwick Camp at Stanwick St. John

Stanwick Camp at Stanwick St. John in Richmondshire, North Yorkshire is an enormous Iron Age hillfort. There are nearly six miles of ditches and ramparts enclosing about 700 acres of land. It was, without doubt, an important Brigantes settlement – so large that it was presumably intended as a statement of power. Sited between Scotch Corner (on the A1) and the River Tees, it may have been the *oppidum* of the rebellious northern Brigantian leader Venutius. An earthwork known as Scots Dyke runs from the Swale to the Tees denoting a boundary and suggesting a 'no-go zone', but Gnaeus Julius Agricola pushed across Stainmore Pass in 80, and it is thought that the rebelling Brigantes eventually retreated across the Pennines. In 1845, a hoard of metal artefacts was discovered at Stanwick, including four sets of harnesses for chariots and a bronze horse head buckle. Sir Mortimer Wheeler excavated the site in 1951 and 1952. He held the opinion that the first enclosure was started in 40 and finally extended in 72. This rather fits the career of the rebel Venutius who was a thorn in the side of the Romans between 51 and 80. It is worth noting the outcome of the Durham University digs from 1981 to 1986 which concluded Stanwick was more likely Cartimandua's estate. This seems to rely on the opinion that the fort would be difficult to defend. While this may be one view, it is generally held that the southern Brigantes cooperated with the Romans, and from the mid-first century, stone structures begin to appear at Isurium. Perhaps Cartimandua and her new consort Vellocatus were already ensconced in their villa and benefitting from treaty arrangements which may have included lead mining. The fort is so vast it is difficult to photograph, and my attempts to gain access to St. John's Church tower failed. Relatively untouched, I am sure this site has more secrets to yield as witnessed by the recently discovered Melsonby hoard.

Artist: G. T. Lowe

Elmet

Edmund Bogg was an enthusiastic Leeds antiquarian who, in 1902, published the *Old Kingdom of Elmet*. He drew maps of the hillfort at Barwick-in-Elmet and the surrounding area long before there were any modern developments. He also commissioned a drawing of the earthworks from the west. Bogg was a self-taught historian who was acutely aware that the environs of Elmet must have played a pivotal role in the early history of the region. The proximity of York and the criss-crossing Roman roads lent ample evidence for the patchwork of history he attempted to interpret through the local landscape. Without attributing the site to Cartimandua, he labels her a 'false Queen, of Cleopatra type' who was spurred on 'by sordid selfish ambition'. His interpretations, though colourful, are reasonable conjecture given his intended readership. In respect of Arthur, he recounts that the 'Scotch Chronicles say that in 521 King Arthur kept Christmas at York surrounded by his courtiers and famed knights of the round table. No other city in Great Britain can dwell on such historic scenes of the past as the ancient city of York'. This is not so much a claim for Arthur, more one for York.

Antiquaries and local historians provide a rich tapestry of folklore woven into the landscape. In Yorkshire alone, we are fortunate to have many such published authors, for example, T. D. Whitaker (1873), Harry Speight (1897), Edmund Bogg (1902), Ella Pontefract with Marie Hartley (1939) and many more. Each of these authors sought, in their own style, to record the folklore, local history and buildings within their landscape and interpret their contribution to Britain's national history. Often more sensitive to impinging industrial development, these authors witnessed the disappearing medieval landscape and recorded many archaeological finds and oddities that would otherwise have been lost. I can only imagine how thrilled Edmund Bogg might have been to learn that Cartimandua was likely evacuated by the Romans from Barwick and that the northern Prince Arthwys may have looked out from the battlements of Wendel Hill.

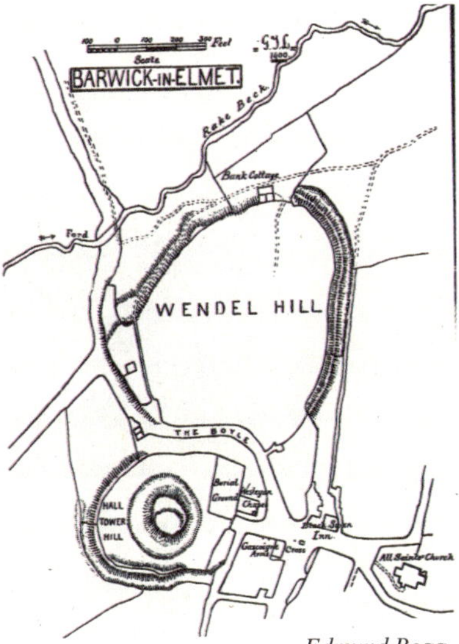

Edmund Bogg

All Saints Church, Ledsham

All Saints Church, Ledsham dates from 700, according to the church pamphlet. Pictured above is the famous south-facing tower doorway. Nikolaus Pevsner, in his series *The Buildings of England*, noted that the doorway was restored in 1871, but he thought it likely that it represented genuine evidence. The church may have been the building referred to by Bede in 731. He tells of a stone altar from an earlier wooden church. It is, nonetheless, the oldest building still in use in the West Riding of Yorkshire

The city of Lincoln
The city of Lincoln sitting upon its defensive hill with commanding views in every direction.

St. Paul in the Bail, Lincoln
Artist's impression of St. Paul in the Bail, Lincoln. An early Christian church built in the forum of Roman Lincoln and dating back to the early fifth century.

Artist David Vale

Swinefleet Ordnance Survey, 1824

A photograph of a section of the first Ordnance Survey map of Hull surveyed in 1824 showing Swinefleet, Whitgift and Goole Moor. Blackwater Dyke and Black Drain in the centre of the map may indicate the original location of the River Dubglass.

The Ouse near Swinefleet

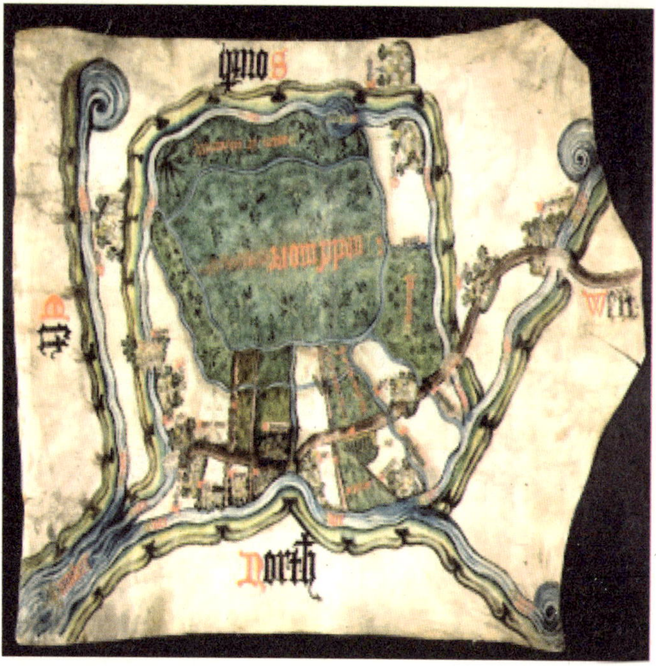

The Inclesmoor Map, circa 1450

The Inclesmoor Map is the National Archives' oldest map. It was drawn in circa 1407 to help resolve a dispute about pasture rights between the Duchy of Lancaster and St. Mary's Abbey, York. It is orientated to the south. The area covered by the map includes Thorne Waste and Hatfield Moor and the region is bounded by the rivers Aire, Ouse, Humber, Trent, Don (Tourne) and old Don (Doen). These lands are quite possibly those granted to Hengist and Horsa by Vortigern and are referred to in the *Historia Brittonum* as their *tenat*. Swinefleet (Ypwinesfleot), mentioned as their landing place in the *Anglo-Saxon Chronicle*, is just beyond the confluence of the Aire and Ouse. Four of Arthur's battles were fought by a river Dubglass, and there are several candidates in this region. Dubglass is usually translated as 'black water', and while the Inclesmoor Map doesn't mention this name, all around this region are water courses named similarly descriptively, such as Blackwater Dyke and Black Drain. An earlier spelling for the area, Inkle Moor, is derived from the inky appearance of the water running across these vast peat moors. Drainage, agricultural development and peat cutting have been constant from early medieval times, taming the rivers and landscape, but the map gives an inkling of what a wild marshy region this must have been in the Dark Ages.

Late Roman military buckles

From the mid-third century the Romans employed ever-increasing numbers of mercenary troops. Following the Barbarian Conspiracy in 367, mercenaries accompanied Theodosius the Elder to Britain to crush the rebellion. In circa 380, Magnus Maximus recruited British and perhaps some Angle tribes to defend the country. Stilicho is thought to have arrived in Britain with mercenaries between 398 and 400 and from 415 to 425; elements of the British ruling classes employed *foederati* (mercenaries) to defend their towns and property from the Irish, Scotti and Pictish raiders – culminating in the *Adventus Saxonum* described by Gildas. One archaeological trace left by these armies and bands is military buckles. These buckles originated on the Continent but in time were copied and made in Britain. A study of Dark Age buckles may one day cast some light on the deployment and positioning of troops during this chaotic period. I do recommend an extremely detailed study by Stuart Laycock and Chris Marshall called 'Late Roman Buckles in Britain' which discusses and lists nine different categories of buckles. The buckles below are three of the more interesting styles recently discovered.

This buckle is of a category originally thought to be linked to Germanic *foederati*. However, while dolphins face each other in the Roman style, the head motif is described as 'enticingly Celtic' suggesting a militia of Roman Britain. The buckle was found in 2013 close by Owston Ferry on the west bank of the Trent. This is in the area where I suggest the battle between Vortigern and the Saxons occurred, known as Rither Gabail or Agelsford.
Image © North Lincolnshire Museum

The horse head buckle alongside was found near Walesby, Market Rasen in Lincolnshire.

A similar buckle was found near Arlesford, Winchester in June 2015. It is thought there may be some political significance to the buckles – the dolphins representing Rome with the horse heads representing another layer of government or political faction. Laycock and Marshall list the areas where there would seem to be concentrations of horse head buckles

– Water Newton, Peterborough, Cirencester, north of Wansdyke and in Wiltshire. They have even been found in Yorkshire. Pure conjecture on my part, but I can't help thinking that these are areas where the armies of the Britons were active. Water Newton in particular was on the border of Saxon territory and probably where the Britons retreated after the battle of Crecganford (Stamford). Two similar buckles have been found in Spain suggesting a link to the militia of Gerontius, the British general of Constantine III who was active in Spain from 408 to 411. It would be extraordinarily interesting if horse head buckles were ever found in the region of Bourge or Déols in France and might help confirm where the army of Riothamus originated.

The Elloe Stone near Whaplode

Pictured right is an easily missed monument placed by a roadside not far from the village of Whaplode, East Anglia. It is known as the Elloe Stone. The inscription on its modern base reads 'The Elloe Stone erected in Anglo-Saxon times to indicate the place of meeting of the Elloe Courts. Presented to Moulton Parish Council by F Dring Esq. and mounted here by public inscription of June 22nd 1911 the day of the coronation of King

George'. Apart from some Saxon fragments in the parish church at Whaplode, there are no other significant Saxon or Roman stones or monuments in the entire region. The Fens are dominated by Norman architecture, the building materials for which were brought from quarries further inland. In Roman times, the sea came much closer to this area. The *Historia Brittonum* records a battle between the Saxons and the Briton Vortimer 'on the plain of the inscribed stone by the shore of the Gaulish sea'. Might the Elloe Stone be this monument? The *Anglo-Saxon Chronicle* calls this battle '*Wippedsfleot*' after a thane called 'Wipped'. Is Whaplode and Fleet a derivation of this name and area? It was a victory for the Britons. Arthur's battle at the mouth of the River Glein, also a victory, may have occurred in this immediate region – the mouth of the River Glen being less than five miles from the Elloe Stone. Do these records all report the same battle and was it unknowingly mentioned twice in the *Historia Brittonum* because the information came from different sources?

The mouth of the River Glen
This peaceful creek is just upstream from the mouth of the River Glen. The river joins the Witham here before reaching the sea, but in the fifth century, the Glen emptied directly into the Wash near this location.

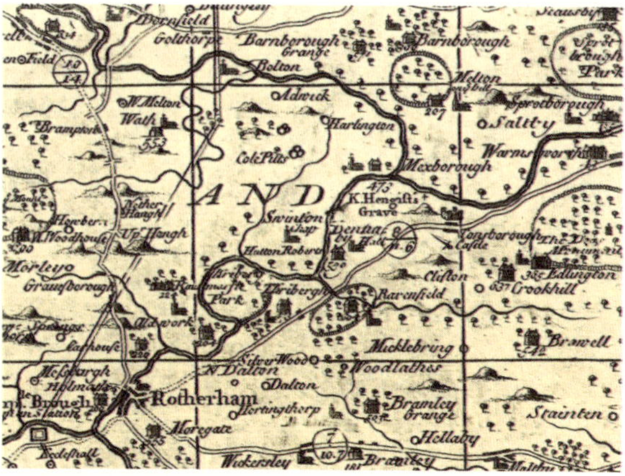

John Warburton's map of 1720 which records 'K Hengist's Grave' by Conisbrough Castle

Looking east from the battlements of Conisbrough Castle over 'Celyddon' with Doncaster in the distance.

The impressive Norman keep of Conisbrough Castle

Arthur depicted at his eighth battle at Castellum Guinnion
A painting by the late Richard Hook taken from the book *Warriors of Arthur* by John Mathews and R. J. Stewart first published in 1987. Arthur is depicted carrying a shield bearing the image of the Virgin Mary. This battle scene pictures Arthur's eighth battle at Castellum Guinnion where there was 'great slaughter'. The uniforms and equipment are perhaps tending towards early medieval rather than those of the British militia, but the artist captures the brutality and chaos of such a battle. Image © Estate of Richard Hook

The Vale of the Trent from Beacon Hill
The view north from Beacon Hill, Charnwood Forest across Trent Vale. In the distance, Ratcliffe-on-Soar Power Station stands out like a sore thumb helpfully way-marking the area where the River Soar joins the mighty Trent which is my conjectured location for Arthur's battle called Tribuit.

Bardon Hill and Charnwood Forest

The above photograph was taken north-west of Bardon Hill at Breedon on the Hill. The top of Bardon Hill is on the right-hand side of the picture. The area known as Battle Flat is on the south-western side and is now heavily industrialised. It is easy to see why Mount Badon was such a commanding position.

Breedon on the Hill

The church of St. Mary and St. Hardulph sitting atop Breedon on the Hill. This photograph was taken from close by Ambro Hill. A history guide written by Brian Williams tells of the monastery that preceded the church which was founded in 675 from lands gifted by Friduricus with Hedda as first abbot. Prior to this, the hill was an Iron Age fort known locally as the Bulwarks. It is an impressive site that dominates this section of Trent Vale. The *Anglo-Saxon Chronicle* refers to the hill as *Briudun.*

Sculptures at Breedon

The church has many 'Saxon' sculptures, the so-called Byzantine Blessing and the Breedon Angel being the most famous. The inhabited vine scroll panels appear to be remnants of a larger frieze and have a distinctly Celtic feel. The mounted warriors are particularly interesting and may have been intended to commemorate battles.

Bardon Hill

An engraving of the view west from Bardon Hill, 1837

Battle Flat to the south-west of Bardon Hill

A legion of solar panels now occupies the area known as Battle Flat to the south-west of Bardon Hill.

The Lake District from Camboglanna
Looking towards the Lake District from Camboglanna near Hadrian's Wall on a bleak January day. It seems likely that this region was central to the activities of Coel Hen and his successors. Carlisle, in particular, has become associated with the Carvetti tribe who may have been a royal branch of the Brigantes, the northern confederation that resisted the Roman advance north. The *Annales Cambriae* record Arthur's death in battle at a place called Camlann and this may have occurred in this vicinity.

Edin's Hall Broch
The best preserved of a clutch of brochs built and occupied during the 2nd-century AD in the lowlands of Scotland. Their presence in this location at this date is a mystery – most of Scotland's brochs were built 500 years earlier in the far north of the country. The close proximity to Newsteads fort near Melrose has led to speculation that a northern tribe may have cooperated with the Romans. Were these lowland brochs the homesteads of the Attacotti who famously rebelled in 367?

St. Pabo's Church, Llanbabo, Anglesey

The above church was founded before the twelfth century but there is little evidence other than its round churchyard and dedication to a sixth-century prince, St. Pabo, who according to the genealogy known as the *Bonedd Ewr Y Gogledd*, was a son of Arthwys and brother to Eliffer, Ceidyn and Cynfelyn. There is no evidence for the church's connection to Pabo except a stone slab showing his image holding a sceptre with an incomplete inscription stating, 'Here lies Pabo pillar of Britain'. 'Llanbabo' translates as the 'enclosure' ('llan') of Pabo ('babo'), but the stone slab is dated to the late fourteenth century. Tradition holds Pabo was driven out of the north and died on Anglesey. When Debbie and I cycled to the church, it was locked so we were unable to see the inscription. The churchyard grass needed cutting, but it was possible to make out the raised circular 'llan' which suggests an early Christian site. This place's connection to Pabo is intriguing and at least suggests early contact between descendants of Coel Hen and the Welsh Kingdom of Gwynedd.

Gwen Ystrat– The White Valley of the River Swale near Richmond

According to medieval Welsh poetry there were two battles near th end of the fifth century that both occurred in the region of North Yorkshire. They are recounted in two poems, *Y Gododdin*, ascribed to Aneirin, and *Gweith Gwen Ystrat*, ascribed to Taliesin. Both poems mention Catraeth, an area of Rheged under the control of a leader named Urien who was part of the Coeling dynasty. *Y Gododdin* is the more famous of the two, and a passing reference to Arthur is often quoted. Modern historians have preferred to consider the battles as separate, Urien fighting northern raiders and the Gododdin fighting the nascent Anglian kingdom of Deira. However, the location, the style of engagement, the names and references, and the seemingly low number of warriors involved all suggest British and Pictish warriors in a regional confrontation. The victors in both poems are the men of Catraeth. Both poems mention fords, ramparts and dynastic friction. The text of *Y Gododdin* seems to have benefitted from bardic improvements, and elegies for early warriors have perhaps been added when they may not have been at the battle. Surely the River Swale is the shingle of Cranwynion described by Taliesin and the river that Ywain, Aneirin's friend, fell into after being killed by a spear?

Scots Dyke, Richmond, North Yorkshire

Scots Dyke runs from the River Swale at Richmond to the River Tees. North of the town, this Iron Age fortification becomes patchy and indistinct, whereas by Richmond itself, it seems to have been refortified. Is this the rampart upon which Gwawrddur 'glutted ravens' in the poem *Y Gododdin* or the low rampart upon which Urien's dejected, tired men witnessed 'the throng of three regions dead' as described in the poem *Gweith Gwen Ystrat*?

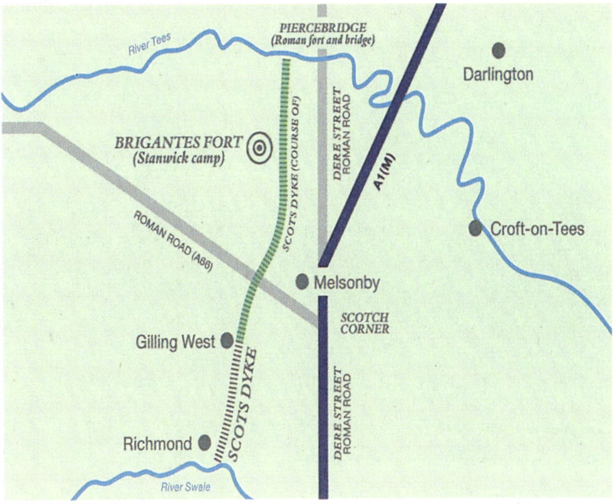

Map of Scots Dyke

The Rock of Dumbarton
Known as the Brittonic kingdom of Alt Clut in the Dark Ages.

The Hillfort of Traprain Law

A Dark Age hillfort to the south of Edinburgh associated with King Lott in legend.

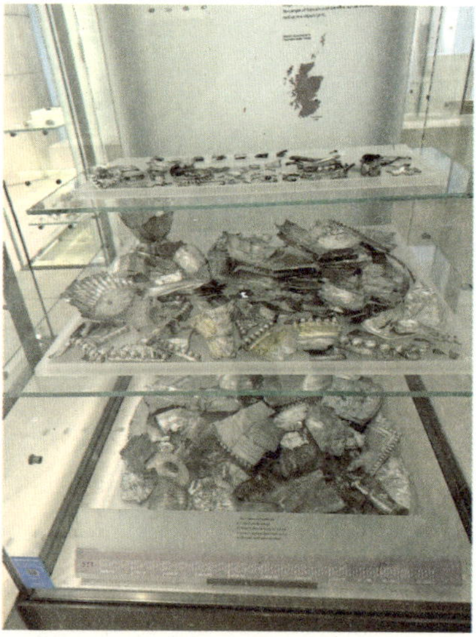

The Traprain Law treasure

A hoard of late Roman hack silver discovered at Traprain Law in 1919 and now on display in the National Museum of Scotland. Modern archaeologists consider the bulk of treasure to be an accumulation of diplomatic gifts.

Important further reading

History

Roman Britain
Peter Salway
A dogged, detailed and accurate history of Roman Britain through to the late fourth century.

Britannia: A History of Roman Britain
Sheppard Frere
A history of Roman Britain. This work is the quintessential balance between history and archaeology. A bit out of date now but easy to read.

Roman Britain and the English Settlements
R. G. Collingwood and J. N. L. Myers
This is a 'must read' for students of the period if only to highlight how much progress there has been with the interpretation of history as a result of advances in archaeology and subsequent discoveries. There is a review on the sleeve by Christopher Dawson of *The Tablet*, a Catholic journal that has endured from 1840 to this day. He says of the book: 'Now at last we have adequate treatment of Roman Britain and of the Dark Age that submerged it, written by specialists who are no less competent in the field of archaeology than in the use of literary sources. The result is that for the first time we have a history of Britain based on sound foundations, a history which paradoxically throws new light on the past by showing us how little we know about it.' This statement is still an accurate reflection of our knowledge of this period.

Pro-Arthur

The Age of Arthur: A History of the British Isles from 350 to 650

John Morris

I read this book cover to cover in the 1990s. Published in 1973, Morris postulates King Arthur as a historical figure towards the end of the fifth century. The book is often portrayed as fantasy, which is wrong. It is an enormous compendium of all the information John Morris assembled in his lifetime about the period, which is a great deal – be that fact, fable, legend or hearsay, rather like the *Historia Brittonum* itself. Morris wrote in a style that is over-positive, but it is easy to set this aside and simply enjoy the detail. However, his academic peers considered his book too misleading. The late David Dumville wrote that Arthur 'owes his place in our history books' to a 'no smoke without fire' school of thought, then added, in an apparent reference to Morris, 'there is no historical evidence about Arthur, we must reject him from our histories and, above all, from titles to our books'. This was particularly damning because Dumville had attained his doctorate in philosophy through a comprehensive thesis on the *Historia Brittonum* and was considered the expert on the primary version which includes the earliest written source for the battles of Arthur. Morris' book was also criticised by two other leading academic contemporaries, namely J. E. Caerwyn Williams and David P. Kirby. I was fortunate to meet David Kirby in 2019 to discuss my first book, and he recalled his article in *Studia Celtica* and how he had worried about criticising a fellow academic. It was, he explained, a matter of academic probity that such published works should not stray into fantasy. This rigid academic approach rather extinguished the embers of a 'real' Arthur, and for almost forty years, historians tiptoed around the subject, sometimes simply explaining the difficulty of pinning down legendary figures to time and space. However, this did not discourage populist authors such as the late Geoffrey Ashe. This former resident of Glastonbury wrote some thirty-five books that mention the legends, ten of which have King Arthur in the title.

The Reign of Arthur: From History to Legend

Christopher Gidlow

An honest and fair-minded attempt to interpret legend and history so as to release Arthur from his detractors' snares.

A Brief History of King Arthur: The Man and the Legend Revealed

Mike Ashley

This is written by a professional writer and it shows. No hang-ups, crammed with detail and some clever thinking and conclusions.

On the fence

Worlds of Arthur: Facts and Fictions of the Dark Ages

Guy Halsall

Interesting and insightful with innovative analysis.

In Search of the Dark Ages

Michael Wood

A popular historian with exceptional communication skills.

King Arthur: Myth-Making and History
N. J. Higham
Professor Higham is highly knowledgeable; his interpretation of the myths must be of huge interest to medieval literature and early Christian studies.

Essential reference

The Earliest English Kings
D. P. Kirby
A highly specialised work on Anglo-Saxon history which provides clarity to the evolution of the heptarchy and the nature and extent of the overlordship exercised by powerful but early kings. Professor Kirby lived in the next village to me, and I am grateful for his guidance, particularly in respect of the caution that should be exercised with the early tradition recounted by Bede.
The Place-Names of Roman Britain
A. L. F. Rivet and Colin Smith
An incomparable study published in 1979 which is still providing insight for historians and authors.
The Towns of Roman Britain
John Wacher
Another magnificent compendium published in the late seventies. Rather out of date but a good baseline.
Late Roman Warlords
Penny MacGeorge
This is an amazing study of mighty Roman generals pursuing their own agenda in a crumbling Roman Empire. Aetius, Marcellinus, Aegidius and Syagrius demonstrate ruthless purpose and in many respects mirror and provide insight to Magnus Maximus, Vortigern, Ambrosius and Riothamus. This is one of my favourite books.

The Age of the Saints in the Early Celtic Church
Nora K. Chadwick
I am fortunate indeed to own a copy of this book. Nora Chadwick, who died in 1972, spent her life in research, primarily on the Celts. The work is a summary of lectures given at the University of Durham in March 1960. The style is easy and displays no academic stiffness; it reads as if it was written recently and brims with a knowledge of its subject.
An Age of Tyrants: Britain and the Britons A.D. 400–600
Christopher A. Snyder
This is a more important work than perhaps it is given credit for. Professor Snyder demonstrates a remarkable understanding of the factions and polities of sub-Roman Britain immediately prior to and during the emergence of early kingship. Roman influence waned much more quickly in Britain compared to the Continent and this book tracks this shift, providing a convincing regional analysis.
The Celtic Heroic Age:
Literary Sources for Ancient Celtic Europe and Early Ireland and Wales
edited by John T. Koch and John Carey
This is a compendium of the literary sources for ancient Celtic Europe, Britain and Ireland. John Koch has occasionally found himself at odds with conventional Anglo-Saxon history and literature. I am a supporter of his views on the dating of *Y Gododdin* and believe his work requires greater attention.

Britain Begins
Barry Cunliffe
A modern, informative guide to the pre-history of Britain right up to the Vikings. Sir Barry is our greatest living archaeologist, and this book brilliantly assembles a mass of the latest evidence for each topic it covers. It should be on the shelf of every student of early British history.
The Fall of the Roman Empire: A Reappraisal
Michael Grant
This has been my easy-to-read reach-for reference on matters pertaining to the wider Roman Empire. The book is crammed with interesting illustrations.

Broader sociological Dark Age subjects

Britain After Rome: The Fall and Rise 400 to 1070
Robin Fleming
A beautifully written treatise on the broader consequences of the events endured by Late Antiquity Britain. This book displays a Frere-esque balance of history and archaeology.
In the Land of Giants: Journeys Through the Dark Ages
Max Adams
This is a highly enjoyable book about significant locations stitched into the likely journeys Dark Age travellers undertook. Adams absolutely nails the difficulties and restrictions of travel at a time when danger lurked everywhere. Insight, knowledge and reflection spill out during each journey.

The Sea Kingdoms: The History of Celtic Britain and Ireland

Alistair Moffat

This is another highly enjoyable book that builds on a vast knowledge of the history, myths and folklore in respect of the western seaboard of Britain and Ireland. Anyone wishing to understand Celtic and Romano-British communication must recognise the significance of these networks particularly with respect to trade, cultural exchange, Christianity, raiding and even slavery.

Bibliography

This bibliography contains works cited as well as texts consulted for my research and to feed my general curiosity in respect of King Arthur. The books recommended for 'Important further reading' are also listed below.

Abdy, Richard Anthony. *Romano-British Coin Hoards*. Princes Risborough: Shire Archaeology, 2002.

Adams, Max. *In the Land of Giants: Journeys Through the Dark Ages*. London: Head of Zeus, 2016.

Alcock, Leslie. *Arthur's Britain: History and Archaeology AD 367–634.* Harmondsworth: Penguin, 1973.

Ashe, Geoffrey. *The Discovery of King Arthur.* London: Book Club Associates/Webb and Bower (Publishers) Ltd, 1985.

Ashley, Mike. *A Brief History of King Arthur: The Man and the Legend Revealed.* London: Robinson, 2010.

Barber, Richard. *King Arthur: Hero and Legend.* Woodbridge: Boydell Press, 1986.

Barker, Phil. *The Armies and Enemies of Imperial Rome*. 4th ed. Goring-by-Sea: Wargames Research Group, 1981.

Bede. *The Ecclesiastical History of the English People.* Edited by Judith McClure and Roger Collins. Translated by Bertram Colgrave. Oxford: Oxford World's Classics, 2008.

Blair, Peter Hunter. *An introduction to Anglo-Saxon England.* Cambridge: Cambridge University Press, 1977.

Bogg, Edmund. *The Old Kingdom of Elmet: The Land 'Twixt Aire and Wharf.* York: John Sampson, 1904.

Burke, John. *Roman England.* London: Book Club Associates/Weidenfeld and Nicolson, 1983.

Castleden, Rodney. *King Arthur: The Truth Behind the Legend.* London: Routledge, 2000.

Chadwick, N. K. *The Age of the Saints in the Early Celtic Church.* London: Oxford University Press, 1961.

Chambers, E. K. *Arthur of Britain: The Story of King Arthur in History and Legend.* London: Sidgwick and Jackson, 1966.

Collingwood, R. G., and J. N. L. Myres. *Roman Britain and the English Settlements*. 2nd ed. Oxford: Clarendon Press, 1937.

Cunliffe, Barry. *Britain Begins*. Oxford: Oxford University Press, 2013.

Dare, M. Paul. *Charnwood Forest and its Environs*. Leicester: Edgar Backus, 1925.

Dark, Ken. *Britain and the End of the Roman Empire*. Stroud: Tempus Publishing, 2000.

Doel, Fran, Geoff Doel and Terry Lloyd. *Worlds of Arthur: King Arthur in History, Legend and Culture*. Stroud: Tempus Publishing, 1998.

Dumville, David N. 'The Textual History of the Welsh-Latin Historia Brittonum'. PhD diss. University of Edinburgh: Edinburgh Research Archive, 1975. https://era.ed.ac.uk/handle/1842/8972.

'Sub-Roman Britain: History and Legend', *Nottingham Medieval Studies*, 62, (1977), 187–88.

Dunning, R. W. *Arthur: The King in the West*. Stroud: Alan Sutton Publishing, 1988.

Faulkner, Neil. *The Decline and Fall of Roman Britain*. Stroud: Tempus Publishing, 2000.

Fife, Graeme. *Arthur the King: The Themes Behind the Legends*. London: BBC Books, 1990.

Fleming, Robin. *Britain after Rome: The Fall and Rise 400 to 1070*. London: Penguin, 2011.

Frere, Sheppard. *Britannia: A History of Roman Britain*. London: Book Club Associates / Routledge and Kegan Paul Limited, 1973.

Geoffrey, of Monmouth. *The History of the Kings of Britain*. Translated by Lewis Thorpe. London: The Folio Society, 1969.

Gibbon, Edward. *The Decline and Fall of the Roman Empire*. Abridged by D. M. Lowe. London: Book Club Associates / Chatto and Windus Ltd, 1972.

Gidlow, Christopher. *The Reign of Arthur: From History to Legend*. Stroud: Sutton Publishing, 2004.

Goodrich, Norma Lorre. *King Arthur*. New York: Franklin Watts Inc, 1986.

Grant, Michael. *The Fall of the Roman Empire: A Reappraisal*. Radnor: The Annenberg School of Communications, 1976.

Green, Caitlin R. 'The British Kingdom of Lindsey', Cambrian Medieval Celtic Studies, 56 (2008), 1–43. https://www.academia. edu/27372761/ The British Kingdom of Lindsey.

Halsall, Guy. *Worlds of Arthur: Facts and Fictions of the Dark Ages*. Oxford: Oxford University Press, 2013.

Higham, N. J. *King Arthur: Myth-Making and History*. London: Routledge, 2002.

Hoskins, W. G. *The Making of the English Landscape*. London: Guild Publishing, 1988.

Jackson, Kenneth. *The Gododdin: The Oldest Scottish Poem*. Edinburgh: Edinburgh University Press, 1969.

Johnson, Stephen. *Later Roman Britain*. London: Book Club Associates / Routledge and Kegan Paul Ltd, 1980.

Keegan, Simon. *Pennine Dragon: The Real King Arthur of the North*. New Haven Publishing, 2016.

Kelly, Christopher. *Attila the Hun: Barbarian Terror and the Fall of the Roman Empire*. London: Bodley Head, 2008.

Kirby, D. P. *The Earliest English Kings*. London: Routledge, 1994.

Koch, John T. and John Carey, eds. *The Celtic Heroic Age: Literary Sources for Ancient Celtic Europe and Early Ireland and Wales*. 3rd ed.

Oakville and Aberystwyth: Celtic Studies Publications, 2000.

Leahy, Kevin and Catherine M. Coutts. *The Lost Kingdom: The Search for Anglo-Saxon Lindsey*. Scunthorpe Borough Museum, 1987.

Lindsay, Jack. *Arthur and His Times*. London: Frederick Muller, 1958.

MacGeorge, Penny. *Late Roman Warlords*. Oxford: Oxford University Press / Oxford Classical Monographs, 2007.

Matthews, John and Bob Stewart. *Warriors of Arthur*. London: Blandford, 1993.

Mee, Arthur ed. *The King's England: Yorkshire West Riding*. London: The Caxton Publishing Company Ltd, 1945.

The King's England: Lincolnshire a County of Infinite Charm. London: Hodder and Stoughton, 1949.

Millar, Ronald. *Will the Real King Arthur Please Stand Up?* London: Cassell, 1978.

Moffat, Alistair. *Arthur and the Lost Kingdoms*. London: Weidenfeld and Nicolson, 1999.

The Sea Kingdoms: The History of Celtic Britain and Ireland. Edinburgh: Birlinn Limited, 2008.

Morris, John. *The Age of Arthur: A History of the British Isles from 350 to 650.* London: Phoenix Giant / Orion, 1998.

Mothersole, Jessie. *The Saxon Shore*. London: John Lane The Bodley Head Limited, 1924.

Oppenheimer, Stephen. *The Origins of the British: A Genetic Detective Story.* London: Constable and Robinson, 2006.

Pace, Edwin. *Arthur and the Fall of Roman Britain: A Narrative History for Fifth Century Britain*. Cheltenham: Invermark Books, 2008.

Reid, Howard. *Arthur the Dragon King: The Barbaric Roots of Britain's Greatest Legend.* London: Headline Book Publishing, 2001.

Rivet, A. L. F and Colin Smith. *The Place-Names of Roman Britain.* London: Book Club Associates/B. T. Batsford Ltd, 1981.

Russell, Miles and Stuart Laycock. *UnRoman Britain: Exposing the Great Myth of Britannia*. Stroud: The History Press Ltd, 2010.

Saklatvala, Beram. *Arthur: Roman Britain's Last Champion*. Newton Abbot: David and Charles Publishers Ltd, 1967.

Salway, Peter. *Roman Britain*. London: Book Club Associates / Oxford University Press, 1982.

Senior, Michael ed. *Sir Thomas Malory's Tales of King Arthur*. London: Guild Publishing, 1980.

Snyder, Christopher A. *An Age of Tyrants: Britain and the Britons A.D. 400–600*. Stroud: Sutton Publishing, 1998.

Steinbeck, John. *The Acts of King Arthur and his Noble Knights: From the Winchester Manuscripts of Thomas Malory and Other Sources*. London: Book Club Associates/William Heineman Ltd, 1977.

Swanton, Michael, trans. and ed. *The Anglo-Saxon Chronicles*. London: Phoenix Press, 2003.

Tacitus: The Annals of Imperial Rome. Edited by Michael Grant. Harmondsworth: Penguin Books, 1959.

Wace and Lawman. *The Life of King Arthur*. London: Everyman Paperback Classics, 1997.

Wacher, John. *The Towns of Roman Britain*. London: Book Club Associates / B. T. Batsford Ltd, 1976.

Webster, Graham. *Rome against Caratacus: The Roman Campaigns in Britain, AD 48–58*. London: Book Club Associates/B. T. Batsford Ltd, 1981.

Whitwell, J. B. *Roman Lincolnshire*. Lincoln: History of Lincolnshire Committee, 1970.

Wildman, S. G. *The Black Horsemen*. London: John Baker, 1971.

Wood, Michael. *In Search of the Dark Ages*. London: BBC Worldwide Limited, 2001.

Glossary of Fifth-century Terms, People and Place Names

Throughout this book I have used authentic place names and terms as necessary. These are gleaned from an array of sources, in particular the annals, and monuments of the Romans and the Britons.

By the early fifth century, Rome had dominated much of western Europe for four hundred years. Latin became the language of the law, the military, religion and culture. Most ethnic languages endured, but the people who lived within or close by the Empire's frontiers came to adopt Latin terms, much like the English language now pervades modern global terms. The written word was mostly Latin, and later, ethnic writing was influenced by the phonetics of Latin speech. The poetry of the earliest bards was likely composed in either common Brittonic or archaic Welsh peppered with Latin. The 'Surrexit Memorandum' in the seventh-century Lichfield Gospels is the best example of this hybrid writing that developed over two centuries. Christianity, in particular, was taught in Latin. During the fifth century, the elites and their militias likely messaged and wrote in Latin but conversed in Brittonic.

Roman Provinces prior to AD 410

Maxima Caesariensis	The south and south-east
Flavia Caesariensis	The East Midlands, East Anglia and Norfolk
Britannia Prima	All territory west of a line from Chester to Dorset
Valentia	The territory between Hadrian's Wall and the Antonine Wall

Senior Roman military and civil appointments (in order of superiority)

patrician	highest class of noble appointed by the Emperor
magister militum	master of soldiers, the most senior general of a region, or if Empire-wide, 'magister utriusque militum'
magister peditum	master of infantry
magister officiorum	head of the civil service
Comes litoris Saxonici	*Count of the Saxon Shore*, general controlling south-east Britannia and the coast of northern Gaul
Comes Britanniarum	Count of the Britons
Dux Britanniarum	Duke of Britain, general controlling northern Britannia
praefectus	prefect, high-ranking officer
decurion	Roman cavalry officer in command of a squadron (ala) consisting of three or more turmae
eques	knight, member of Roman equestrian order
optio	junior officer, similar to a lieutenant

Tribes and peoples

Alans	a tribe which allied with the Romans and were settled in central Gaul

Angles	one of the Germanic peoples who settled in Britain during the Roman period
Attacotti	obscure highland tribe
Belgae	large Brittonic southern tribe
Bretons	Britons who emigrated to Armorica (Brittany)
Brigantes	large Brittonic northern tribe
Burgundians	Germanic tribe from the middle Rhine region
Carvetti	Brittonic tribe living in Cumbria, north-west Britannia
Cornovii	large Brittonic midland tribe
Cymry	a cultural grouping of Brittonic tribes some of whom, prior to AD 410 were Roman citizens – a modern-day translation is 'the Welsh'
Damnonii	Brittonic people who lived in the Kingdom of Strathclyde
Deisi	a tribe of people from ancient Ireland who settled in Wales
Dobunni	large south-west Brittonic tribe, based around Gloucester
Franks	Germanic tribe from the east bank of the lower Rhine
Frisians	coastal tribe from around the Rhine estuary
Gaels	group native to Ireland, who migrated to western Scotland and the Isle of Man

Gaini	Frank or Frisian tribe which occupied the east bank of the Trent
Goths	The collective name for Germanic people who originated from Poland and the western Steppes and migrated as different tribes to the Roman Empire
Gododdin	Brittonic-speaking people of north-eastern Britannia (now southern Scotland)
Huns	nomadic people who lived in Central Asia and the Caucasus who grew by conquest to become as powerful as the Roman Empire
Jutes	Germanic people from Jutland who emigrated to Britannia
Novantae	tribe who lived in Galloway, south-west Scotland
Parisi	Brittonic tribe located in the east of Yorkshire
Picts	tribes who lived in Scotland north of the Forth–Clyde isthmus
Scotti	Irish raiders who colonised western Scotland
Suebi	Germanic people from the Elbe river region, now Germany and the Czech Republic

Syagrii	famous Roman family of which Aegidius is assumed a descendant
Vandals	Germanic people from southern Poland who swept across Europe and colonised North Africa
Visigoths	Germanic tribe first noted in the Balkans who eventually colonised southern Gaul

Other references

Agnes Dei	a liturgical chant 'Lamb of God'
atrium	a large open-air reception space
bacaudae	groups of populist insurgents
basilica	a large building for civic use
bucellari	barbarian escort troops
Caledfwich	famous sword known in legend as Excalibur
castrum	stone turret or watchtower
cena	dinner
Chi Rho	Ancient Christian symbol
cives	citizens
civitas	town
Coeling	descendants of Coel Hen
colonae	areas of settlement
culdeis	partners of God, Church-appointed representatives
Damnatio memoriae	Latin phrase meaning 'condemnation of memory', indicating that a person be excluded from official

	accounts, often applied to executed usurpers
foederati	barbarian tribes bound to provide military assistance under treaty to Rome, also known as foedus
Gallic	the culture of Roman northern France
gladius	type of sword used by infantry
gorchan	a poetic elegy, commemorating fallen warriors
labarum	a Christian banner and the imperial standard of Constantine the Great
Limes Germanicus	line of frontier fortifications stretching along the Rhine and the Danube dividing the Roman Empire and the Germanic tribes
lorica	a prayer for protection in Irish monastic tradition, associated with St Patrick
lusoria	Roman vessel used as a troop transporter
mansio	a large house used as a hotel or guest house
Pascha	the Christian festival of Easter
patria, the Patria	native country or homeland
peristylium	open inner courtyard surrounded by a row of columns

Praetorian Guard	the Emperor's guard
praetorium	headquarters of a Roman official
primogeniture	the right of succession of the firstborn child
publicanus	tax collector
Romanitas	Roman identity and culture
Saturnalia	an ancient Roman festival and holiday in honour of the god Saturn, held 17–23 December
seax	Saxon knife with a single cutting edge and a long, tapering point
siliquae	small, thin Roman silver coins produced in the fourth and early fifth century AD
solidi	pure gold coins issued in the late Roman Empire.
spatha	a straight, long sword used by cavalry
tanet	an area of land allocated for settlement
the Purple	the epithet for the position of Roman Emperor
thegn	Anglo-Saxon leader/landowner
tribune	an official leading a region
turma	a cavalry unit, usually thirty strong
Verbeia	a water goddess
vicus	village or part of a town
Wealas	Anglo-Saxon term for Britons, translates as foreigner or sometimes slave

Place names, Britannia

Afon Menai	Menai Straits
Alauna	Roman fort, just north of Maryport
Alt Clut	Brittonic fortress, capital of the kingdom of Strathclyde
Ambro Hill	hill in Leicestershire overlooking Breedon on the Hill
Axholme	island to the west of the Trent now drained
Badon	Bardon Hill, Leicestershire
Banna	Birdoswald Fort, Hadrian's Wall
Blencathra	mountain in the northern part of the Lake District
Breguoin	Breedon on the Hill in Leicestershire
Bremetennacum	Roman fort, Ribchester
Britannia	Roman Britain
Brovacum	Brougham Castle near Penrith
Bryneich	Brittonic name for Bernicia land between the Tyne and the Tweed, mostly Northumbria
Caint	modern-day Kent
Caledonia	Scotland, north of the Forth
Calleva	Silchester
Cambodunum	possibly Barwick-in-Elmet
Camulodunum	Colchester
Candida Casa	monastery at Whithorn
Cataractonium	Catterick

Catraeth	assumed later name for Catterick
Causennis	Saltersford, Little Ponton
Celyddon	the northern part of the Great Forest near the river Don
Cheviot	a mountain between the rivers Tyne and the Tweed
Clausentum	Roman port, Bitterne, Southampton
Corieltauvorum	Leicester
Corinium	Cirencester
Corstopitum (Coria)	Corbridge
Crecganford	present day Stamford Bridge
Danum	Doncaster
Derventio	a fort, Little Chester, Derby
Deva	Chester
Din Eidyn	Edinburgh
Din Guarie	Bamburgh fort, Northumberland
Dumnonia	Cornwall, Devon and part of Somerset
Dunnad	Scotti hillfort near Lochgilphead
Dunragit	fort of Reged, near Glenluce and Stranraer
Durnovaria	Dorchester
Durobrivae	Water Newton, Peterborough
Durovernum	Canterbury
Dyfed	county in south-western Wales
Eboracum	York
Elmet	the kingdom of Elmet, now part of northern England

Episford	ferry on the River Trent, also known in Welsh as Rither Gabail
Erechwyd	the region of the Lake District
Flavia	Roman province of central Britain sometimes called Flavia Caesariensis
Fortriu	Pictish kingdom
Gainnion	stronghold of the Gaini, Gainsborough
Gaulish Sea	the North Sea beyond the Wash
Glevum	Gloucester
Great Forest	the largest forest in Britannia, incorporating Charnwood, Sherwood, Elmet and Galtres, stretching from Leicester to beyond York
Guoloph	battle site, Nether Wallop, Hampshire
Gwynedd	region in the north-west of Wales
Hibernia	Ireland
Insula Manavia	Isle of Man, also known as Mannin
Isca Augusta	Caerleon, South Wales
Isca Dumnoniorum	Exeter
Isurium (Brigantum)	Aldborough, Boroughbridge, North Yorkshire
Itunocelum	Roman naval fort, Ravenglass, Cumbria
Lactodurum	Towcester

Lavatris	Bowes, County Durham
Letocetum	Wall, Lichfield
Lindinis	Ilchester, Somerset
Lindum	Lincoln
Linnuis	the kingdom of Lindsey, a large area of North Lincolnshire
Londinium	London
Luguvalium	Carlisle
Maglona	Old Carlisle, Wigton
Magna	Roman fort at Whin Sill on Hadrian's Wall
Mamucium	Manchester
Mona	Anglesey
Mons Badonicus	Bardon Hill, Leicestershire
Novomagus	Chichester
Orcades	the Orkney Islands
Pons Aelius	Newcastle upon Tyne
Ratae (Corieltauvorum)	Leicester
Reged	northern kingdom, covering north-west England and south-west Scotland
Rither Gabail	ferry on the River Trent, also known as Episford
Roman turf wall	the Antonine wall built between the Clyde and the Firth of Forth
Rutupiae	Richborough
Ryknild (Via)	northern part of the Roman road known as Icknield Street

Saxon Shore	military command of the Roman Empire consisting of a series of fortifications on both sides of the English Channel
Segontium	Caernarfon
Sorviodunum	Old Sarum, Salisbury
Traprain Law	Gododdin fortress, Lothian, Scotland
Tribruit	the shore of the Trent, near the junction with the Soar
Valentia	the fifth province of Britannia between Hadrian's Wall and the Antonine Wall
Vectis	Isle of Wight
Venonis	High Cross, Lutterworth
Venta Belgarum	Winchester
Venta Icenorum	Caistor St Edmund
Verbeia	Roman fort, Ilkley, West Yorkshire
Verulamium	St Albans
Vinovia	Binchester, Bishop Auckland
Viroconium	Wroxeter
Wall, the	Hadrian's Wall, Northumberland
Whithorn	location of the monastery known as Candida Casa
Wippeds Fleot	Surfleet Seas End near the Wash
Ypwines Fleot	Swinefleet near Goole on the Humber
Yr Wyddfa	Snowdon

Place names, Roman Empire

Aletum	St Malo, France
Ambianensium	Amiens, France
Aquitania	Roman province in south-west France
Armorica	Brittany, France
Arvernis	the Auvergne region around Clermont-Ferrand, France
Aurelianum	Orléans, France
Autissiodorum	Auxerre, France
Avaricum	Bourges, France
Belgica Secunda	Roman province that combined Belgium and northern France
Bononia	Boulogne, France
Carthage	Roman city and port, now the capital of Tunisia
Chalons	the region between Reims and Troyes where Aetius fought Attila
Constantinople	Istanbul, Turkey
Dalmatia	historical region on the eastern shore of the Adriatic Sea in Croatia, sometimes known as Illyricum
Déols	ancient town in eastern central France
Gallaecia	northern Portugal
Gaul	France
Germania	Roman province bordering the Rhine and the Danube
Hispania	Roman name for the Iberian Peninsula

Illyricum	eastern shore of the Adriatic, sometimes called Dalmatia
Juliomagus	Angers, western France
Lake Lemanus	Lake Geneva, Switzerland
Lutetia	Paris, France
Mare Nostrum	Mediterranean Sea
Noviodunum	Soissons, northern France
Pannonia	Roman province in the Balkans
Ravenna	fortified imperial palace, Emelia–Romagna province, Italy
Salona	ancient city and capital of the province of Dalmatia (Illyricum)
Tolosa	Toulouse, France
Treverorum	Trier, Germany
Turonum	Tours, France

River names

Aire	tributary of the River Humber
Bassas	River Torne (or Thorne)
Dergeuntid	River Derwent near Derby, tributary to the Trent
Don	tributary of the River Trent
Eden	flows into the Solway Firth
Ellen	flows into the Solway Firth at Maryport
Esk	flows into the sea at Ravenglass
Garonne	flows through Toulouse to the Gironde estuary

Glen	flows into the River Welland
Humber	estuary, flows into the North Sea
Irthing	tributary of the River Eden
Loire	longest river in France, flows into the Atlantic Ocean at the Bay of Biscay
Skell	tributary of the River Don
Soar	tributary of the River Trent
Swale	tributary of the River Ouse
Teme	tributary of the River Severn
Trent	tributary of the River Humber
Welland	flows into The Wash

INDEX

A

B

C

D

E

F

G

H

I

J

L

M

N

O

P

R

S

T

U

V

W

Y

Z

Historical fiction titles by Alistair Hall

The first title in this series: *The Genesis of Arthwys*

The year is 412 AD. The Roman legions have all withdrawn from Britannia. The cives and tribes who remain no longer have the might of Rome at their backs or her foot on their throats. They must rally to fill the power vacuum and defend themselves against an array of seaborne enemies attracted by prosperous lands lightly defended. Meanwhile, the Picts of Caledonia seize their opportunity to invade and so begins sixty years of strife for the Britons. This is a story of those warlords that became kings and valiantly defended their religion and culture, ensuring their deeds passed down the ages into legend. The last Roman appointed Duke of Britain, Coel Hen, not only defended the North but also gave rise to a dynasty that would extend its grip on power, shaping kingdoms whilst facing the gathering tide of invasion from across the sea. *The Genesis of Arthwys* tells the story behind the rise of this illustrious northern dynasty. There is a prophecy that a serpent will come from the east, and the men of the North must be ready or risk losing all that they hold dear… only the Bear will defeat it.

The second title in the series: *The Rise of Arthwys*

The year is 446 AD. The beleaguered Britons have endured a debilitating plague and are surrounded by enemies. A surprising and shocking Saxon rebellion has been contained by King Vortimer but an entire province has been lost and the south and west are now in danger. An appeal by the council of Britons to the Roman high command in Gaul has been ignored and all hope seems lost. All that is left is a faith in God and an old prophecy that the Brigantes Bear will defeat the serpent in the east. Meanwhile in Gaul the Romans face conquest by the Huns and the empire teeters on the edge of destruction as city after city falls to the barbarians.

This is a story of devotion to God, to duty and to each other. History records the imperial palace intrigue and treachery but the legends tell of the bravery of the last generation that held the line against the gathering storm facing impossible odds whilst enduring immense personal loss.